MODERN
OPERA HOUSES
AND THEATRES

MODERN
OPERA HOUSES
AND THEATRES

BY

EDWIN O. SACHS

ARCHITECT,

AND

ERNEST A. E. WOODROW,

A.R.I.B.A.

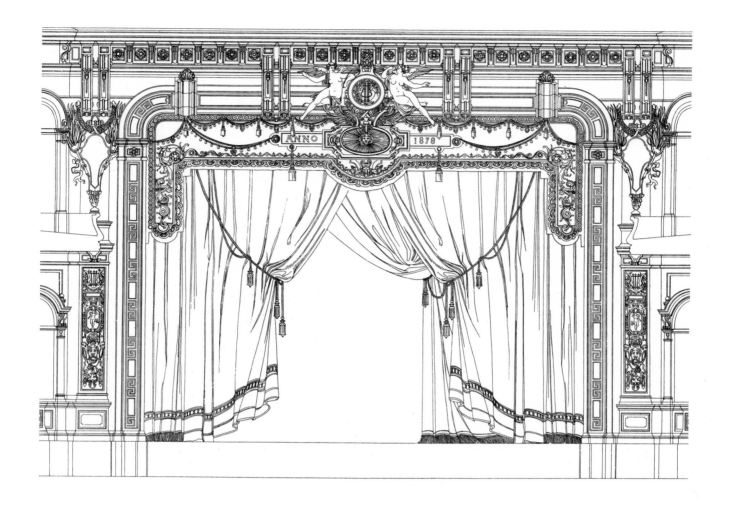

VOLUME II.

WITH ONE HUNDRED PLATES

AND

NINETY FIVE ILLUSTRATIONS IN THE TEXT.

ARNO PRESS

A NEW YORK TIMES COMPANY
NEW YORK, 1981

Reprint edition 1981 by Arno Press, Inc.

Volumes 1, 2, 3 first published in
London 1896, 1897, 1898 respectively

LC81-43132

ISBN 0-405-14256-0

Manufactured in the United States of America

Printed in U.S.A. by
NOBLE OFFSET PRINTERS, INC.
NEW YORK 3, N. Y.

LIST OF ORIGINAL SUBSCRIBERS.

THE ART LIBRARY, SCIENCE & ART DEPARTMENT, SOUTH KENSINGTON MUSEUM, LONDON.

H.M. PATENT OFFICE, LONDON.

THE ARCHITECTURAL SCHOOLS, PRUSSIAN ROYAL ACADEMY, BERLIN.

THE LONDON COUNTY COUNCIL.

THE MITCHELL LIBRARY, GLASGOW.   *THE PUBLIC LIBRARY, LIVERPOOL.*

THE IMPERIAL TECHNICAL COLLEGE, VIENNA.

THE ASTOR LIBRARY, NEW YORK, U.S.A.   *THE PUBLIC LIBRARY, TORONTO.*

THE ENGINEER'S DEPARTMENT TO THE GAEKWAR OF BARODA.

THE BOARD OF WORKS, HAMBURG.   *THE POLICE ADMINISTRATION, HAMBURG.*

THE IMPERIAL ENGINEERING COLLEGE, TOKIO.

THE CITY FIRE BRIGADE, ALTONA.   *THE CITY FIRE BRIGADE, BREMEN.*

THE CITY FIRE BRIGADE, HAMBURG.

THE IMPERIAL UNIVERSITY LIBRARY, STRASSBURG.

THE TECHNICAL SCHOOLS, LEMBERG.   *THE TECHNICAL SCHOOLS, MAGDEBURG.*

THE ROYAL TECHNICAL AND COMMERCIAL LIBRARY, STUTTGART.

THE CORNELL UNIVERSITY LIBRARY, ITHACA, U.S.A.

THE PUBLIC LIBRARY, CINCINNATI, U.S.A.   *THE PUBLIC LIBRARY, DETROIT, U.S.A.*

THE ATHENÆUM LIBRARY, MINNEAPOLIS, U.S.A.

THE FOREIGN ARCHITECTURAL BOOK CLUB, LONDON.

THE ALHAMBRA THEATRE DIRECTORATE,
   By A. Moul, Esq., London.

PROFESSOR ERNESTO BASILE, Teatro Massimo, Palermo.

FRANK R. BENSON, Esq., Maidenhead.

JOHN CAMPBELL, Esq., F.R.I.B.A., The Fort, Bombay.

ARTHUR CAREY, Esq., A.M.I.C.E., Rosary Gardens, S.W.

J. CHARLTON, Esq., Huntley, U.S.A.

R. CHISHOLME, Esq., Heidelberg.

MAX CLARKE, Esq., A.R.I.B.A., Queen's Square, W.C.

HENRY IVES COBB, Chicago.

ISAAC COHEN, Esq., Pavilion Theatre, Mile End, E.

A. O. COLLARD, Esq., A.R.I.B.A., Craig's Court, Charing Cross, S.W.

T. E. COLLCUTT, Esq., F.R.I.B.A., Bloomsbury Square, W.C.

AUGUSTIN DALY, Esq., Daly's Theatre, W.C.

ALFRED DARBYSHIRE, Esq., F.S.A., F.R.I.B.A., College Chambers, Manchester.

JAMES B. DUNN, Esq., George Street, Edinburgh.

WALTER EMDEN, Esq., Strand, W.C.

THE EMPIRE THEATRE DIRECTORATE,
   By A. W. Tennant, Esq., London.

H. ERNST, Esq., Zurich.

H. L. FLORENCE, Esq., F.R.I.B.A., Verulam Buildings, Gray's Inn, W.C.

H. FORTLAGE, Esq., College Road, Dulwich, S.E.

Messrs. GREEN & WICKS, Buffalo, U.S.A.

J. T. HAMP, Esq., High Holborn, W.C.

SIR AUGUSTUS HARRIS, Theatre Royal, Drury Lane.

W. HANCOCK, Esq., Wardrobe Chambers, E.C.

JOHN HEBB, Esq., F.R.I.B.A., Assistant Architect, London County Council.

H. AWDUS HILL, Esq., Theatres Department, London County Council.

WALTER HILL, Esq., Southampton Row, W.C.

EMIL HOLLÆNDER, Esq., Dresdener Bank, Berlin.

J. CHARLTON HUMPHREYS, Esq., Knightsbridge, W.

SIR HENRY IRVING, The Lyceum Theatre, W.C.

II.—b

LEOPOLD JACOBI, Esq., Ferdinandstrasse, Hamburg.

Messrs. KAYE & SONS, High Holborn, W.C.

Messrs. KAYSER & VON GROSSHEIM, Berlin.

BOLOSSY KIRALFY, Esq., Olympia, S.W.

IMRE KIRALFY, Esq., Earl's Court, S.W.

T. E. KNIGHTLEY, Esq., F.R.I.B.A., Cannon Street, E.C.

Mrs. LANE, The Britannia Theatre, Hoxton, N.

CHARLES LONG, Esq., A.R.I.B.A., Rosslyn Hill, Hampstead, N.W.

Messrs. MAPLE & CO., Tottenham Court Road, W.C.

PROFESSOR OTTO MARCH, Charlottenburg.

FRANK MATCHAM, Esq., Warwick Court, W.C.

CARL MEYER, Esq., Hill Street, Berkeley Square, W.

A. MŒLLMANN, Esq., Woodsome Lodge, Weybridge.

T. B. MULHOLLAND, Esq., Theatre Métropole, Camberwell, S.E.

ALBERT OCHS, Esq., Hyde Park Street, W.

J. TAVENOR PERRY, Esq., F.R.I.B.A., The Grove, South Kensington, S.W.

C. J. PHIPPS, Esq., F.S.A., F.R.I.B.A., Mecklenburgh Square, W.C.

P. E. PILDITCH, Esq., F.S.I., Parliament Street, S.W.

FRANZ VON RAICHL, Esq., Buda-Pesth.

ERNEST RÜNTZ, Esq., Moorgate Street, E.C.

F. H. REED, Esq., A.R.I.B.A., Grove Villa, Lee, S.E.

GUSTAV SACHS, Esq., Marlborough Hill, N.W.

ALBERT SAMSON, Esq., Avenue Louise, Brussels.

GUSTAV SAMSON, Esq., Cottbus.

F. BENNETT SMITH, Esq., F.R.I.B.A., Manchester.

W. G. R. SPRAGUE, Esq., Arundel Street, Strand, W.C.

HERBERT SPRAKE, Esq., Collins' Music Hall, London.

PROFESSOR IMRE STEINDL, Hon. Corr. Mem. R.I.B.A., Houses of Parliament, Buda-Pesth.

SYDNEY STENT, Esq., F.R.I.B.A., Cape Town.

INIGO TASKER, Esq., John Street, Bedford Row, W.C.

BRANDON THOMAS, Esq., Cadogan Terrace, S.W.

FRANK T. VERITY, Esq., A.R.I.B.A., Surveyor to the Lord Chamberlain, Jermyn Street, W.

LUDWIG WAGNER, Esq., North Finchley, N.

RICHARD WIENER, Esq., Bendlerstrasse, Berlin.

Messrs. WILLIAMSON & MUSGROVE, Princess Theatre, Melbourne.

CHARLES WILMOT, Esq., The Grand Theatre, Islington, N.

MAJOR WINSTANLEY, Royal Opera House, Leicester.

OSWALD C. WYLSON, Esq., F.R.I.B.A., King William Street, W.C.

PROFESSOR JOS. ZITEK, Imperial Technical College, Prague.

BALINT ZOLTAN, Esq., Buda-Pesth.

Mr. E. G. ALLEN, London.

Messrs. CALVE, Prague.

Messrs. FLOR & FINDELI, Florence.

Mr. GLAISHER, London.

Mr. T. HENRY, Toronto.

Messrs. HESSLING & SPIELMEYER, New York.

Messrs. LANSON & WALLIN, Stockholm.

Messrs. LEHMANN & WENTZEL, Vienna.

Messrs. VAN NOSTRAND & CO., New York.

Mr. Y. J. PENTLAND, London.

Messrs. G. P. PUTNAM'S SONS, London.

Messrs. SCHUSTER & BUFLEB, Berlin.

Messrs. SCRIBNERS' SONS, New York.

Messrs. SIMPKIN, MARSHALL & CO., London.

Messrs. B. F. STEVENS, London.

SUPPLEMENTARY LIST.

THE CITY FIRE BRIGADE, AMSTERDAM.

THE PUBLIC LIBRARY, BOSTON.

THE AMERY LIBRARY, NEW YORK.

THE FREE LIBRARY, CARDIFF.

THE PUBLIC LIBRARY, WIGAN.

H. J. BLANE, Esq., Edinburgh.

Messrs. A. G. BROWN & CO., London.

R. H. BRUNTON, Esq., London.

ARTHUR CATES, Esq., F.R.I.B.A., London.

BERTIE CREWE, Esq., London.

C. B. DUNHAM, Esq., Boston, U.S.A.

THOMAS ELSLEY, Esq., London.

W. S. GILBERT, Esq., Harrow Weald.

WILLIAM GREET, Esq., Lyric Theatre, London.

Messrs. H. GREVEL & CO., London.

Miss ALICE HALGARTEN, Hamburg.

E. D. HEINEMANN, Esq., Chicago.

W. HOPE, Esq., North Shields.

J. MURRAY, Esq., A.R.I.B.A., London.

SIR DAVID SALOMONS, Bart., Tunbridge Wells.

A. SELIM, Esq., London.

Messrs. SHOOLBRED & CO., London.

SYDNEY STOTT, Esq., Oldham.

G. F. WARD, Esq., Birmingham.

Mr. M. HOEPLI, Milan.

iv

NOTE TO VOLUME II.

THE encouraging manner in which the first volume of this work has been received compels me, on the issue of the second, to express my great appreciation of the interest which has been shown in the undertaking, and I trust that those in whose eyes the first volume found favour will not be disappointed with the succeeding ones. It affords me special pleasure to be able to record that experts and others particularly associated with the Theatre have in every way supported my efforts. The reception by architects, engineers and public officials has been equally cordial, while playgoers and the general public, as represented by the Press, have not been ungenerous in their approval. I would add that owing to the Subscribers' edition of the first volume having been exhausted a further issue of that part has been found necessary, and the number of copies of this present volume accordingly increased.

In the original Preface I remarked on the length of time over which the compilation of the work had been spread, for, whilst I commenced to map out these two volumes early in 1890, they only saw their completion during 1896 and 1897. In consequence of this lapse of time it was practically impossible for me to keep strictly to my scheme as first conceived, or even to follow in every detail the definite programme made public in 1895. For, on the one hand, the favourable reception of the first volume has enabled me to considerably extend the scope of the work, whilst, on the other, the enormous variety of material collected has compelled me either to abbreviate or entirely omit much I should like to have included. In so long a period, too, there have been great changes among those who have assisted me in the compilation, and I would particularly mention that, much to my regret, Ernest A. E. Woodrow, who during the short period of our professional association was always ready to help, has been unable to co-operate in the execution of the work as was originally anticipated. I believe, however, that the circumstances referred to have had but little effect on the general treatment of the subject, and, taken as a whole, I trust it will be found that it has been dealt with even more comprehensively than was promised.

I would call attention to the fact that, whilst in this volume also I have adhered to the original idea of presenting all plans on a uniform scale, I have not considered absolute similarity in the reproduction of sections to be of the same importance. Where it has been possible, I have adopted the same reduction; but in the case of smaller theatres, where much of the detail would have been lost, a different scale has been introduced. I have attempted, as in the previous volume, to present the various plans and sections in a uniform manner, showing the main features of the respective buildings by a few geometrical lines. The illustrations in the text, which are necessarily limited in number, are, as before mentioned, still only intended to assist in the appreciation of the architectural or decorative features, whilst the letterpress is solely confined to recording facts, or to directing attention to noteworthy characteristics.

There is one point, however, which I wish to emphasise. This work aims at continuing the valuable Atlas on earlier Theatres, published by Contant in 1842, and reprinted in 1860. Hence, it has not been my intention to notice buildings, however famous, previous to that date. These volumes, as may be seen from the title, deal essentially with modern structures, and, as a matter of fact, the earliest buildings treated of are the Paris Opera House and the Vienna Opera House, which were opened, respectively, in 1875 and in 1869, the designs for which, however, were prepared in 1861.

I would here repeat what I said in my Preface regarding watchfulness to avoid errors in illustrations, text and tables. For any discrepancies that may be found I again crave indulgence, in view of the wide scope of the enterprise, and of the fact that it has not been found practicable to submit proofs to the various persons interested.

Let me again take the opportunity of conveying to all who have so kindly assisted me in the issue of this work, my cordial thanks for their help and advice.

E. O. S.

11 WATERLOO PLACE, PALL MALL, LONDON, S.W.

June 3, 1897.

"HER MAJESTY'S" THEATRE, LONDON.
General View.

LIST OF EXAMPLES ILLUSTRATED

IN

VOLUME II.

II.—c

ILLUSTRATIONS DERIVED FROM OTHER PUBLICATIONS.

———————

THE PHOTOGRAPHS OF "HER MAJESTY'S" THEATRE, THE "GARRICK" THEATRE, AND THE "EMPIRE" VARIETY THEATRE, LONDON, ARE BY ALFRED ELLIS;
THE PHOTOGRAPHS OF THE SHAKESPEARE MEMORIAL THEATRE, STRATFORD-ON-AVON, ARE BY THE LONDON STEREOSCOPIC COMPANY, LIMITED.
IN OTHER INSTANCES THE NAMES OF THE PHOTOGRAPHERS HAVE NOT BEEN OBTAINABLE.

"EDEN" VARIETY THEATRE, PARIS.
DETAIL OF ELEVATION.

LIST OF ILLUSTRATIONS

PART I.

FRANCE.

NATIONAL OPERA HOUSE, PARIS.

NATIONAL "OPÉRA COMIQUE," PARIS.

"EDEN" VARIETY THEATRE, PARIS.

MONACO.

CASINO THEATRE, MONTE CARLO.

ITALY.

MUNICIPAL THEATRE, PALERMO.

"LIRICO" THEATRE, MILAN.

PEOPLE'S THEATRE, TURIN.

SPAIN.

MUNICIPAL THEATRE, BILBAO.

PART II.

AUSTRIA AND HUNGARY.

COURT OPERA HOUSE, VIENNA.

CZECH NATIONAL THEATRE, PRAGUE.

MUNICIPAL THEATRE, SALZBURG.

MUNICIPAL THEATRE, LAIBACH.

II.—d

MUNICIPAL THEATRE, GENEVA.

MUNICIPAL THEATRE, ZÜRICH.

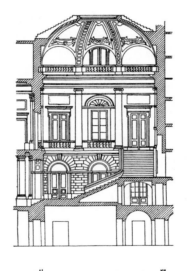

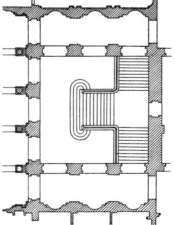

MUNICIPAL THEATRE, BORDEAUX.
GRAND STAIRCASE.

SHAKESPEARE MEMORIAL THEATRE, STRATFORD-ON-AVON.
VIEW OF TOWER.

MODERN
OPERA HOUSES AND THEATRES.

VOLUME II.

INTRODUCTION.

In preparing the first volume, I purposely limited the contents to a selection of playhouses recently erected in Great Britain, Germany, Austria, Russia, Scandinavia and the Netherlands, with the view of keeping together all structures where the influences apparent are either of Teutonic or Anglo-Saxon origin. I had intended to devote the second volume to theatres of Latin countries, since their individuality is similarly distinct. But, in arranging my material, I found that, whilst the latter countries no doubt made a great epoch in theatre construction during the first half of the present century, comparatively few playhouses had been recently erected showing any great progress either in plan, architectural rendering or construction. Little, if anything, is to be learnt from modern theatres in France, Italy and Spain. Taken generally, the examples from countries subject to Teutonic and Anglo-Saxon influences alone show a marked development in theatre construction. Among these countries I should, perhaps, add that Greece and Roumania have been included, for the same reasons that the Russian playhouse was placed with this group in the first volume.

It was owing to the fact of finding so few theatres of interest in the Latin countries that I decided to devote only a section of the second volume to examples from these localities, retaining the other section for the further illustration of more instructive work. It will now be found that this volume is divided into two parts, the first comprising examples from France, Italy, Monaco and Spain, the second representing Austria, Germany, Great Britain, Greece, Holland, Roumania and Switzerland.

In my former Introduction an attempt was made to explain briefly the various circumstances under which playhouses exist in Europe, for I considered it essential to the right appreciation of the buildings to know the intentions which have guided their erection and the purposes for which they were built. Though generalising for the whole of Europe, my remarks were offered perhaps more particularly in connection with the examples dealt with in the first volume. It should be emphasised that what I have said there holds good for the examples of Latin countries, and I will only supplement those particulars with a few additional notes respecting local peculiarities.

It will be remembered that I divided all theatres into the five following classes, namely :—Court Theatres, National and Government Theatres, Municipal and District Theatres, Subscription Theatres—with or without Court, Government or Municipal subsidy—and Private Theatres, with or without such assistance.

Firstly, I must now point out that in the same manner as the Court Theatre is a particular feature of the German Empire, so in France, or, to be exact, in Paris, there exists the peculiarity of the state-subsidised Theatre, over which a manager or lessee is appointed by the Government. Subscription Theatres proper are unknown in France, and the Municipal Theatre is only to be found in the Provinces.

Further, I would call attention to the fact that similarly, as England is essentially the home of the Private Theatre,

Spain also now holds, to a lesser degree, this reputation.   Moreover, there is a likeness between the objects for which the audiences assemble in the two countries, the desire being more for amusement than for instruction; whilst, it will be remembered, the people of Germany and Austria generally regard the playhouse as a kind of educational institution.   A feature of the smaller Spanish theatre, peculiar to that country, is the nightly production of several minor plays, each of short duration, and for which there is a considerable change in the audience, separate tickets being issued for each individual presentation.   An arrangement of this description, it will readily be understood, to some extent influences the planning.

Then, as regards Italy, it is well to bear in mind that the theatre fulfils functions of a quite unique character.   In the first place it is a *rendezvous;* a playhouse only in the second, the performance itself, as a rule, receiving but limited attention.   The system of box-holdings is particularly developed, and accounts for much in the plan, whilst the essentially different purposes of the accommodation devoted to stalls and pit likewise call for a different treatment in the design.   The private theatre managed on commercial principles, I may mention, appears of late to be becoming a common adjunct to the more important Italian towns.

Since the issue of the first volume, in which I pointed out that the latest development of the Subscription Theatre had taken the form at Worms of a People's Theatre, subscribed for and managed on democratic lines, a further evolution has been heralded by the proposed presentation of a playhouse to a rural community in the neighbourhood of our metropolis.   Here, if I may say so, the subscriptions take the form of an individual donation, and the gift will certainly be a remarkable one in the history of English theatres.   To-day the Free Library is one of our favourite objects of munificence.   Why should not the People's Theatre become equally popular among our would-be benefactors?

I have remarked before on the great difference of feeling common to individual Continental countries respecting the suitable housing of Dramatic Art: I have called attention to the absence of interest in theatre architecture common to this country.   A London audience will rest content if it can hear and see well and is comfortably seated: the architectural rendering of their surroundings is considered immaterial.   I would now emphasise the fact that certain Continental countries, in their enthusiasm for a suitable framing for their plays, even go to the extreme of attempting such exact distinctions as the definition of a Palace of Art and a Temple of Art.   Reference to the plans illustrated in these volumes will assist an appreciation of the meaning of these terms, for there is no difficulty in seeing how the Paris Opera House may be considered to figure as a Palace, whilst the evident cold severity of a so-called Temple of Art will also be found embodied in various examples.   I hold, however, that it appears almost trivial to English eyes when such fine distinctions become the matter of controversy; for the purpose should be defined at the outset, and the architectural rendering should be a characteristic expression of the original intention.   The excessive attention given to such artificial distinctions distracts the architect, and even leads to regrettable technical omissions.   What, for instance, is the value of a well-known Austrian critic's opinion that the grand "Hofburg" Theatre at Vienna should be classified as a Temple of Art, when, on the other hand, we have the lamentable fact that the acoustics of the auditorium are defective and the sight-lines unsatisfactory?   Perhaps I should here add that these faults, of which complaint was made in the first volume, have actually been found so serious as to necessitate considerable alterations being taken in hand and a heavy expenditure incurred.

It is not my intention here to dwell on the development of theatre planning, but, as I pointed out in the preceding volume, it is essential to bear in mind such evolutions in theatre design as were there so forcibly illustrated by the gradual changes in the arrangement of certain playhouses, culminating in the design of the proposed Opera House for St. Petersburg.   A diagram illustrating the principal stairs of the old theatre of Bordeaux will now again show the origin of such a well-known feature as the Grand Staircase of the Paris Opera House.   I cannot but impress upon those who seriously study modern theatre architecture the value of carefully examining the gradual progress so evident in kindred examples of consecutive dates, for the most successful designs are doubtless the result of evolutions in which some distinct idea has been developed.   Such development may have been brought about by a number of architects aspiring to the same purpose, or, as is more commonly the case, by an individual member of the profession who has had sufficient opportunity to gradually evolve certain schemes.   Gottfried Semper had such opportunities, as has already been shown, and so have Ferdinand Fellner and Hermann Helmer at Vienna, Heinrich Seeling at Berlin, Victor Schroeter at St. Petersburg.   In this country, though theatre design has generally been in a few individual hands, I am afraid I cannot speak of the development of ideals in theatre planning by any particular architect, though a certain growth of special features in theatre construction—as, for instance, the cantilever gallery or the double staircase—is quite evident.   We can only boast of improvement in certain practical features as distinct from a specific evolution in the general design of our playhouses.

The contents of these volumes undoubtedly emphasise the advantages of designing with purpose to end and with an ideal.   Our theatre architecture would, I am sure, greatly benefit if this were kept in mind.

NATIONAL OPERA HOUSE, PARIS. GENERAL VIEW.

PART I.

FRANCE.

NATIONAL OPERA HOUSE, PARIS.

CHARLES GARNIER.

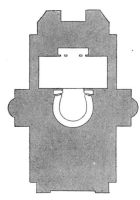

BLOCK PLAN.

THE first volume of this work opened with a description of the "Hofburg" Theatre at Vienna, and in the same way as that institution claimed priority in every respect among the examples selected from countries where Teutonic and Anglo-Saxon influences predominate, so too there can be no doubt that the National Opera House at Paris occupies the most eminent position among playhouses subject to Latin influence.

The present volume, as I have mentioned, is divided into two parts, according to the different tendencies prevailing, but I think it will readily be acknowledged that the Paris Opera House takes precedence of all buildings presented here, including the Opera House at Vienna, which stands at the head of the second part. It is, however, more than doubtful whether the Paris Opera House should be placed before all the theatres illustrated in this work as a whole, for, although, as a structure, it is the largest and most important that has so far seen completion, still it cannot compare favourably from a technical point of view with so essentially a modern institution as the "Hofburg" Theatre at Vienna. In the eyes of the world, it is true the Paris Opera House is considered the most unique building of its kind, and has generally been accorded the first position among playhouses. For my part, I should, nevertheless, be inclined to place the "Hofburg" Theatre far higher as an example of modern theatre construction.

The word "National," prefixed to the title of the Opera House in Paris, must in no way be considered meaningless, for we have in it an institution that is in every respect national. Owned as it is by the State, its managers, though not actually officials of the Government, are under its control, while the doors of the building are thrown open on all occasions of great national festivity, the works presented are chiefly of French origin, and French art is primarily encouraged. The Paris Opera House is one of the "show places" of Paris, and is undoubtedly the pride of the French nation. We may even go further and say that it is also the pride of the civilised world, or, at least, of that world which regards Paris as the chief centre of art. So elaborate and costly a monument has, as yet, nowhere else been devoted to the interests of any one special branch of art, and the only structure in which a possible rival may some day be found for it is the great Opera House at St. Petersburg, which has been so long under consideration, and the original plans for which were presented in the foregoing volume.

It was during the execution of the great street improvements in Paris, introduced by Napoleon III. and his minister Baron Haussmann, that, by an Imperial decree dated December 29, 1860, a competition was opened for the great Opera House. In spite of the fact that only a few weeks were given to the competing architects to prepare their plans, no less than one hundred and seventy designs were sent in. By a process of selection on the part of the assessors this number was successively reduced to forty-three and to seven, but, no final choice having been made, a second limited competition was immediately instituted. It was in this latter competition that Charles Garnier was unanimously declared the victor. The author of the successful design was still a young man and as yet unknown to fame, but the

commission for this great undertaking, its masterly execution, and also the controversies which arose about many of its archi-tectural features, soon brought him a world-wide celebrity. Before com-mencing his task, however, Garnier determined to make a tour through Euro-pean countries for the purpose of studying the theatre in all its aspects. After thoroughly investi-gating the Italian and German methods of theatre construction, he came to the conclusion that the so-called French type of auditorium was the one most adapted to modern requirements. His views on the subject, based on the results of this early research, have been em-bodied in a treatise entitled 'Le Théâtre.'

NATIONAL OPERA HOUSE, PARIS. GENERAL VIEW OF GRAND STAIRCASE.

The foundations of the new structure were begun as early as August 1861, an important fact to be borne in mind when we judge the general concep-tion of the Paris scheme; since it shows that very little time was allowed for maturing the general de-sign and laying out the principal lines, which no amount of attention sub-sequently given to detail could materially alter. In works of such a monumen-tal character it will be re-membered that quite a number of years frequently elapse between the com-petition and the commence-ment of the building.

From the very out-set of the operations it was perceived that, owing to the excessive depth of the foundations, nearly seventy feet, considerable difficulties would have to be encountered with the water, and for a whole year the work consisted almost solely in securing a solid bottom and adopting the necessary precautions to prevent the earth from shifting. From March to October, 1862, no less than eight large pumps were kept working day and night, until, at the end of this period, the site was sufficiently free from water to enable a start to be made. It was not until 1863 that the foundation-stone was laid. The ground covered is about 450,000 square metres in extent, and the quantities of materials for the building can be fairly well gauged by the dimensions of the walls shown in the plans and sections. In the year 1869 the enormous mass of brickwork and masonry was already sufficiently forward to receive the roof, but then the disturbances of the Franco-German War of 1870 and 1871 intervened and hindered further progress. The carcase was successively converted into a hospital and a military store, and during this latter period it is thought that part of the construction must have been strained through being subjected to the great weight of arms, etc. At the time of the investment of Paris, also, a semaphore station was erected and worked on the roof by the naval authorities, and a portion of the interior was used as a prison, while at a later date again the building was occupied by the Communists. Although, in the midst of these vicissitudes, the Opera was luckily saved from irreparable damage, a sum of 12,000l. was afterwards required to make good the injuries inflicted by the uses to which the house had been put.

Soon after Paris had recovered from these disturbances, building operations were again quietly commenced, and the completion of the building was promised by Garnier for 1876. The destruction of the old Opera by fire, however, made it necessary to push on with the work as rapidly as possible, and Garnier, by dint of great energy and application, succeeded in placing the fabric in the hands of the administration on January 5, 1875, the opening performance taking place that day.

So much has been written about the work of Charles Garnier, and the Opera House has been so excellently illustrated and described in his monumental volumes entitled 'Le Nouvel Opéra de Paris,' that it is difficult for me to add anything of much value to the literature of the subject. In the volumes referred to Garnier gives expression to his views on this building, and furnishes a defence of the points upon which he was attacked. There is one feature, however, which though characteristic of his work has not been generally recognised, namely, that Garnier designed with a very distinct purpose in mind, that every line in his sketches and drawings was based on a system, and what may appear eccentric or even ill-advised in the architectural rendering was in no case the outcome of an unthinking mood. We find in Garnier, in fact, an architect who most studiously examined the requirements of his client, and the public taste of the period for which he had to cater. He was no mere talented artist who, as is often the case, designs spontaneously but without method. The very fact of his tour of inspection immediately after obtaining the commission speaks forcibly on this point. Combined with his natural genius and his great facility with the pencil was a power of application and, further, a strict regard for business. It is this combination that has given him the position which he holds to-day. It may appear curious to have to state so simple a fact here, but general opinion, particularly in art circles, has been disinclined to accord to Garnier anything but great talent. He has always been regarded as an artist of genius, and rarely as an architect in the fullest sense of the term, who gave equal attention to the three aspects of architecture—the business, the scientific and the art sides. Anyone who has followed the history of the Paris Opera House closely will comprehend what infinite pains the architect expended upon the most trivial technical details, and what amount of thought was, for instance, given to

NATIONAL OPERA HOUSE, PARIS.
DETAIL OF ELEVATION.

stage machinery, a department too generally relegated to other hands than those of the designer. It may indeed be news to some that official documents show that Charles Garnier was actually considering the resignation of his commission should the Government, his client, compel him to use in the auditorium *strapontins*, a kind of seat which he deemed a dangerous obstruction in the gangways in the event of a panic.

We have heard much, on the one hand, of Garnier's grand conception of the Opera House, and, on the other, of the novelty of his architectural rendering. It will now be well to remind his admirers and opponents that the building was designed and executed not only in a most painstaking manner, but also under exceptional difficulties. These were not merely of a technical character, but arose from circumstances so frequently found on the Continent when great Government works are entrusted to outsiders, to the envy of the official architects or surveyors. Even political difficulties had to be encountered, for the archives contain letters, dated September 4, 1870, from two leading officials, ordering Garnier, from political motives, to remove certain imperial emblems from the façade, a demand to which he gave an unqualified refusal. The history of the National Opera House is in many respects unique, but especially, perhaps, is it a record of the firmness and independence of the architect.

NATIONAL OPERA HOUSE, PARIS. SIDE VIEW.

Speaking of the purposes for which the Opera House was designed, it must not be forgotten that the original intentions were to provide Paris with a home for its opera which should also be a national memorial of the position accorded to music during the *régime* of Napoleon III., while perpetuating, by means of an important structure, the architecture characteristic of the same reign. It was distinctly defined that, in size, in design, and in elaboration, the building should take the leading position in its class for some considerable time, and by it the prominence of the new Vienna Opera House, which had already been decided on in 1860, was to be overshadowed. Further, the Paris Opera House was to lend itself to such special national receptions as have from time to time been associated with it since its erection. It is scarcely too much even to say that it was the intention of those in authority to give to the world that which in its way would be an eighth wonder.

As to the manner in which the original purposes of 1860 were fulfilled, the building on its opening in 1875 showed that the architect had in every way grasped the desired idea, and though Paris was a very different city after the war, as regards its requirements and capacity for pleasure, from what it was in the sixties, there is no doubt that the building in every way embodied the sentiment of the time in which it was conceived, and was a brilliant memorial of the *régime* of the then reigning monarch.

NATIONAL OPERA HOUSE, PARIS. VIEW OF LOUNGE.

The site, on which so much depended for the carrying out of the idea, was not, perhaps, the most suitable that could be wished for, and I hold that Garnier had reason to complain, since he was thus materially hindered from giving his building the breadth necessary for a monument of this description. The block is decidedly hemmed in, and though a fine aspect is obtainable for the central feature of the principal elevation, much of the grandeur is lost by the close proximity of the surrounding buildings. If the whole frontage as shown in the geometrical elevation were unobstructed, the noble proportions of the building would be far better appreciated. The site, too, was not by any means a level one, and this materially affected the general dispositions of the plan.

As in the first volume, no lengthy description of the examples presented is attempted, and in each case I am limiting my remarks to some comments on features of particular importance. In the case of the Paris Opera House, it would in fact be worse than injudicious to try to fully explain the plans, for those especially interested will, as I have remarked, find in Garnier's own writings on this building an amount of information which it would be impossible to present, even in the briefest form, in a work of this description.

I have already touched on the requirements which governed the general conception of the block and would only add that the principle with which the plan is identified is the adoption of what I will term the "central" system with one grand staircase as distinct from Semper's so-called "radial" system with its two main stairs. The idea which has found embodiment is no doubt adapted from some of the older playhouses of the Continent, whilst the actual lines of the grand staircase show, as I have already explained, a development of those at the Bordeaux Theatre, of which an illustration is presented. The manner in which this particularly effective "central" arrangement has been obtained, in such a way as to allow an extensive vista in nearly every direction, is one of the greatest achievements ever accomplished in the planning of a public building, and the beauty of the scheme can, I think, be most appreciated when the structure is employed for some great official function, with a larger number of visitors on the stairs than is the case at an ordinary performance. If there is any fault in this fine production, it is, perhaps, the excessive amount of space accorded to this part of the building, for the individual is dwarfed, and appears quite lost in the large halls at his disposal. Here I would, however, suggest that the audience and its entertainment perhaps only had a subsidiary place in the general conception of the Opera House, for I contend that the grand staircase, with its surroundings, speaks far too forcibly of having been designed mainly with an eye to state functions, regardless of the comfort of the playgoer. As for the architectural rendering of the grand staircase, the lounge and its loggia, the almost barbaric splendour of the decorations and the richness of the colour-study are too well known to call for comment, and I would merely repeat that Garnier only too thoroughly understood the requirements of the nation at the time of his design, and if he erred in excessive lavishness, it was through a belief that the national taste for luxury in the early sixties would increase as the completion of the building drew near, whilst, as a matter of fact, the reverse was the case. As regards the general proportions I must say that the fault throughout is the accentuated height of every section, and in the case of the long and narrow lounge this is especially observable. Garnier seems to have delighted in stilted proportions, to the material detriment of some of his most interesting features.

Of the other passages and general offices in the "front of the house," with the endless lobbies, vestibules and saloons, I can only say that in their extent they have no precedent. It is only to be regretted that, where so much space was at the disposal of the architect, the requirements of 1860 did not include a liberal supply of staircases for the upper tiers, since the stairs of the Opera House are unsatisfactory in plan as well as in dimensions, and the separation of the different parts of the audience for purposes of entry and exit has been disregarded.

The principal feature of the auditorium is the manner in which the ceiling is supported by columns, to the disadvantage of the "sighting" in various parts of the house. The all too logical method of dealing with the ceiling has further compelled the architect to place that part of the audience which is situated on the uppermost tier in a "well," a particularly unsatisfactory makeshift for a building of this class. As to the "back of the house," the ballet-room specially calls for remark on account of its elaborate architectural treatment. The same roominess which characterises the "front of the house" is also found behind the curtain, for the offices and dressing-rooms with their passages are very ample, and the stage is simply immense. The equipment, however, throughout is, unfortunately, not in accord with the requirements of to-day, for the general installations at the time of opening did not comprise the latest achievements of science, nor have any important improvements been since introduced. As to the stage appliances, these will be described elsewhere.

Of the exterior, it may be said that the grouping on the whole is particularly satisfactory, with the exception only of the manner in which the cupola over the auditorium is joined to the block containing the stage. In judging the architectural rendering of the façades, I cannot but insist that the requirements which were made of the architect should be borne in mind. The Paris Opera House, it should always be remembered, is not essentially a playhouse. It is, primarily, to borrow the Continental expression already referred to, a "Palace of Art," in which the auditorium supplies indeed the official *raison d'être*, but is by no means the sole object of the erection. Garnier's design reveals this to the full; and were this not so—had he striven merely to present the idea of a theatre by his treatment—his conception of the elevations must have been pronounced a failure.

In conclusion, I would only remark that the total expenditure on the Paris Opera House is believed to have been nearly 1,500,000*l.*; nevertheless, this building is, perhaps, in a worse state of repair than any of the larger theatres which I have seen. Much in the equipment appears extremely defective, and the decorations require thorough renovation. There have even been fatal accidents on account of this condition of affairs. It would indeed seem a pity if so grand a monument were to practically fall into a state of ruin from lack of careful attention:

APPROXIMATE DIMENSIONS.

Width of Proscenium Opening at Curtain Line	52' 6"	16·00 m.
Height of Proscenium Opening at Curtain Line	45' 0"	13·75 m.

AUDITORIUM.

Curtain Line to Front of First Tier . .	83' 6"	25·50 m.
Curtain Line to Front of Third Tier . .	84' 6"	25·75 m.
Curtain Line to Furthest Seat . . .	101' 9"	31·00 m.
Sunlight Opening above Area . . .	67' 3"	20·50 m.
Highest Seat above Street	72' 3"	22·00 m.
Lowest Seat above Street	20' 6"	6·25 m.

STAGE.

Width inside Containing Walls . . .	173' 0"	52·75 m.
Curtain Line to Containing Back Wall .	86' 9"	26·50 m.
Curtain Line to Furthest Wall of Back Stage	156' 9"	47·75 m.
Gridiron Floor above Stage at Curtain Line	119' 0"	36·25 m.
Cellar Floor below Stage at Curtain Line .	46' 9"	14·25 m.
Stage Floor at Curtain Line above Street .	24' 6"	7·50 m.

NATIONAL OPERA HOUSE, PARIS. LOWER PART OF GRAND STAIRCASE.

NATIONAL OPÉRA COMIQUE, PARIS.

LOUIS BERNIER.

BLOCK PLAN.

THE lamentable loss of life on the occasion of the fire at the Opéra Comique, Paris, was one of those calamities which have, unfortunately, from time to time been associated with places of public amusement throughout the world. The particulars of the catastrophe will be found in the supplement to Volume III. of this work, dealing with Theatre Fires, and it need only be mentioned here that the conflagration took place on May 25, 1887, and that the number of those who succumbed to the fire exceeded one hundred. This establishment, it should at once be said, is one of the subsidised theatres of Paris, the structure being the property of the nation, while the lessees, who are responsible for the management, are appointed by the Government.

No less than ten years have elapsed since that conflagration, but owing to considerable delays Paris has not yet been able to open its new Opéra Comique. The building has, in fact, only been recently taken in hand, and it will not reach a state of completion until next year. By some curious lack of sentiment quite uncommon to Paris, the site of this house of gaiety—unsatisfactory as it is for a National institution, being in a narrow square of secondary importance—will be the same as that of its unfortunate predecessor. Several proposals for a new theatre had already been made soon after the fire, but none seemed to find favour, and when, in February, 1889, the Chamber of Deputies suggested an open competition for the design, their scheme was rejected by the Senate. The matter then remained in abeyance until 1892, when the Government apparently entered into some provisional agreement with a firm of contractors to erect a new playhouse from the plans of Dutret and Charpentier. But even this arrangement failed to gain acceptance from the Senate, for the latter body now chose to reverse its earlier decision, and recommended the competition scheme. Eventually, this method was resorted to, a sum of 1200*l.* being set aside for premiums, and the conditions for the competitors were framed on the basis of providing seating accommodation in the auditorium for 1500, while the total expenditure was limited to 140,000*l.* Unfortunately, however, the designs put before the assessors were most disappointing, the work being quite below the average, and no new features of any practical value being apparent. The award of the first premium to Louis Bernier, of Paris, in whose hands the commission was ultimately placed, cannot be termed popular.

It would be premature to speak of the details, the equipment or the execution of the new Opéra Comique at this date, when it is merely in carcase, but on reference to the plans taken from the architect's working drawings, and a view of the exterior furnished in the competition design, the general characteristics of the building will be sufficiently apparent. To my regret, however, I do not feel justified in saying anything in favour even of the general lines of this most recent example of French theatre construction. As I have indicated elsewhere, there has been little or no progress in France since the erection of the Paris Opera House, and Bernier's work shows, if anything, a retrograde movement. One would almost imagine on looking at the plan that the architect was unacquainted with the advance which has been made in other countries during the last few decades, and that he had overlooked the fact that his site had been the scene of a terrible fire. The isolation of staircases and the separation of the audience into sections, which are the most elementary features of a modern theatre plan, have been neglected, although the ground offered fair opportunities for skilful planning in this direction. As to the academic rendering of the exterior, its mediocre treatment can only be termed regrettable.

In the selection of the site, and in permitting this design to be carried out, the French Government has, for once, given us an exception to the good traditions which are usually connected with the architecture of its public buildings.

APPROXIMATE DIMENSIONS.

Width of Proscenium Opening at Curtain Line .	33' 9"	10·25 m.
Height of Proscenium Opening at Curtain Line .	42' 9"	13·00 m.

AUDITORIUM.

Curtain Line to Front of First Tier .	49' 3"	15·00 m.
Curtain Line to Front of Third Tier .	55' 9"	17·00 m.
Curtain Line to Furthest Seat .	73' 9"	22·50 m.
Ceiling Centre above Area .	57' 3"	17·50 m.
Highest Seat above Street .	68' 9'	21·00 m.
Lowest Seat above Street .	15' 6	4·75 m.

STAGE.

Width inside Containing Walls .	57' 6"	17·50 m.
Curtain Line to Containing Back Wall .	42' 9"	13·00 m.
Gridiron Floor above Stage at Curtain Line	73' 0"	22·25 m.
Cellar Floor below Stage at Curtain Line .	23' 0"	7·00 m.
Stage Floor at Curtain Line above Street .	18' 0"	5·50 m.

"EDEN" VARIETY THEATRE, PARIS.

W. KLEIN, A. DUCLOS.

THERE is no doubt that the "Eden" Variety Theatre at Paris was the most important building that has ever been devoted to a form of entertainment comprising, primarily, great spectacular ballets, and in the second place the many kinds of performances more particularly associated with the music-hall of old. Unfortunately, the enterprise of the promoters, whose plans were highly ambitious, was attended with failure, and the structure after only having been in use for a few years had to be demolished. At the present time, an hotel is being erected on the site which it occupied.

Though the building is no longer in existence, I considered that this institution should rightly be included in my work on account of its conception, its plan, and its architectural rendering, and because many of its technical details have considerably influenced the design of other buildings erected for somewhat similar purposes. The "Eden" Theatre at Paris marked the commencement of a new epoch in the history of Variety establishments, and its characteristic features found considerable favour in other countries, leading to various adaptations and imitations on a smaller and less lavish scale. To the influence of this Paris theatre is due much that is found in the "Linden" Variety Theatre at Berlin, illustrated in my first volume, and its sister establishments at Vienna and Buda-Pesth, as well as much which we now see at our own "Empire" and "Alhambra" Variety Theatres, also presented in this work. It is, indeed, a matter for regret that so important an example, in the history of theatre construction, as the "Eden" Theatre, has had such a brief existence, though I trust that its inclusion among my illustrations will help to prevent its lines from being altogether forgotten.

The task entrusted to the architects of this building was to construct a house suitable for small variety shows as well as for most elaborate spectacular performances. Moreover, all such facilities as promenades, smoking-rooms, bars, etc., had to be provided. At the time of its erection no variety theatre of any architectural pretensions existed elsewhere.

The conception of W. Klein and the late A. Duclos was undoubtedly novel, and their design showed a breadth which was in every respect praiseworthy, especially as the ground, though having a frontage on an important thoroughfare, possessed none of the advantages of a detached site, and was to a certain degree irregular. The architects commenced operations in January, 1881, and completed their task in January 1883, the total cost of the block amounting to 220,000*l.* The structure may be said to have consisted of an iron skeleton clothed in cement and plaster, and as such was a pioneer in this special form of construction, in fact the only portions built of masonry and brickwork were the containing walls and the principal façade, the latter being in Scotch granite. The style which prevailed in the rendering may be termed Indian, but though the details were very carefully worked out, the effect was rather heavy. The colour study was excellent, and the workmanship much above the average.

"EDEN" VARIETY THEATRE, PARIS. GENERAL VIEW.

Among the main features of the "Eden" Theatre, the arrangement of the vestibule and the staircase calls for particular notice; and attention should also be paid to the manner in which the promenades, lounges, and refreshment rooms were planned. The only fault in connection with the lounges is that the performance could not be viewed from them, and it seems curious that no staircase accommodation beyond the principal flights should have been provided from the first tier, especially when it is remembered that the work here was carried out shortly after the theatre fires at Vienna and Nice. The seating capacity of the house included about 350 places in the area, and 450 places on the first tier, and, as may be seen from the plans, there were numerous boxes. In an establishment of this description the actual number of seats available or occupied is small when compared with the number of the audience as a whole, since those using the standing room, together with the visitors to the parts of the house other than the area and first tier, form a large proportion of the total. The back part of the house included accommodation for a staff of six hundred.

Taken generally, the "Eden" Variety Theatre is certainly the most interesting example of theatre construction executed in France since the completion of the Paris Opera House. In the first place, the building was a pioneer for a certain "type" of playhouse, and in the second, a forerunner in so-called skeleton construction. In many respects it showed a marked advance, and afforded the one instance during the last decades where two French architects have been able to prove themselves alive to the evolution of modern requirements in theatres. I am sorry that I cannot say this of any other French architect engaged in theatre work. It is not that there has been a lack of opportunity, since the preceding example of the Paris Opéra Comique is only too plainly an instance where a talented and studious architect might have distinguished himself. I am afraid that the splendours of Garnier's Opera House have prevented his French confrères from going outside their own country for examples of modern theatre construction. At the most the playhouse of Italy may have been visited by some of them, and, as will be illustrated, that country affords, as far as recent theatre architecture is concerned, but little deserving of study, except, perhaps, in a negative sense. Probably, however, when a change is made, and Charles Garnier's notable journey on receiving his commission is imitated, the home of the French drama will again make rapid progress, and French architects will produce work equal to, if not better, than that of their contemporaries in other countries. In conclusion, I would remark that the "Eden" Theatre has shown to what extent the abode of the Variety Entertainment may be elevated by an enterprising management, assisted by thoughtful and talented experts.

APPROXIMATE DIMENSIONS.

| Width of Proscenium Opening at Curtain Line . | . . . . . . 37' 9" | 11·50 m. |
| Height of Proscenium Opening at Curtain Line . | . . . . . . 37' 9" | 11·50 m. |

AUDITORIUM.			*STAGE.*		
Curtain Line to Front of First Tier . .	65' 6"	20·00 m.	Width inside Containing Walls . . .	101' 9"	31·00 m.
Curtain Line to Furthest Seat . . .	78' 9"	24·00 m.	Curtain Line to Containing Back Wall .	78' 9"	24·00 m.
Sunlight Opening above Area . . .	64' 9"	19·75 m.	Gridiron Floor above Stage at Curtain Line	67' 3"	20·50 m.
Highest Seat above Street	18' 9"	5·75 m.	Cellar Floor below Stage at Curtain Line .	18' 0"	5·50 m.
Lowest Seat above Street	2' 6"	0·75 m.	Stage Floor at Curtain Line above Street .	1' 6"	0·50 m.

CASINO THEATRE, MONTE CARLO. General View.

MONACO.

CASINO THEATRE, MONTE CARLO.

CHARLES GARNIER.

IT was a matter of some difficulty to decide whether or not the Casino Theatre at Monte Carlo should be included among these examples, since though the building was primarily intended to fulfil the purposes of a small playhouse in connection with the great gambling establishment of the Riviera, the object of its construction was also to afford suitable accommodation for concerts and the lesser forms of entertainment customary at a fashionable

BLOCK PLAN. winter resort. It appeared to me doubtful whether the Monte Carlo Theatre should not be rather classified among the minor private establishments, such as the Theatre at Craig-y-nos, the Castle Theatre at Totis, and similar structures, to be dealt with in the third volume. But, taking into consideration the fact that the performances are essentially of a public character, and that plan and execution alike speak forcibly of the designer's intention of making this hall primarily the home of the opera and the drama, rather than a concert or assembly room, I concluded that it might not inappropriately be placed among the few examples which I have thought advisable to present in this volume, as illustrating work subject to the influence of Latin countries. Though small, the Monte Carlo Theatre, to my mind, holds a prominent position in modern theatre architecture, owing to the clever fulfilment of the unusual requirements of a miniature play-house, and to an architectural treatment which is thoroughly adapted to its purpose as well as being of considerable merit.

The mere mention of the fact that Charles Garnier is the architect of this building, and that it was erected by him whilst still under the inspiration of his great work, the Paris Opera House, will go far to explain to what an extent the sentiment of the theatre pervades the Casino hall, and how all other purposes for which this auditorium was erected are made subservient to its main object. Garnier's individuality in theatre design is strongly evident throughout the plans, the façade, and the interior decorations, as it is in nearly all his public work. No doubt everything is on a miniature scale, but Garnier's characteristics are as conspicuous here as in the National Opera House at

CASINO THEATRE, MONTE CARLO. VIEW OF AUDITORIUM.

Paris, and are particularly noticeable in the colour study and in the detail of the auditorium; the difference, if any, lying only in the direction of a greater refinement in the mouldings. To this improvement in detail is due the fact that many architects prefer Garnier's work as shown at Monte Carlo to that in his greater undertaking.

As regards situation, the Monte Carlo Theatre certainly has a unique position, for it is placed high up on the Casino grounds overlooking the Mediterranean. As viewed from the sea it thus partly screens the halls of the gambling establishment proper, while serving to mark the position of the whole institution in the landscape. The floor of the auditorium is practically on the same level as that of the gaming saloons, and can, in fact, be used in conjunction with the main establishment, there being the necessary communication from the central hall of the Casino either to the lobby of the theatre or direct to its area. The plan, however, admits of the building being used quite separately, since it has its own main entrance and vestibule, with independent staircases to the small balconies which serve as a first tier.

Very great care is visible in the manner in which the planning is adapted to the limited space the architect had at his disposal; and it is noticeable that the stage, with its various offices, is thoroughly well equipped.

As regards the architectural rendering, this will be sufficiently explained by the illustrations, but attention should be directed to the fact that the walls of the stage exhibit a treatment almost identical with that of the auditorium proper; while the green-room also shows considerable elaboration. The effect of the colour study, largely dependent on the use of gold, bronze, yellow ochre and red, though exceedingly rich, is fully in keeping with the objects of the institution and the purposes for which it is frequented. I have before had occasion to remark that the requirements of the audience in the matter of architectural treatment should not be overlooked, and I have indicated how a system of decoration in Rococo style would be inconsistent for a theatre in a small provincial town. In a locality frequented by all nations, alike by visitors on pleasure bent, and by habitués of the gambling saloons, desiring some form of distraction, this luxurious and highly decorated piece of work is not only very appropriate but particularly agreeable, and the architect is to be congratulated on the manner in which he has understood the interests of his client and the taste of the people for whom the building is intended.

Of course, it would be quite correct to speak of the Principality of Monaco being represented by a playhouse of peculiar interest, for the Casino Theatre stands in that small state, and the work which Charles Garnier executed at Monte Carlo can no more be included among the buildings of France than the theatres of Fellner and Helmer at Berlin, Odessa and Zürich can be classed among the structures of Austria. Nevertheless, the individuality of the architect, and the influence of a French management, are much more palpable in the Monte Carlo example than the individuality of the Viennese architects and Austrian influence are observable in, say, the Municipal Theatre of Odessa. The Casino Theatre is essentially a French production, and it will be generally regarded as such, no matter what the geographical or technical distinctions may be.

APPROXIMATE DIMENSIONS.

Width of Proscenium Opening at Curtain Line	. . . . .	39' 3"	12·00 m.
Height of Proscenium Opening at Curtain Line	. . . . .	31' 3"	9·50 m.

AUDITORIUM.				*STAGE.*			
Curtain Line to Front of First Tier	.	64' 0"	19·50 m.	Width inside Containing Walls	. . .	44' 0"	13·50 m.
Curtain Line to Furthest Seat	. .	78' 9"	24·50 m.	Curtain Line to Containing Back Wall	.	26' 3"	8·00 m.
Sunlight Opening above Area	. .	62' 3"	19·00 m.	Cellar Floor below Stage at Curtain Line	.	17' 3"	5·25 m.
Highest Seat above Street	. .	33' 6"	10·25 m.	Stage Floor at Curtain Line above Terrace	12' 0"	3·75 m.
Lowest Seat above Street	. .	9' 9"	3·00 m.				

CASINO THEATRE, MONTE CARLO. VIEW OF CASINO ENTRANCE.

ITALY.

MUNICIPAL THEATRE, PALERMO.

G. B. FILIPPO BASILE, ERNESTO BASILE.

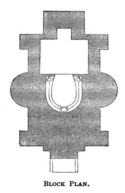

BLOCK PLAN.

DURING the period under consideration in these volumes, few theatres of any importance have been erected in Italy, and in those establishments which have been opened little or no progress has been visible, either in the general planning or in the equipment of the building. As a matter of fact, the ignorance usually displayed in the fulfilment of even the most elementary requirements (as, for example, the safety of the audience) has been remarkable. A visit to many of the modern Italian playhouses is extremely disheartening, for a structure of recent date usually reveals, if anything, a retrogressive tendency, whilst in no instance have I been able to discover the slightest sign of any advance. In the early part of this century—an important epoch in theatre construction in Italy—the designs, though not in accordance with the requirements of to-day, were at least impressive, owing to a certain breadth of treatment, and one seldom discovered examples of theatre-architecture actually displeasing to the eye. To-day, however, we do not even meet with such redeeming features as characterised the old Italian theatre. With few exceptions, everything pertaining to the modern playhouse in Italy is far from satisfactory.

It is not my purpose here to examine the causes of this deterioration, since such a discussion would lead too far, and I merely record the unfortunate fact. As a rule, however, it is not so much the Italian architect who is responsible for this lamentable condition of the playhouse in his country, as the speculative builders, in whose hands are placed the commissions to design and erect theatres for a stipulated payment, and who dispense with the services of an expert. These "master-builders," as they are popularly called in Italy, have as little idea of either architectural design or modern theatre construction as they are notoriously conversant with all the most contemptible forms of "jerry-building."

To my mind, the only exception to the general inefficiency of the modern Italian playhouse is to be found at Palermo, where a Municipal Theatre has been erected which in many respects ranks among the most important examples of Europe. In size this building comes next to the great Opera Houses at Paris and Vienna. It is true that it cannot in any way be classed with such a modern building as the "Hofburg" Theatre in respect to the manner in which it fulfils the later day requirements of plan and equipment. This is chiefly due to the circumstances of its erection, for the design dates back as far as 1865, though the inauguration of the building was only witnessed last year. But, taken as a whole, this theatre is a remarkable piece of architecture, and stands

MUNICIPAL THEATRE, PALERMO. VIEW OF CENTRAL FEATURE.

as a monument to the energy and enterprise of the Sicilians, headed by their leading architect, the late Filippo Basile.

In 1864 the Municipality of Palermo resolved to erect a monumental playhouse. A competition was opened for the design of a building on a grand scale, the sum of 4500*l.* being set aside for premiums. The finest site in Palermo, near the Porta Macqueda, was chosen for the block, and great enthusiasm prevailed throughout Sicily, the proposed structure being regarded as a kind of National Monument. A jury, presided over by Gottfried Semper, selected the design of Filippo Basile, of Palermo, who was entrusted with the execution of the work. Building operations were, however, not commenced until January, 1875, and then frequent interruptions occurred owing to lack of funds, while between 1882 to 1889 little or nothing was accomplished. In 1890, however, the works were again seriously taken up, but in 1891, soon after their resumption, Basile died. The completion of the undertaking was then placed in the hands of his son, Ernesto Basile, who, after further delays, placed the building at the disposal of the authorities in 1896.

In size, as I have said, this example ranks next to the Opera Houses of Paris and Vienna, whilst the seating accommodation is for an audience of 3200, and the total outlay on the structure has almost reached 270,000*l*. The plan of the auditorium is typically Italian. The area has the usual small number of stalls, and an exceedingly large pit, the main approach to the latter being through a spacious central lobby. There are no less than five tiers of boxes arranged on the so-called "pigeon-hole" system, and above these is a small gallery. The ceiling is almost flat, whilst the "fall" of the area floor is reduced to a minimum. A State Box, it will be observed, has been provided over the entrance to the pit. The grand vestibule and also the main lobbies are on the same level as the area, whilst the level of the principal lounge and the various saloons is that of the State Box. Accommodation for a club which enjoys certain privileges had to be provided on one side of the building, and some large boxes are reserved for its members. The general arrangement of the block, however, as I have indicated, is scarcely in keeping with modern requirements, and this fact is very noticeable in the unsatisfactory planning of the staircases. The severe style of architecture adopted is impressive, but, if anything, too sombre in a building for public entertainment. The principal feature of the façade is its main entrance, which, with its flight of steps and the grand portico, is most imposing, while the excellent effect of the masonry should also be commented on. The method of joining the cupola to the block containing the stage, is, however, a weak point in the grouping. In conclusion, I would particularly emphasise that the Palermo Theatre must be judged with reference to the date of the design, and not to that of its completion.

APPROXIMATE DIMENSIONS.

Width of Proscenium Opening at Curtain Line	43' 6"	13·25 m.
Height of Proscenium Opening at Curtain Line	48' 3"	14·75 m.

AUDITORIUM.			*STAGE.*		
Curtain Line to Front of State Box . .	86' 9"	26·50 m.	Width inside Containing Walls . . .	119' 6"	36·50 m.
Curtain Line to Front of Third Tier .	86' 9"	26·50 m.	Curtain Line to Containing Back Wall .	91' 3"	27·75 m.
Curtain Line to Furthest Seat . .	98' 6"	30·00 m.	Curtain Line to Furthest Wall of Back Stage	119' 6"	36·50 m.
Ceiling Centre above Area . . .	64' 6"	19·75 m.	Gridiron Floor above Stage at Curtain Line	106' 0"	32·25 m.
Highest Seat above Street . . .	70' 6"	21·50 m.	Cellar Floor below Stage at Curtain Line .	37' 0"	11·25 m.
Lowest Seat above Street . . .	14' 9"	4·50 m.	Stage Floor at Curtain Line above Street .	20' 6"	6·25 m.

MUNICIPAL THEATRE, PALERMO. General View.

"LIRICO" THEATRE, MILAN.

ACHILLE SFONDRINI.

BLOCK PLAN.

THE "Teatro Lirico Internazionale" of Milan, which was opened in 1894, takes the place of the old Canobiana Theatre, and its erection is due to the initiative of Edoardo Sonzogno, who, being a man of considerable wealth and much interested in theatrical matters, provided the necessary funds. It has been difficult to ascertain whether this playhouse is intended to fulfil the purposes of commercial enterprise, or whether it should be regarded, to a certain extent, in the light of an institution for providing entertainment at popular prices, in which any deficit is made up by the owner in the interests of his hobby. I am inclined to think that the latter idea predominated at the time of its erection. At all events, the work was taken in hand under the sole direction of Edoardo Sonzogno; his requirements were embodied in the building, and he has since managed the establishment regardless of conventional business methods. No architect, however, was employed to design the theatre, the commission for the execution of the block being entrusted to a "master-builder," whose terms included the preparation of the design; and what I have already indicated regarding the execution of work on such lines practically holds good here.

The "master-builder" in this case was named Achille Sfondrini, a specialist who travels from town to town erecting theatres and other places of public entertainment. He is certainly quite an extraordinary character, and one cannot but be struck, on the one hand, by his remarkable ability in directing his men and managing his work, and, on the other, by his ignorance of the most elementary principles of design and the necessities of modern theatre construction. In the instance of his Milan theatre, I understand that a surveyor of some experience assisted in setting out the main lines, and also provided some sketches for the façades and interior decorations; but, otherwise, the block was practically carried out without any plan, as has been the case with Sfondrini's other buildings. To construct a playhouse of this size under consider-

"LIRICO" THEATRE, MILAN. GENERAL VIEW.

able difficulties, without any of the facilities afforded by draughtsmanship, and without even the knowledge afforded by ordinary school education or elementary technical instruction, is no mean achievement in the annals of this age of progress.

I have selected this particular example because I consider it to be one of the best of its class, and because the auditorium shows several features, especially in the arrangement of the tiers and the ceiling, which are not usually found in Italian theatres. In other respects the requirements of former generations have apparently been carefully fulfilled without much consideration for the necessities of the present age. The planning of the staircases, in particular, calls for comment owing to the entire disregard of the safety of the audience; and it is surprising that in a city like Milan such arrangements should be permitted in a new playhouse. When examining the plans, it should be noted that some of the walls of the previous building had to be utilised. The treatment of the façades, which are in plaster, is above the average for work of this description.

APPROXIMATE DIMENSIONS.

Width of Proscenium Opening at Curtain Line	41' 0"	12·50 m.
Height of Proscenium Opening at Curtain Line	30' 6"	9·25 m.

AUDITORIUM.

Curtain Line to Front of First Tier	67' 3"	20·50 m.
Curtain Line to Front of Third Tier	71' 3"	21·75 m.
Curtain Line to Furthest Seat	83' 9"	25·50 m.
Sunlight Opening above Area	79' 6"	24·25 m.
Highest Seat above Street	46' 9"	14·25 m.
Lowest Seat below Street	2' 6"	0·75 m.

STAGE.

Width inside Containing Walls	65' 6"	20·00 m.
Curtain Line to Containing Back Wall	72' 3"	22·00 m.
Gridiron Floor above Stage at Curtain Line	60' 6"	18·50 m.
Cellar Floor below Stage at Curtain Line	11' 6"	3·50 m.
Stage Floor at Curtain Line above Street	5' 9"	1·75 m.

PEOPLE'S THEATRE, TURIN.

CAMILLO RICCIO.

BLOCK PLAN.

IT has been necessary to call attention to the unfortunate lack of progress shown in the architecture of modern playhouses of Italy, and my remarks will have indicated why this country should be so poorly represented in these volumes. The examples in this section only include three Italian theatres, for, as I must again emphasise, the great epoch in Italian theatre construction belongs to a much earlier part of the century than that with which this work deals. The buildings of the last few decades call for but little comment. The most important structure of the modern era which I have selected is that of the Municipal Theatre at Palermo, designed by one of the leading architects of Italy. The "Lirico" Theatre, on the preceding page, affords one of the best instances of a comparatively large block designed and executed by a "master-builder." I will now add a building at Turin, designed and executed by an architect in private practice, which, though small compared with the two preceding theatres, exhibits by far the best plan among recent Italian playhouses, and fulfils present day requirements to a greater extent than is the case elsewhere in Italy. This theatre even has a certain individuality in its rendering which is interesting and instructive, while the workmanship shown is better than that customarily found in theatres of this country.

The People's Theatre at Turin is an institution where plays are rendered at popular prices, but otherwise it has nothing in common with the *bonâ fide* People's Theatre, such as we find at Worms. The plan shows how, on an irregular site, the superficial area available has been utilised to the utmost advantage without in any way interfering with the clearness of the arrangements or the facilities of exit. It is true that the auditorium has only one tier, and the difficulties which frequently attend the provision of staircase accommodation are thus lessened, but, as will have been observed, one-tier houses, even when standing on their own ground, only too frequently show little regard for the most elementary rules governing the safety of the audience.

The principal features of the structure are the breadth of the auditorium, the presence of only one tier, the architectural treatment of the proscenium, and the section of the ceiling with its lantern light. It is also worthy of notice that there are six broad exits from the pit, three of which lead directly into the open and three into lobbies, and the stalls have two exits. The first tier has two staircases, one on each side of the block, as well as "emergency" balconies. The exterior, it is true, scarcely gives the impression of masking a playhouse, although, in an unostentatious manner, it fulfils the purpose of indicating the public character of the building. Camillo Riccio is the name of the architect who held the commission, and if all modern theatres of Italy had been planned with as much forethought as that at Turin, there would be little reason to raise any complaints against them as a whole.

APPROXIMATE DIMENSIONS.

Width of Proscenium Opening at Curtain Line	32' 9"	10·00 m.
Height of Proscenium Opening at Curtain Line	25' 6"	7·75 m.

AUDITORIUM.			*STAGE.*		
Curtain Line to Front of First Tier . .	55' 9"	17·00 m.	Width inside Containing Walls . . .	50' 9"	15·50 m.
Curtain Line to Furthest Seat . . .	68' 9"	21·00 m.	Curtain Line to Containing Back Wall .	27' 9"	8·50 m.
Sunlight Opening above Area . . .	49' 3"	15·00 m.	Gridiron Floor above Stage at Curtain Line	42' 6"	13·00 m.
Highest Seat above Street . . .	17' 0"	5·25 m.	Cellar Floor below Stage at Curtain Line .	13' 0"	4·00 m.
Lowest Seat below Street . . .	1' 6"	0·50 m.	Stage Floor at Curtain Line below Street .	4' 0"	1·25 m.

SPAIN.

MUNICIPAL THEATRE, BILBAO.

JOAQUIN RUCOBA.

BLOCK PLAN.

IN my Introduction, I indicated that various purposes have to be fulfilled by theatres erected in countries subject to Latin influences, and I mentioned how, in Italy, for instance, the playhouse is regarded as a *rendezvous* in the first place, and as a theatre only in the second. I also pointed out the distinguishing features of the Spanish Theatre in regard to its entertainment. The general public in Spain favours the custom of attending one or two of the several performances given nightly at private theatres at intervals of an hour, each play occupying only about forty minutes, for which separate tickets are sold. The Spaniards treat their theatres in a similar fashion to that in which our music halls and variety theatres are used—that is to say, they avoid the restraint of a seat booked for a play which absorbs the whole evening. It is only at two or three of the older theatres that the opera or drama is presented in the same way as it is in this country, and even in these isolated instances, the Italian method of using the playhouse as a social centre, particularly on the part of the governing classes, is greatly in vogue. The performances which attain to the greatest popularity in the last named institutions are those of a light character, such as operettas or comedies which do no more than amuse ; for the Spaniard, unlike the German, attends his theatre not so much as a matter of education as merely from a desire to be entertained.

To my knowledge, there are only two first-class playhouses at Madrid—the Teatro Real and the Teatro Español—both of which are owned by the Municipality. The former is used for opera, and the latter for drama. Though a municipal institution, the Teatro Real is annually leased to an impresario, who makes the highest bid for the privilege of running an opera season ; whilst the Teatro Español, which is associated more with the classic drama, is in the hands of a manager, who receives a subsidy from the Government in order to cover the deficiency arising from the production of a species of play which, as a rule, is particularly unfavourably received.

The other theatres in Madrid, and for the most part those in the provinces, are institutions run solely on commercial lines, which cater for an ever-increasing taste for the lighter forms of amusement. The buildings are generally erected by syndicates, and, as a rule, a well-known architect is employed to prepare the design. This was the case with the Bilbao Theatre, now under consideration, which, although denominated—and to a certain extent

MUNICIPAL THEATRE, BILBAO. GENERAL VIEW.

rightly—a " municipal " playhouse, fulfils that function to about the same extent as do the so-called " Stadt " theatres of Germany mentioned in the Introduction to the preceding volume. The municipality has supported the enterprise only to the extent of providing a site, which is granted under certain conditions, not unlike those which governed the erection of the theatre at Amsterdam, and including one by which the building becomes the property of the ratepayers on the expiration of the term of ninety-two years.   As a matter of fact, the management is a limited liability company, and the commission was given by its direction to the city architect, Joaquin Rucoba.

With regard to the size of the building, the auditorium has been planned to accommodate an audience of 1600 persons, whilst the superficial area covered by the building is 1675 square metres.   Its total cost, including furniture and a stock of scenery, amounted to over 40,000*l.*, and the time occupied in its construction extended from July, 1886, to May, 1890, the inaugural ceremony taking place on the last day of that month.   Though the theatre stands on an isolated site, it is a matter for regret that a considerable portion of the ground-floor level has been devoted to shop premises and to restaurant accommodation.

On examining the plan it will be seen that there is in the arrangement of this theatre much similarity to that of the Théâtre de la Renaissance at Paris, and, unfortunately, the defects of that structure have been reproduced in the present example.   In the first place, the area level of the building is on the second floor, and the lowest seat of the auditorium is as much as twenty-six feet above the street.   Owing to the arrangement of the shops and restaurant, the facilities for ascent and descent are most unsatisfactory, three out of the four staircases being even curvilinear in plan.   There are, moreover, but four staircases for the joint use of the area and the four tiers, which prevents the necessary isolation of the different sections of the audience.   It is curious that the authorities at Bilbao should have permitted such dangerous planning, more especially in view of the serious fire by which the theatre at Oporto was destroyed in the month of March, 1888, when over 170 people were killed—an incident occurring whilst building operations were in progress.

The principal characteristic of the structure is, if I may say so, the aforesaid position of the auditorium at so high a level above the street, and I would also call attention to the manner in which the superficial area available has been utilised for an auditorium of such considerable breadth.   The outline of the latter is distinctly observable in the front elevation, a clever piece of designing on this irregular site.   The central feature of the principal façade, curvilinear in plan, flanked first by two turrets containing staircases, and again by two wings of less height than the main block marking the position of the lounges, is a conception that would do credit to any architect.   Joaquin Rucoba must be congratulated on the very pleasing effect produced by the grouping of the block.   Unfortunately, however, the details of his mouldings are not up to the same standard.   With regard to the division of the auditorium, it will be observed that there are two tiers of partly open boxes, and two tiers of galleries, the uppermost seats of which are almost on ceiling level.   On either side of the auditorium the lounges just referred to have been placed, and a very effective appearance has been obtained by allowing these halls to cut through two tiers, and by so constructing small galleries as to overlook them.   The corridors are of ample width, and I notice that two lifts have been provided to assist the visitors in reaching their seats.

So far as theatre construction in Spain is concerned, little progress has been made during recent years, although it is curious to observe in the case of the Bilbao Theatre that, while the general arrangement of the staircases and the position of the auditorium are so unsatisfactory, the treatment of the façade has been executed in a manner which not only shows great skill, but is also quite in accordance with the most recent ideas of designing with a set purpose.   In closing, I would say that, in spite of the absence of any new features in this example, I consider it to be the only one of interest among Spanish theatres of the modern epoch.

APPROXIMATE DIMENSIONS.

Width of Proscenium Opening at Curtain Line .	.	.	.	.	.	52' 6"	16·00 m.
Height of Proscenium Opening at Curtain Line .	.	.	.	.	37' 9"	11·50 m.

AUDITORIUM.			*STAGE.*		
Curtain Line to Front of First Tier .	.	55' 9"	17·00 m.	Width inside Containing Walls .	.	.	78' 9"	24·00 m.
Curtain Line to Front of Third Tier .	.	55' 9"	17·00 m.	Curtain Line to Containing Back Wall	.	55' 9"	17·00 m.
Curtain Line to Furthest Seat .	.	74' 9"	22·75 m.	Curtain Line to Furthest Wall of Back Stage	79' 6"	24·25 m.
Sunlight Opening above Area	.	.	49' 3"	15·00 m.	Gridiron Floor above Stage at Curtain Line	62' 3"	19·00 m.
Highest Seat above Street .	.	.	75' 6"	23·00 m.	Cellar Floor below Stage at Curtain Line .	27' 9"	8·50 m.
Lowest Seat above Street .	.	.	26' 3"	8·00 m.	Stage Floor at Curtain Line above Street .	29' 6"	9·00 m.

COURT OPERA HOUSE, VIENNA. General View.

PART II.

AUSTRIA AND HUNGARY.

COURT OPERA HOUSE, VIENNA.

VAN DER NÜLL, SICCARDSBURG.

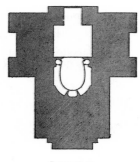

Block Plan.

One of the results of the proclamation of the Emperor of Austria, in 1858, directing that the fortifications of Vienna should be destroyed and large boulevards established in their place, was the growth of a brilliant school of architects whose works have made Vienna a formidable rival to Paris. It is seldom that such an exceptional opportunity as the development of a city occurs for the display of talent, and the Ringstrasse, with its stately buildings, testifies to the wisdom which has distinguished the Viennese in taking full advantage of the occasion. Among the first buildings to be designed and completed was the great Court Opera House at Vienna, now before us. This block, which ranks in size next to the Paris Opera House, may, perhaps, be said to belong to the same epoch that saw the creation of the latter and also that of the Municipal Theatre at Palermo, since the original designs for these buildings were all prepared at approximately the same time, i.e. early in the sixties. Of these three examples it occupies the second place, and though, as I have already declared, I consider the "Hofburg" Theatre, presented in Volume I., to be of greater architectural importance than either of the others, there is much in the Vienna Opera House which gives it a most prominent position among recent playhouses, and its technical equipment more particularly makes it a pioneer in certain directions.

It was originally intended that the new Court Opera House should occupy the square in front of the old Kärtner Gate, but as the general grouping of the new buildings was evolved, the present site, which is far more spacious and appropriate, was allotted to this purpose. A competition for the design was opened in 1860, and resulted in the commission being entrusted to Van der Nüll and Siccardsburg, architects who had been prominently associated with the scheme for laying out the Ringstrasse. The necessary alteration of their competition plans, consequent upon the change of site just referred to, however, prevented building operations from being commenced before the beginning of 1862. Owing to the illness of Siccardsburg in 1867, the supervision of the work was temporarily relegated to G. Gugitz, who, after the decease of the former, and the subsequent death of Van der Nüll, was permanently appointed in their place, with J. Stork as his collaborator in the decorative work. But it would be an injustice to the original authors not to state most emphatically that the conception of the Opera House, even to the veriest detail, was practically completed before their decease, and that the chief work devolving upon their successors consisted in attending to the execution of the plans.

The ceremony of laying the foundation stone only took place in 1863, some fifteen months after the commencement of the work, and the first performance was given in May 1869. The total cost of the building amounted to about 500,000*l.*, and while the actual seating accommodation is limited to seventeen hundred and twenty, the total number of persons for whom space can be provided, if the standing room is fully utilised, is two thousand eight hundred and eighty.

As regards the purposes of the building, there is little doubt that, although no inclination was shown towards that ostentation which characterised the Paris Opera House, conceived during the *régime* of Napoleon III., still the Emperor of Austria intended to make the block a monument worthy of the position occupied by operatic art in Vienna at the time, besides serving as a suitable place for receptions or special entertainments arranged for his Court. The administration of the institution is identical with that of the "Hofburg" Theatre, as its management falls under the same department—that of the Lord Chamberlain. There was no intention of making the building a National Monument in the sense in which the Paris Opera House is regarded, for, as in the case of the "Hofburg" Theatre, its purpose is essentially that of a Court playhouse, where the head of the State passes a considerable part of his leisure, and also entertains his guests on different occasions. The Vienna Opera House, as I have said, was one of the first buildings to appear during the great evolution of the main boulevards of Vienna; hence it is not surprising to learn that the architects of this building had far greater financial difficulties to contend with, especially with regard to the outlay on the architectural rendering, than was

COURT OPERA HOUSE, VIENNA.   View of Central Feature.

the case at a later period, when one monumental building after another had arisen at Vienna in a kind of friendly rivalry. One might almost say that the principal difficulty which the architects had to face was a somewhat niggardly spirit on the part of those who controlled the exchequer, and much that cannot be understood at first sight in a building conceived on such broad lines must be attributed to this parsimony.

As in the case of the "Hofburg" Theatre, I regret to say that this building has been the subject of a considerable amount of criticism and controversy, which, however, has fortunately been outlived, and both design and execution are now deservedly accorded general approbation. What is, perhaps, the most

pleasing feature considering the date of erection, and at the same time an idea which has since been most favoured in the development of Continental theatre construction, is the very distinct manner in which the various parts of the block are grouped round the main body containing the auditorium and the stage. It is only to be regretted that the architects did not see their way to go a step further at the time and make a greater distinction between that part of the structure which holds the audience, and that which is used for the presentation of the drama. Nevertheless, the individuality shown in the grouping is of considerable merit, and, undoubtedly, the façades plainly mark the different divisions of the structure. Next to the general arrangement of the building, a feature of considerable interest is the large amount of space devoted to storage purposes and to the various offices of the stage.

Taken as a whole, the Vienna Opera House is an example of the application of the so-called "central" system of planning, which was likewise adopted for the Paris Opera House, for here again we find the arrangement of the grand central staircase distinct from the two main staircases, so characteristic of Gottfried Semper's designs. It will, however, be at once observed that, in this instance, the central staircase is not given the same significance as at the Paris Opera House, for, with the different foyers, saloons and lobbies, it takes an essentially subsidiary position in relation to the auditorium. The latter, together with the stage, unmistakeably occupies the principal place in the building, and even the portions reserved for the Court are of less prominence in their architectural treatment than the auditorium proper. If I may say so, the building embodies the practical qualities, the dignity and unassuming demeanour for which its Imperial owner is noted, without, however, in any way being too sombre for its purpose. In the same manner as the Opera House at Paris is representative of a special period, so in every way the Vienna example reflects the characteristics of the Imperial Court to which it belongs.

On examining the plans in detail there is little that calls for comment, except perhaps that in so important a building, where space had to be so little considered, there is a marked lack of staircase accommodation. This, however, is easily explained when we remember that the structure was opened in 1868, before much thought was given to the subject of the safety of the public. A feature demanding attention is, perhaps, the great open Loggia in front of the principal public lounge, to which an unusual amount of space has been given. The situation of the ante-room to the State Box, only to be reached by crossing a passage, which rightly should be open to the public, calls for remark as being a somewhat unsatisfactory arrangement, though this form of planning can scarcely be avoided on account of the central position of the grand staircase. It should, however, be remembered that, as a rule, the side proscenium boxes are used by the Emperor and Court, and that when the State Box is occupied, practically the whole of the building is reserved for the Emperor and his guests. At such times, perhaps, only a small section of the house, such as a few rows of the stalls or an upper gallery, is available for public use. At the back of the house, as I have said, the accommodation provided for offices is very unusual, whilst as to the spacious scene-stores, I must repeat that I hold them to be dangerous. With regard to protective measures against fire in this part of the house, I would here take the opportunity of remarking that the two sets of corridors on either side of the stage already show the slots for working hydrants referred to elsewhere. From a technical point of view the general equipment of the block shows much forethought; while the ventilation and heating apparatus are unique. It would lead too far to go into detail here as to the various appliances used, but I would again emphasise what a very high state of efficiency is shown, more particularly when the time of erection is considered.

Speaking, in conclusion, of the architectural rendering, I would only say that I consider the treatment of the façades particularly successful, while there is much that is novel in their design and in the execution of the masonry. The mouldings and other details of the façades are thoroughly harmonious, and the group as seen from different points is always effective. In the interior the decoration, though frequently sombre in colour, is most pleasing. The building reflects Renaissance feeling, and, taken as a whole, the treatment of this example is worthy of considerable study.

APPROXIMATE DIMENSIONS.

Width of Proscenium Opening at Curtain Line	47' 6"	14·50 m.
Height of Proscenium Opening at Curtain Line	39' 3"	12·00 m.

AUDITORIUM.

Curtain Line to Front of State Box . .	87' 0"	26·50 m.
Curtain Line to Front of Third Tier . .	87' 0"	26·50 m.
Curtain Line to Furthest Seat . . .	101' 9"	31·00 m.
Sunlight Opening above Area . . .	64' 0"	19·50 m.
Highest Seat above Street . . .	64' 0"	19·50 m.
Lowest Seat above Street . . .	9' 9"	3·00 m.

STAGE.

Width inside Containing Walls . . .	98' 6"	30·00 m.
Curtain Line to Containing Back Wall .	85' 3"	26·00 m.
Curtain Line to Furthest Wall of Back Stage	164' 3"	50·00 m.
Gridiron Floor above Stage at Curtain Line	85' 3"	26·00 m.
Cellar Floor below Stage at Curtain Line .	39' 3"	12·00 m.
Stage Floor at Curtain Line above Street .	14' 9"	4·50 m.

COURT OPERA HOUSE, VIENNA. View of Auditorium.

CZECH NATIONAL THEATRE, PRAGUE.

JOSEPH ZITEK, JOSEPH SCHULZ.

BLOCK PLAN.

IT is notorious how exceedingly enthusiastic all classes of the Czech race are in maintaining the traditions of the old Kingdom of Bohemia, and the various institutions pertaining to their nationality. Among the methods which they favour for a retention of their individuality, not the least has been the institution of so-called national theatres, established both at Prague and other Czech towns. The Czech National Theatre in the capital of Bohemia is regarded by many as possessing the character of a monument, not merely in a national sense, but also as a means of perpetuating their native tongue.

In the previous volume I have referred to the origin of the new "German" playhouse at Prague, erected by an essentially German society. Similarly, the National Theatre is the outcome of the energy of a private association of prominent members of the Czech community specially formed in 1850 with the view of encouraging the Czech drama. It was this association to which belonged the old Czech Theatre of Prague, a structure but ill-adapted to their requirements. The executive, however, did not rest content with that building, for already in 1868 the erection of a new playhouse was decided on, and the foundation stone for the building actually laid in that year. With this ceremony and some preliminary works the progress of the structure had, unfortunately, for a time to come practically to an end, there being considerable difficulty at the outset in obtaining the necessary funds. Not until quite a number of years afterwards was more rapid progress made, and it was 1881 before the building saw its opening performance. Though not quite finished as far as interior decorations were concerned, the formal inauguration of the institution took place with some ceremony in August of that year, shortly after which a few plays were presented. Unfortunately,

CZECH NATIONAL THEATRE, PRAGUE. GENERAL VIEW.

however, only eleven performances in all were destined to be given, for, owing to some yet unexplained reason, the structure, on which so much labour and skill had been bestowed, was destroyed by fire on the 12th of the following month. Only the principal containing walls remained after the conflagration, and I am glad to say their façades were only slightly damaged. The duty of planning and executing this national theatre had been entrusted to Joseph Zitek, an architect of considerable local standing, and it is interesting to observe that the amount of money expended under his direction was about 135,000*l.*

Nothing daunted by this disaster, the Czech people with indomitable energy succeeded in raising, by voluntary subscription, a sum of 94,000*l.*, in the short space of six weeks, and within two years of that date they had the satisfaction of seeing the second opening of their new National Play-

house. For this work of reconstruction, however, the architect who had in the first instance been responsible for the plans was not again employed, for Zitek had to make room for Joseph Schulz, also an architect of considerable position in Prague. The precise reasons for this change I have been unable to discover, as the reports are contradictory, but I am afraid I must here notice that the fact of two architects having been engaged has again given rise to much controversial literature as to the responsibility for the building as it now stands. On careful examination of both the original set of plans which Zitek had prepared and the working drawings of Schulz for the reconstruction, and after a comparison of photographs of the original building and its condition after the fire, and a later personal examination on the spot, I have come to the conclusion that the fairest method will be to bracket the names of the two architects as collaborators. If I place Joseph Zitek's name first, I do so because I consider that the general conception of the block must be attributed to this architect, no

matter what alterations and extensions were subsequently made. It was at first my intention to present a plan explaining the building as it stood in 1881 and indicating what had been done after the fire, but I have since thought it better merely to illustrate the building as it is at the present day. Much that appears anomalous, both in plans and sections, must, however, be attributed to the somewhat extraordinary experiences of the block. It would be unfair to judge it in the same manner as we should if it were a theatre designed and executed by one architect without any obstacles of the character alluded to.

The situation chosen for the Czech National Theatre at Prague is exceedingly picturesque, for the block stands on the banks of the Moldau, with its principal elevation facing the main thoroughfare of the city, and its side elevation overlooking that river.' It has thoroughfares also on its other two sides. The building comprises the theatre proper,

CZECH NATIONAL THEATRE, PRAGUE. VIEW OF AUDITORIUM.

which occupied exactly the same site used on the first occasion, as well as a block of offices at the back, which was afterwards added on some adjoining ground. As regards seating capacity, the audience is considered to be limited to seventeen hundred, but with standing accommodation, room can be found for two thousand. As I have said, the structure involved an outlay of 135,000*l.* up to the date when it was destroyed by fire; the reconstruction actually cost 108,000*l.* more.

On examining the plans as the building now stands, and without in any way considering the fact that it is a structure which has seen two phases of erection, it will in the first place call for comment that the great irregularity of the site must have given the architects no little trouble in laying out the principal lines. As regards the theatre proper, I hold that the arrangement of the grand entrance, the main vestibule, with the staircases on either side, and of the large lounge above, has been very cleverly managed in spite of unfavourable circumstances. Further, I contend that the superficial area available has been extremely well utilised by the way in which the auditorium has been planned. There have not, however, been difficulties only in planning, but also in the elevation, on account of the site having different levels; in fact, the deep slope to which the building had to be worked from front to back, was not at all helpful to the monumental rendering desired. On glancing at the views of the building the difficulties which had to be encountered will be fully appreciated, but it will be noted that the grouping as a whole has been very satisfactory. As a matter of fact, the difference of angle to the various corners of the block is scarcely observable to the eye, owing to the ingenious way in which the various parts of the building have been set out. It will be perceived that, as in the case of the Vienna Opera House, an attempt has been made to draw distinctions between the architectural rendering of the part which holds the auditorium with the stage proper, and the surrounding sections containing the foyers, saloons and offices. It is only regrettable that here, as at Vienna, it was impossible for the architect to make a variation in the treatment of the exterior of the auditorium from that of the stage.

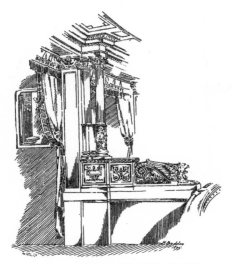

CZECH NATIONAL THEATRE, PRAGUE.
DETAIL OF BOX DIVISION.

There are no special features in the building such as those I have been able to point out in many other instances, but the arrangement of the auditorium with its two tiers of side boxes with central balconies, its third tier entirely occupied by a balcony, and its fourth tier in the form of a gallery set back on to the main containing-wall, the ceiling being supported by columns, has a particularly pleasing effect. Nor is there anything of importance that calls for adverse criticism, except, perhaps, that the upper gallery seats are in a well, which is a fault I have already had occasion to condemn; and, further, that the staircase accommodation is scarcely adequate for modern requirements, a defect due, no doubt, to the early date at which the building was first conceived. The arrangement of the doors of the main entrance and main vestibule, as well as those of the side carriage entrance, is specially advantageous to the occupants of the stalls and the first tier, and the manner in which a box on the right-hand side of the auditorium has been reserved for Royal visitors, with its own approach and ante-rooms, is very convenient.

As regards the architectural rendering of the building, I think the illustrations sufficiently explain this, and I would only add that the dignity of the principal loggia in front of the lounge is exceedingly impressive. The colour study of the interior is pleasing, and were I to select any detail of the decoration for special remark, it would be the treatment of the Royal rooms, on which considerable skill, particularly in plaster work, has been bestowed.

Taken as a whole, the building amply fulfils the requirements of a national institution for the Czech community resident in Prague. In judging its design we should not forget the early date at which the building was planned, and how irregular was the site chosen for its erection, and we should also bear in mind the experiences this theatre passed through before it was finally completed.

APPROXIMATE DIMENSIONS.

Width of Proscenium Opening at Curtain Line	36' 9"	11·25 m.
Height of Proscenium Opening at Curtain Line	39' 3"	12·00 m.

AUDITORIUM.

Curtain Line to Front of First Tier . .	60' 9"	18·50 m.
Curtain Line to Front of Third Tier . .	64' 0"	19·50 m.
Curtain Line to Furthest Seat . . .	91' 0"	27·75 m.
Sunlight Opening above Area . . .	69' 6"	21·25 m.
Highest Seat above Street . . .	75' 6"	23·00 m.
Lowest Seat above Street . . .	7' 3"	2·25 m.

STAGE.

Width inside Containing Walls . . .	68' 9"	21·00 m.
Curtain Line to Containing Back Wall .	44' 3"	13·50 m.
Curtain Line to Furthest Wall of Back Stage	62' 3"	19·00 m.
Gridiron Floor above Stage at Curtain Line	88' 6"	27·00 m.
Cellar Floor below Stage at Curtain Line .	32' 9"	10·00 m.
Stage Floor at Curtain Line above Street .	10' 6"	3·25 m.

CZECH NATIONAL THEATRE, PRAGUE. SIDE VIEW.

MUNICIPAL THEATRE, SALZBURG.

FERDINAND FELLNER, HERMANN HELMER.

BLOCK PLAN.

IN the first volume I had frequent occasion to refer to the work carried out by the Austrian architects, Ferdinand Fellner and Hermann Helmer, and in this volume two further examples of their designs are given. As I have remarked, these architects, who, to my mind, must be considered the leading specialists of Austria, have executed several fixed "types" of buildings, and there is a certain sameness between their one-tier theatres, their two-tier theatres, etc. Though, in some cases, their playhouses may be to a large extent mere variations of one model, all, however, possess some particular feature that calls for comment, and many are interesting examples of modern theatre construction. While in each production the individuality of the architects is exhibited in excellence of plan, in general equipment, and in the satisfactory treatment of the interior, I regret to have to repeat that practically all, however, reveal that same mediocrity in the architectural rendering of their exterior which I have already condemned.

The example here under consideration is a small two-tier house for a provincial town well known as a summer resort, and may practically be considered a Municipal institution. The structure, like the majority of Fellner and Helmer's theatres, occupies an isolated site.

As will be seen from the plans, the site was a tri-angular one, and the architects have overcome the difficulties they had to encounter, arising from this unusual outline, with considerable skill, for the arrangement of the semi-circular grand vestibule, with its two staircases on either side leading to the first and second tiers respectively, is not only very practical, but most effective. The second-tier staircases, as will be seen, have also been so set out as to have their own exits directly into the open, besides those through the principal vestibule. The auditorium is a typical example of the work of the Vienna architects, except that it is perhaps unusual to find the whole of their first tier given up to boxes.

MUNICIPAL THEATRE, SALZBURG. GENERAL VIEW.

The decoration of both the auditorium and vestibule, as well as of the lounge, is almost identical with that of other buildings erected by the same firm. The seating accommodation is for 630 and there is additional standing room for 370. Comparatively small as the establishment is, a suitable vestibule, staircase and ante-room have been provided for a royal box on the first tier; and it is noticeable that the cloak-room conveniences are specially well placed. It should be emphasised, however, that the arrangement of the vestibule and staircases at the apex of a triangular site remains the chief characteristic of this building.

In conclusion, I would say that the Salzburg Municipal Theatre, as a whole, fulfils its purpose in a most admirable manner, while its equipment accords in every respect with our most recent requirements. The scene-store, it may be added, has been wisely relegated to another building, instead of having a position found for it under the same roof as the auditorium. The cost of the institution, exclusive of the scene-store, amounted to about 25,000*l*.

APPROXIMATE DIMENSIONS.

Width of Proscenium Opening at Curtain Line	32' 0"	9·75 m.
Height of Proscenium Opening at Curtain Line	24' 6"	7·50 m.

AUDITORIUM.			*STAGE.*		
Curtain Line to Front of First Tier . .	50' 9"	15·50 m.	Width inside Containing Walls	68' 9"	21·00 m.
Curtain Line to Front of Second Tier .	51' 9"	15·75 m.	Curtain Line to Containing Back Wall .	29' 6"	9·00 m.
Curtain Line to Furthest Seat . . .	65' 6"	20·00 m.	Curtain Line to Furthest Wall of Back Stage	50' 9"	15·50 m
Sunlight Opening above Area . . .	38' 6"	11·75 m.	Gridiron Floor above Stage at Curtain Line	50' 9"	15·50 m.
Highest Seat above Street . . .	26' 3"	8·0 m.	Cellar Floor below Stage at Curtain Line .	9' 9"	3·00 m.
Lowest Seat above Street . . .	2' 6"	0·75 m.	Stage Floor at Curtain Line above Street .	5' 9"	1·75 m.

MUNICIPAL THEATRE, LAIBACH.

J. VLAD. HRÁSKY, ANT. HRÚBY.

BLOCK PLAN.

THE Municipal Theatre at Laibach plays as important a *rôle* in the life of the Slav community which predominates in the division of Carniola, as does the National Theatre at Prague in that of the Czechs. The entertainments at this theatre are intended essentially to foster a certain sentiment of patriotism in which the members of Slav nations much delight. The new Laibach Theatre takes the place of the old building destroyed by fire in 1887, and its erection is in a great measure due to the liberality of the various local authorities. The design is the result of a commission placed, in 1889, in the hands of the local architects, Hrásky and Hrúby, for a set of provisional plans. The accommodation to be provided was for an audience of one thousand, and the cost was limited to 20,000*l*. It was not, however, until August, 1890, that the foundations were commenced, and the building was completed in the year 1892.

In examining the plans for this theatre I would lay emphasis on the fact that, like the National Theatre at Prague, this structure was designed by local architects, who had but little experience in work of this class. The manner in which the building has been grouped is in the first place noticeable as following the lead of structures of far greater importance, for the architects have indicated the outline of their auditorium by a curvilinear façade, in which the central feature marks the main entrance and grand foyer, while two towers, one on either side, serve to show the position of the principal staircases and the two side entrances. Though the building is by no means of particular architectural merit so far as the rendering of the exterior goes—in fact, much of the detail is unsatisfactory—I would remark that this general grouping is deserving of attention, and again affords an example where, by careful study of the development of other work, a satisfactory result has been obtained. The plan

MUNICIPAL THEATRE, LAIBACH.   GENERAL VIEW.

is particularly clear in its main lines, and, from an English point of view, it is noticeable as one of the few instances of Continental theatre building where two sets of stairs, overlapping one another, have been constructed within the same containing walls. The auditorium has also been very effectively contrived, though the arrangement of the boxes on the second tier should certainly not be imitated. Both in cloak-room accommodation and in the arrangement of the offices at the back of the house, our most recent requirements have been fully considered, and we also again find that the principal scene-stores are not in the same block as the auditorium, but are located in a detached building not far distant.

In conclusion, I would only say that, though making no pretensions as an architectural achievement, this theatre, in a small town of some thirty thousand inhabitants, does credit to those who have conceived it.

APPROXIMATE DIMENSIONS.

Width of Proscenium Opening at Curtain Line	31' 0"	9·50 m.	
Height of Proscenium Opening at Curtain Line	31' 0"	9·50 m.	

AUDITORIUM.			*STAGE.*		
Curtain Line to Front of First Tier . .	46' 0"	14·00 m.	Width inside Containing Walls . . .	39' 0"	18·00 m.
Curtain Line to Front of Second Tier .	46' 9"	14·25 m.	Curtain Line to Containing Back Wall .	32' 0"	9·75 m.
Curtain Line to Furthest Seat . . .	67' 0"	20·50 m.	Curtain Line to Furthest Wall of Back Stage	49' 3"	15·00 m.
Sunlight Opening above Area . . .	40' 0"	12·25 m.	Gridiron Floor above Stage at Curtain Line	54' 0"	16·50 m.
Highest Seat above Street	34' 3"	10·50 m.	Cellar Floor below Stage at Curtain Line .	16' 3"	5·00 m.
Lowest Seat above Street	3' 3"	1·00 m.	Stage Floor at Curtain Line above Street .	6' 6"	2·00 m.

"RAIMUND" THEATRE, VIENNA.

FRANZ ROTH.

IN speaking of the "Grand" Theatre at Islington, in my first volume, I remarked how that establishment was practically the pioneer of suburban theatrical enterprise. The application of the idea of giving the outlying districts of a metropolis separate playhouses has not only been most markedly developed of late in London, but the principle, as I have already had occasion to observe, has found considerable favour in various Continental cities. There are several foreign capitals in which such institutions have lately been opened. Berlin, for instance, has only recently seen the inauguration of a theatre equipped on a most lavish scale in one of its western suburbs, and the example at Vienna, here under consideration, though, at present, the only one of its kind in Austria, is already being followed by similar ventures.

The "Raimund" Theatre at Vienna is essentially a suburban theatre; I might almost call it a suburban People's Theatre, for it is an institution where plays of a popular character are given at popular prices, and, though the subscriptions for its erection were not raised from every part of the community for which it was particularly intended, as was the case with the *bona fide* People's Theatre at Worms, its erection is nevertheless largely due to the co-operation of all classes, and the support accorded to it is of an essentially democratic character. Besides being the first suburban theatre of a Continental capital, and fulfilling the idea of a people's playhouse, the "Raimund" Theatre at Vienna also holds a prominent position on account of the fact that it embodies, to a great extent, the principles of theatre construction promoted under the name of the "Asphaleia" system. This system, which was propounded in 1882, directly after the great catastrophe of the "Ring" Theatre fire, included in its programme an almost entire reform in all parts of the building, though no doubt more particularly in regard to the equipment of the stage. Of the latter I shall speak at some length in the third volume, whilst the general scheme will also receive attention in my chapter on types of theatre planning. The "Asphaleia" scheme, as I have said, dates from 1882, but it was not until 1893, when the "Raimund" Theatre was opened, that the principles brought forward were actually applied to a structure of considerable dimensions. As a matter of interest, I would mention that, though a comparatively large superficial area is covered by the block, the total expenditure on its erection did not exceed 37,500*l.*, and that the time occupied in carrying out the contract was the remarkably short period of six months. The architect was Franz Roth, who had been long associated with those who proposed a material alteration in the arrangement of our places of entertainment.

As to the position of the theatre, it is in a populous suburb, and occupies a prominent site at the junction of several thoroughfares. Three of the frontages overlook streets, whilst at

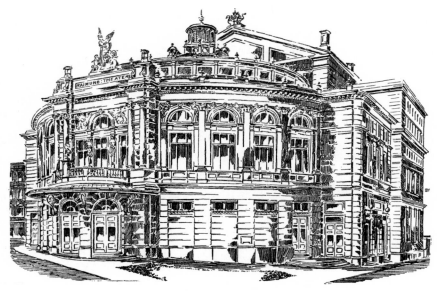

"RAIMUND" THEATRE, VIENNA. GENERAL VIEW.

the rear a yard of comparatively large proportions separates the block from the adjoining property. Here again, as in the case of the Laibach Theatre—the example given on the preceding page—we have an instance where the auditorium finds full expression in the grouping of the building generally, and particularly in the outline of the principal façade. Reference to the third volume, in which the original plan of the so-called model "Asphaleia" theatre is presented, will show the basis on which the design was conceived. Next in importance to the expression of the exterior is the auditorium, which calls for special notice on account of its very deep tiers, its peculiar ceiling, and the unusual form of its proscenium opening, all tending, I consider, to make the building a notable one in the annals of theatre construction.

The shape of the ceiling is due to the adoption of certain theories of acoustics, and certainly the hearing qualities of the building are of a very satisfactory nature. The depth of the tiers has its origin in an attempt to imitate the section of the amphitheatre of old; and though the sighting is satisfactory throughout, and on the upper tier the accommodation is all that can be desired, I regret to find that the overhanging galleries are extremely oppressive both to the occupants of the first tier and to that part of the audience in the area which is not seated in the "well" of the house. The effect of these heavy galleries as they appear from the stalls, I must add, is somewhat unhappy, for the fronts of the tiers are brought too close to the proscenium to allow for any semblance of dignity or breadth in the auditorium. The device, too, of introducing boxes into a plan of this description is by no means pleasing, for they seem to be entirely out of scale in comparison with the general proportions of the interior. It would, in fact, have been preferable if the proscenium boxes had

"RAIMUND" THEATRE, VIENNA. VIEW OF PROSCENIUM.

been cancelled in the design. The framing of the proscenium proper is, to a certain extent, governed by an experiment in lighting the stage on an improved method, with powerful side lights. These are hidden from the audience by a very clever arrangement of the principal mouldings, and I consider that this new form of illuminating the scenes is a great improvement on the antiquated footlights. But here, again, I must not dilate on this point, as the question of stage lighting is dealt with elsewhere. As regards the halls or promenades which have been placed round the auditorium, they are certainly spacious, and, as far as cloak-room accommodation is concerned, very convenient. The staircases are ample, though, as at Laibach, it is observable that two stairs to different tiers are placed within the same walls. The purposes of the "Asphaleia" system of construction will, as I have said, be dealt with in detail in Volume III., and, hence, I need not indulge here in any discussion of the theories involved.

In conclusion, I would only say that the equipment of the building is thoroughly practical, but as regards the architectural rendering of the exterior and the decoration of the interior, unfortunately, nothing favourable can be said. It is remarkable that in this particular instance, where an experiment in theatre construction of considerable interest was attempted, the building had to be carried out with such great rapidity that the architect had but little time for the development and necessary maturing of his plans. With more thought accorded to questions of detail in regard to the plan, better results would no doubt have been obtained. This refers primarily to the arrangement of the auditorium, but the same remark is applicable to the position of the staircases, which, though spacious, do not appear to fit in well with the architect's general scheme. With more time at his disposal, moreover, Franz Roth, I am sure, would scarcely have left the architectural treatment of the exterior in its present condition, and he would have availed himself of the great possibilities for interior decoration. The "Raimund" Theatre, to repeat, embodies an experiment, and as such deserves careful study. It is not a beautiful playhouse, but it exhibits much that is of interest to those associated with theatre construction.

APPROXIMATE DIMENSIONS.

Width of Proscenium Opening at Curtain Line	47' 6"	14·50 m.
Height of Proscenium Opening at Curtain Line	36' 9"	11·25 m.

AUDITORIUM.			*STAGE.*		
Curtain Line to Front of First Tier .	41' 0"	12·50 m.	Width inside Containing Walls . . .	78' 0"	23·75 m.
Curtain Line to Front of Second Tier .	46' 0"	14·00 m.	Curtain Line to Containing Back Wall .	39' 3"	12·00 m.
Curtain Line to Furthest Seat . .	75' 6"	23·00 m.	Gridiron Floor above Stage at Curtain Line	78' 9"	24·00 m.
Ceiling Centre above Area . . .	59' 0"	18·00 m.	Cellar Floor below Stage at Curtain Line .	19' 9"	6·00 m.
Highest Seat above Street . . .	42' 6"	13·00 m.	Stage Floor at Curtain Line level with Street.		
Lowest Seat below Street . . .	3' 3"	1·00 m.			

GERMANY.

MUNICIPAL OPERA HOUSE, FRANKFORT.

LUCAE, BECKER, GIESENBERG.

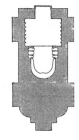

BLOCK PLAN.

IN the Frankfort Opera House we find a typical example of an institution which, though essentially a Subscription Theatre in the first instance, is considered a municipal establishment and known as a "Stadt" theatre, owing to the support accorded to it by the local authorities and the fact that the management is practically carried on under their auspices. Instead of the Municipality, or, perhaps, some society granting the funds for this playhouse, which would have been the more usual procedure in Germany, the erection of this remarkable building is mainly due to the efforts of private citizens, for in the year 1870 a number of prominent men offered the town a very considerable sum for the erection of a theatre, merely stipulating that they should have the first refusal of tickets for certain boxes in the principal tier and a specified number of stalls. The offer was at once accepted by the Municipality, who, on behalf of the ratepayers, responded by presenting a site on the "Rahmhof" and by further contributing to the fund, which was managed under their direction on lines similar to that of a company, i.e. by a directorate elected from among the subscribers, whose votes are proportionate to their share in the capital. A limited competition for the design of the Opera House between the architects Lucae and Strack of Berlin, Brueckwald of Leipsic, Bordiau of Brussels, and Bernitz of Frankfort, was then instituted, and Lucae was declared successful and obtained the commission. Soon after this competition, however, the site was changed from the "Rahmhof" to a yet more suitable spot on the boulevard near the Bockenheim Gate, and it became necessary for Lucae to prepare new plans, so that it was not until the Spring of 1873 that the work was actually commenced. Four years later, when only the carcase of the building had been roofed in, Lucae died, and the completion of the work was transferred to Albrecht Becker and E. Giesenberg, both of whom had been employed in the office of the deceased for some considerable time. The opening ceremony was performed by the Emperor on the 20th November, 1880.

In examining the plans of the Frankfort Opera House, it would be

MUNICIPAL OPERA HOUSE, FRANKFORT. GENERAL VIEW.

well again to bear in mind that the design for this example dates back as far as 1870, and if one remembers this, the comparative excellence of the arrangements for a building of that date will be more perceptible. I know of no playhouse, completed prior to that of Frankfort, in which the same clearness of plan and the same grasp of the requirements of the audience, as regards accommodation, are to be found as in the case before us. The general conception of the scheme stands particularly high, and as an example of "central" planning as distinct from "radial" planning, the structure is also remarkable.

As will be seen, there is a main entrance leading into the grand vestibule, and there are also two side vestibules. This main entrance is particularly convenient for that part of the audience reaching the building by carriage, whilst the side vestibules afford facilities for the entrance of foot passengers without their having to cross the line of vehicular traffic. The conception of the grand staircase is peculiarly satisfactory, and what is more, there is no undue waste of space in obtaining the vistas which are so important a feature for stairs of this description. The manner in which the latter can be overlooked from the grand lounge on the one hand, and from corridors surrounding the auditorium proper, on the other, is extremely clever. The staircases to the upper tiers have been very suitably arranged on either side. The entire planning of these vestibules, staircases and passages is essentially academic in feeling, and it is only right to say at once that the same classical influence is apparent in their decoration.

In the auditorium, which has four tiers, the principal feature is an exceedingly deep proscenium. The architectural rendering shows the same treatment as is observable in other parts of the building.

In the equipment at the back of the house and also in that of the "front" the Frankfort Opera House is far ahead of any other building completed about the same time, excepting only the Vienna Opera House, already referred to. The appliances for ventilation and heating and for the distribution of water are particularly noticeable, and one of the chief items in the equipment is the electric intercommunication which has been installed between all parts of the structure, for use either in the event of an outbreak of fire or for the general purposes of the establishment. More exhaustive remarks upon this point will be found in the third volume. Considering the date of the erection, it is not surprising that no very considerable use has been made of iron; in fact, practically everything on the stage and in the roof is of timber. In other respects, however, a fair amount of attention appears to have been given to the prevention of a spread of fire by the employment of so-called fire-resisting construction in the floors, and by the introduction of such special appliances as "sprinklers."

As to the exterior, the grouping is very successful, for the methods which have been used with such marked effect at the Vienna Opera House and the Czech National Theatre at Prague have been applied here. There is again a distinct separation of the block which contains the auditorium and stage from the surrounding parts holding the lounge, offices and various adjuncts. It is further observable that the treatment of these reveals a greater endeavour to express the interior than has been the case elsewhere, for the side elevation is an instance where the situation of the dressing-rooms and minor offices are clearly indicated on the façades. The arrangement of the two circular entrances on either side of the central feature of the front elevation has a very pleasing effect. The classic rendering of the exterior, with its excellent detail, gives the Frankfort Opera House a certain dignity which is very impressive, and the structure certainly has the semblance of what has been called a "Temple of Dramatic Art," as aspired to by the original donors.

In conclusion, I would only say that the scene-store had, even at that date, been wisely located in a detached building, although in close proximity to the opera house. As a matter of fact, it faces one side of the square in which the theatre is situated, being connected with it by a subway. Most of the machinery has also been placed in this house, and the necessary pipes and wires pass through an underground passage to the main building.

The total outlay on the Frankfort Opera House was approximately 230,000*l.*, and it is interesting to observe that although the work according to the original competition design was not to exceed a cost of 60,000*l.*, after various alterations and additions, the Municipality finally accepted an estimate for 200,000*l.*, and this sum was again exceeded by 30,000*l.* In this country we cannot imagine work being taken in hand in such a manner.

APPROXIMATE DIMENSIONS.

Width of Proscenium Opening at Curtain Line	40' 0"	12·25 m.
Height of Proscenium Opening at Curtain Line	32' 0"	9·75 m.

AUDITORIUM.			*STAGE.*		
Curtain Line to Front of First Tier .	68' 9"	21·00 m.	Width inside Containing Walls . . .	63' 9"	19·50 m.
Curtain Line to Front of Second Tier .	72' 3"	22·00 m.	Curtain Line to Containing Back Wall .	34' 3"	10·50 m.
Curtain Line to Furthest Seat . .	78' 9"	24·00 m.	Gridiron Floor above Stage at Curtain Line	46' 9"	14·25 m.
Sunlight Opening above Area . .	50' 9"	15·50 m.	Cellar Floor below Stage at Curtain Line .	10' 6"	3·25 m.
Highest Seat above Street . . .	21' 3"	6·50 m.	Stage Floor at Curtain Line above Street .	4' 9"	1·50 m.
Lowest Seat above Street . . .	1' 6"	0·50 m.			

MUNICIPAL THEATRE, ESSEN.

HEINRICH SEELING.

BLOCK PLAN.

IN presenting no less than three further examples of playhouses designed by Heinrich Seeling, I am guided by the fact that the work of this architect, to whom I have alluded as the theatre-specialist of Germany, merits particular attention from all interested in modern theatre construction. I have, in the first volume, dealt with his Municipal Theatre at Halle, and the private establishment erected from his drawings at Berlin. The former, it will be remembered, was described as being a pioneer of particular importance, and the second as an example of unusual interest. I now present illustrations of the municipal theatres erected at Essen, Rostock and Bromberg respectively; and though, no doubt, each block exhibits the individuality of the designer, there is not observable in Seeling's work, as I have already indicated, that tendency to follow one model or type of building which has so frequently distinguished the productions of other architects. To assist the study of these examples, I would particularly request reference to my previous remarks in connection with the theatres at Halle and Berlin.

Heinrich Seeling obtained the commission for the Municipal Theatre at Essen in an open competition held during 1889, for which the requirements were laid down in considerable detail. The expenditure was not to exceed 20,000*l.*, and, whilst the number of the audience was to be eight hundred, there were specific restrictions in regard to the distribution of the seats, a limitation no doubt attributable to the fact that Essen is a manufacturing town, in which a special class of spectator had to be catered for. The principal accommodation had to be provided in the upper tier, or, in other words, the seats for which the smallest charge is made were to predominate. Hence, without going into detail, I would at once say that the Municipal Theatre at Essen chiefly calls for attention as a two-tier house, with an unusual seating capacity in the upper tier, and an exceptionally small area. The lines of the auditorium show that no part of the first-tier gallery over-hangs the stalls, and the area exhibits the novel arrangement of a row of open boxes at the back. There are none of the usual half-open side boxes so common in the German playhouse, while the closed boxes are limited to two in the proscenium.

MUNICIPAL THEATRE, ESSEN. GENERAL VIEW.

The plan is a model of clearness, and though the facilities for approach to the actual seats from the spacious corridors do not attain that very high standard which we are accustomed to find in Seeling's work, there is no great cause for complaint. Whilst there is here a marked difference in plan from other playhouses by this designer, the architectural treatment of the exterior and the decoration of the auditorium possess considerable similarity. In equipment the building in every way fulfils modern requirements.

APPROXIMATE DIMENSIONS.

Width of Proscenium Opening at Curtain Line	24' 6"	7·50 m.
Height of Proscenium Opening at Curtain Line	23' 0"	7·00 m.

AUDITORIUM.			*STAGE.*		
Curtain Line to Front of First Tier . .	48' 6"	14·75 m.	Width inside Containing Walls . . .	55' 9"	17·00 m.
Curtain Line to Front of Second Tier	50' 9"	15·50 m.	Curtain Line to Containing Back Wall .	42' 6"	13·00 m.
Curtain Line to Furthest Seat . .	76' 9"	24·00 m.	Gridiron Floor above Stage at Curtain Line	62' 3"	19·00 m.
Ceiling Centre above Area . . .	44' 3"	13·50 m.	Cellar Floor below Stage at Curtain Line .	14' 9"	4·50 m.
Highest Seat above Street . . .	44' 3"	13·50 m.	Stage Floor at Curtain Line above Street .	6' 6"	2·00 m.
Lowest Seat above Street . . .	3' 3"	1·00 m.			

MUNICIPAL THEATRE, ROSTOCK.

HEINRICH SEELING.

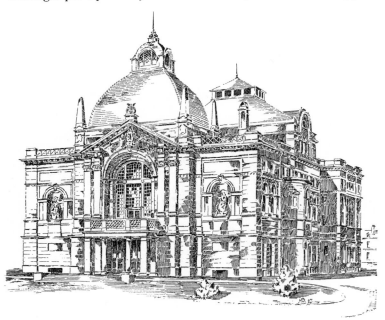

BLOCK PLAN.

IN the Municipal Theatre, Rostock, we have another specimen of Seeling's work, but in this case the building is a three-tier house. The commission was again obtained in competition, the accommodation required being for an audience of one thousand, at a total cost of not more than 21,500*l*. As a matter of fact, however, the elaboration of the design during its execution, and the fuller equipment of the building, involved an extra expenditure, bringing the total outlay to nearly 30,000*l*.

As regards the auditorium, generally so ably dealt with by this architect, I cannot but say that it is here below the average of his work, not only in its lines, but also in its decoration. To my mind, it is mainly in the area that Seeling's principles fully assert themselves, the method of approach to the different rows of seats exhibiting all the advantages to which I have referred in speaking of the Halle Theatre. In clearness of plan, again, there is nothing to be desired, while all passage and staircase accommodation is as ample and as well arranged as usual If any adverse criticism is made, it should be in connection with the two flights of winding stairs to the first tier, which in no way accord with recent ideas of safety, and are quite at variance with the architect's usual forethought for the protection of the audience. The disadvantage of these stairs is the more marked here, in that there appears to have been no particular reason why the flights should not have been set out without " winders." As to the proscenium boxes, there are in this instance three pairs, and, further, we find several open boxes on either side of the first tier, besides several half-open boxes placed at the back of that level. These latter, by a simple arrangement of movable partitions, can be provisionally converted into a large state box for use at official functions. As

MUNICIPAL THEATRE, ROSTOCK. GENERAL VIEW.

regards the architectural rendering of the exterior, I need only refer to my remarks on Seeling's work in the first volume, adding that the treatment of the interior decorations is considerably simpler than in other playhouses by the same architect. The grouping of the block and the central feature of the front elevation call for notice. The general equipment of this theatre is of a high standard.

APPROXIMATE DIMENSIONS.

Width of Proscenium Opening at Curtain Line	32' 9"	10·00 m.
Height of Proscenium Opening at Curtain Line	24' 6"	7·50 m.

AUDITORIUM.			*STAGE.*		
Curtain Line to Front of First Tier . .	47' 6"	14·50 m.	Width inside Containing Walls . . .	62' 3"	19·00 m.
Curtain Line to Front of Third Tier .	53' 3"	16·25 m.	Curtain Line to Containing Back Wall .	44' 3"	13·50 m.
Curtain Line to Furthest Seat . .	68' 9"	21·00 m.	Curtain Line to Furthest Wall of Back Stage	57' 3"	17·50 m.
Sunlight Opening above Area . .	44' 3"	13·50 m.	Gridiron Floor above Stage at Curtain Line	57' 3"	17·50 m.
Highest Seat above Street . . .	42' 6"	13·00 m.	Cellar Floor below Stage at Curtain Line .	15' 6"	4·75 m.
Lowest Seat above Street . . .	1' 6"	0·50 m.	Stage Floor at Curtain Line above Street .	4' 9"	1·50 m.

MUNICIPAL THEATRE, BROMBERG.

HEINRICH SEELING.

THE Bromberg Municipal Theatre, which replaces a structure destroyed by fire in 1889, is, to my mind, one of Heinrich Seeling's happiest efforts. The work here was carried out in accordance with a commission given him by the municipal authorities. The actual building operations only extended over some eighteen months, namely, from May, 1895, to October, 1896, the total cost of the structure amounting to 23,000*l*.

In this instance again, the clearness of the plan is so evident that comment appears quite unnecessary. The manner in which the vestibule, the staircases on either side, and the broad passages with the cloak-counters have been arranged, is as satisfactory as it at first sight appears simple. It is only regrettable that, for some reason, the dangerous "winders" are again used in the lower flights of the several staircases, and it is inexplicable that they should have been permitted in a country where the regulations governing the construction of theatres are particularly stringent as regards the safety of the audience. Speaking of the auditorium, I would only say that the distribution of seats in this instance shows the more customary division of the audience and allows of full use being made of the area. In this theatre, however, we find, for the first time, that there is no proscenium as we generally understand it. There are two pairs of proscenium boxes, but these are built into the auditorium independent of the general lines of the ceiling. This latest departure in a design by Seeling certainly deserves attention. In his Berlin example, it will be remembered that there was only a narrow proscenium, several boxes being built up irrespective of the main framing, whilst in other playhouses by this architect a proscenium of ordinary depth was adopted.

MUNICIPAL THEATRE, BROMBERG.
VIEW OF TURRET.

As regards the architectural rendering of the block, I consider it to be the most successful of Seeling's work. The grouping is particularly effective, whilst the detail is far above the average. The manner of framing the central feature of the principal façade by two turrets, marking the position of the staircases, is worthy of imitation. There is much similarity of treatment in the interior decoration to that of the Berlin theatre, more particularly in the detail of the mouldings ; and, without being unnecessarily ostentatious, or displaying a richness that would be incongruous in a small provincial town, the effect obtained is pleasing.

Altogether, Heinrich Seeling's work takes a leading position among the smaller theatres of the Continent, and particularly deserves the attention of English architects, as many of the features which distinguish his buildings could, subject, of course, to modifications, be adapted to the requirements of larger private establishments in this country.

APPROXIMATE DIMENSIONS.

Width of Proscenium Opening at Curtain Line	27' 9"	8·50 m.
Height of Proscenium Opening at Curtain Line	31' 3"	9·50 m.

AUDITORIUM.			*STAGE.*		
Curtain Line to Front of First Tier . .	42' 6"	13·00 m.	Width inside Containing Walls . . .	51' 9"	15·75 m.
Curtain Line to Front of Second Tier	45' 0"	13·75 m.	Curtain Line to Containing Back Wall .	44' 3"	13·50 m.
Curtain Line to Furthest Seat . . .	65' 6"	20·00 m.	Curtain Line to Furthest Wall of Back Stage	59' 0"	18·00 m.
Ceiling Centre above Area . . .	39' 3"	12·00 m.	Gridiron Floor above Stage at Curtain Line	52' 6"	16·00 m.
Highest Seat above Street . . .	36' 0"	11·00 m.	Cellar Floor below Stage at Curtain Line .	14' 9"	4·50 m.
Lowest Seat above Street . . .	0' 9"	0·25 m.	Stage Floor at Curtain Line above Street .	3' 3"	1·00 m.

"LESSING" THEATRE, BERLIN.

H. VON DER HUDE, J. HENNICKE.

BLOCK PLAN.

IN the preceding volume I have had occasion to refer to the "New" Theatre at Berlin as an establishment managed essentially on commercial lines, and as the result of private enterprise. The opening of that building took place in 1892, some years after the very stringent regulations which now govern the construction of places of entertainment at Berlin had come into force. The "Lessing" Theatre is similarly established only as a money-making concern, and owes its existence to an enterprising playwright, who erected it chiefly with the view of producing comedy. As the regulations referred to only came into force in 1890, whilst this building was opened two years previously, the requirements of that code did not affect it; nevertheless, through the selection of an excellent site, open on all sides, and the owner's distinct purpose of making his theatre as safe as possible, even more was done for the public than would now be demanded, the building, thereby, becoming a model of its class. This is a lesson for us in England, for I am afraid that neither the owners nor the architects of our theatres vie with one another in making the Metropolitan playhouses any roomier or safer than our London County Council regulations require. If anything, as I have already said, the tendency is in the opposite direction.

In the Spring of 1887 the commission was entrusted to H. Von der Hude, an architect of considerable local standing, who was assisted by his partner, the late J. Hennicke. There was some delay in beginning the work, but directly the founda-

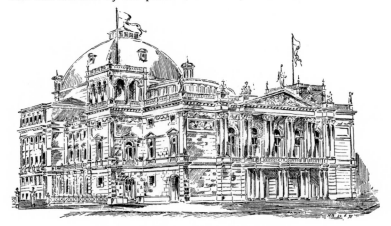

"LESSING" THEATRE, BERLIN. GENERAL VIEW.

tions were taken in hand the rapidity with which the building was completed did credit to all concerned, for the time between the commencement of the excavations and the inauguration was only some twelve months. The exact date of the opening performance was the 11th of September, 1888. Accommodation had to be provided for an audience of 1160, including standing room for sixty, whilst the total expenditure on the block amounted to nearly 40,000*l*.

The plans of the "Lessing" Theatre are worthy of favourable notice on account of the very clear arrangement of the vestibule, the principal passages, and the staircases, and the ease with which the audience can reach the open in case of emergency. The auditorium calls for remark on account of its flat ceiling, and its decoration, I may add, is very pleasing, the effect mainly depending on some fine plaster-work with a light colour-study. As for the "back of the house" and the equipment of the building generally, I can but say that the most recent methods and appliances have been adopted throughout. The only unsatisfactory part is the exterior, which is commonplace and displeasing in detail, though the grouping of the block is by no means so bad. Taken as a whole, however, the "Lessing" Theatre again shows us that a well-equipped playhouse abroad is not necessarily subsidised, or the property of a Court or public body.

APPROXIMATE DIMENSIONS.

Width of Proscenium Opening at Curtain Line	32' 0"	9·75 m.
Height of Proscenium Opening at Curtain Line	32' 9"	10·00 m.

AUDITORIUM.

Curtain Line to Front of First Tier . .	52' 6"	16·00 m.
Curtain Line to Front of Second Tier .	57' 3"	17·50 m.
Curtain Line to Furthest Seat . . .	78' 9"	24·00 m.
Sunlight Opening above Area . . .	39' 3"	12·00 m.
Highest Seat above Street	34' 3"	10·50 m.
Lowest Seat above Street	0' 9"	0·25 m.

STAGE.

Width inside Containing Walls . . .	64' 9"	19·75 m.
Curtain Line to Containing Back Wall .	59' 0"	18·00 m.
Gridiron Floor above Stage at Curtain Line	59' 9"	18·25 m.
Cellar Floor below Stage at Curtain Line .	16' 3"	5·00 m.
Stage Floor at Curtain Line above Street .	4' 0"	1·25 m.

GREAT BRITAIN.

"HER MAJESTY'S" THEATRE, LONDON.

C. J. PHIPPS.

BLOCK PLAN.

IN the preceding volume I had frequent occasion to refer to the spirit in which theatres are generally built in this country, and I referred to the unfortunate disregard of architectural rendering in its higher sense. I mentioned, however, that D'Oyly Carte's Opera House was an exception among the theatres of London, and there is a further exception illustrated in this work, namely, that of the Shakespeare Memorial Theatre. Of playhouses planned to fulfil the usual requirements of the metropolis, i.e. those of a commercial establishment where the architect is restricted by financial considerations, the example now before us, known as "Her Majesty's," no doubt takes the leading position. It is, in fact, the most complete embodiment of the customary demand for economic planning and modern equipment with due regard to our local regulations. I have already spoken of the work of C. J. Phipps in connection with his theatre at Wolverhampton, and I observed that quite forty theatres had been erected from his designs.

In "Her Majesty's" Theatre he has, however, undoubtedly surpassed all his previous efforts, and while founding for himself a monument likely to perpetuate his name with a class of structure with which he was particularly familiar, he has also furnished London with a playhouse so admirable in arrangement that it will long be considered a model of its kind. Since the issue of the first volume, C. J. Phipps, our leading specialist, has, unfortunately, gone from among us—as a matter of fact, but a few weeks after the opening of the building here reproduced. With his departure we have lost a man who has excelled in his speciality to an extent that can scarcely be understood by an outsider. He had been able to satisfy the requirements of the typical theatrical speculator, who primarily demands the greatest accommodation in a limited space at as low a cost as possible, and what is more, he enjoyed full confidence, since no one had cause to fear any inclination on his part to incur expenditure merely in the interests of art. I hold that the deceased could have achieved far better work from an artist's point of view, but, had he sought to do this, his large practice would have dwindled, and he would not have retained the support of those whose financial aid was necessary for the development of his schemes. It is, alas, a sad fact, but one that is only too

"HER MAJESTY'S" THEATRE, LONDON.   VIEW OF PROSCENIUM.

true. The theatre architect who aspires to treat his work from a more ideal standpoint, would not, in London at least, find favour with those promoters who are responsible for the origin of the majority of our playhouses, unless they were convinced that the higher standard of work cost neither extra time nor money, or, that, if put to a greater expense, they would be amply recouped by the greater popularity of the house with the general public.

"Her Majesty's" Theatre is the outcome of the practical financial ability of the late C. J. Phipps, for the development of the large site of which the theatre only occupies a section, is practically due to his management. The playhouse,

II.—K

as it now stands, was executed to meet the requirements of Herbert Beerbohm Tree, whose success as an actor-manager is well known, and there is no doubt that he had considerable influence in the planning of the building as well as in its decoration. The date of the opening was April 28th, 1897, the work of erection having been completed in a remarkably short space of time. The exact cost is not yet available, but it is generally assumed that the structure has involved an outlay of some 60,000*l*. The site on which it stands has long been associated with theatrical enterprise, and fronts the broad thoroughfare known as the Haymarket. There is another street on one side, and an arcade at the back; while, on its remaining side, high party-walls separate it from other sections of the property. The building accommodates an audience of about fifteen hundred.

On examining the plans, in the first place we find what is exceptional for London, namely, the area practically on the same level as the pavement. The arrangement of the entrances with the main vestibule is no doubt one of the most ingenious instances of planning associated with a modern theatre, and I would particularly call attention to what I consider the brilliant manner in which the box office has been placed, so as to allow every section of the audience to purchase its tickets from different sides of the same room. No doubt the plan is not of the most academic character, and the lines of the façades can scarcely be said to agree with the divisions of the structure; but for practical purposes and for this class of building, the arrangement of the vestibules, passages and staircases very nearly approaches perfection. As regards the auditorium, I would only say that there are two tiers, the second of which includes accommodation for a comparatively large proportion of the audience. This part of the house presents a dignity and breadth which is very striking, but the decorations, though above the average, are, to my mind, far too small in scale for an interior of such dimensions. In the offices and general equipment the most recent requirements have been fulfilled, and, of the various appliances, those adopted for electric lighting call for special remark. The stage floor, I would add, has no gradient.

As for the rendering of the exterior, the theatre, through forming part of a large block, has peculiarities which would otherwise not be comprehensible, the waste of space above the lounge being quite anomalous in view of other economies effected. The treatment is considered to be in the French Renaissance style, and stone has been used throughout. The detail cannot, however, be termed satisfactory, nor does the exterior architecturally express the purposes of the building.

APPROXIMATE DIMENSIONS.

Width of Proscenium Opening at Curtain Line	35' 0"	10·75 m.
Height of Proscenium Opening at Curtain Line	29' 6"	9·00 m.

AUDITORIUM.			*STAGE.*		
Curtain Line to Front of First Tier . .	34' 0"	10 25 m.	Width inside Containing Walls . . .	69' 6"	21·25 m.
Curtain Line to Front of Second Tier .	40' 0"	12·25 m.	Curtain Line to Containing Back Wall .	49' 0"	15·00 m.
Curtain Line to Furthest Seat . .	79' 0"	24·00 m.	Gridiron Floor above Stage at Curtain Line	54' 0"	16·50 m.
Sunlight Opening above Area . .	50' 0"	15·25 m.	Cellar Floor below Stage at Curtain Line .	19' 9"	6·00 m.
Highest Seat above Street . . .	45' 0"	13·75 m.	Stage Floor at Curtain Line above Street .	2' 6"	0·75 m.
Lowest Seat below Street . . .	0' 9"	0·25 m.			

"HER MAJESTY'S" THEATRE, LONDON. Front Elevation of Block.

"LYRIC" THEATRE, LONDON.

C. J. PHIPPS.

IN the same way that the Wolverhampton Theatre is a typical example of the provincial playhouses designed by C. J. Phipps, so the "Lyric" Theatre in London must stand as a type of his work in the metropolis, for, as I have said, the preceding example, "Her Majesty's," was an instance wherein this architect achieved a work far above the average found in his other buildings. The "Lyric" Theatre, which may be considered one of our most popular modern establishments, was built to fulfil the requirements of Comic Opera, with a capacity for an audience of 1600. The total outlay on the structure was 43,000*l*., and it was opened in December, 1888, having been erected in the short space of ten months.

The irregularity of the site is most marked, and occasioned considerable difficulties to the architect, especially as accommodation for offices and chambers had to be provided, in order to augment the renting capacities of the property. These offices, it must be said, mar the general arrangement of the building to a great extent, as the space they occupy would have been far better utilised in connection with the theatre proper. As to the auditorium, the stalls and pit have their customary position below the level of the street. There are three tiers, and the seats at the back of the uppermost level are again in a "well" constructed in the manner I have so frequently condemned. Features calling for comment are the depth of the different tiers and the variety shown in the lines of the box fronts. The planning of the staircases, passages, etc., is no doubt exceedingly clever, but owing to undue intricacies the scheme, as a whole, loses in clearness. Perhaps, one of the most noticeable arrangements in this part of the building is the manner in which the semicircular main entrance has been contrived, for the approach to the vestibule is far more effective than might have been expected on such an irregular piece of ground.

"LYRIC" THEATRE, LONDON. GENERAL VIEW.

Regarding the decoration of the interior, and the rendering of the exterior, the less said about them the better, while as to the equipment of the building I would only note that the structure was one of the first in which hydraulic stage machinery was applied in London, a set of "bridges" worked by water power having been provided.

Taken as a whole, the example no doubt merits the attention of those who have to overcome special difficulties in the planning of playhouses on unfavourable sites, while it is certainly most characteristic of the class of structure it represents.

APPROXIMATE DIMENSIONS.

Width of Proscenium Opening at Curtain Line .	. . . . .	30' 0"	9·00 m.
Height of Proscenium Opening at Curtain Line .	. . . . .	28' 0"	8·50 m.

AUDITORIUM.			*STAGE.*		
Curtain Line to Front of First Tier .	.	38' 0"	11·50 m.	Width inside Containing Walls . . .	70' 0"	21·25 m.
Curtain Line to Front of Third Tier .	.	47' 6"	14·50 m.	Curtain Line to Containing Back Wall .	40' 0"	12·00 m.
Curtain Line to Furthest Seat .	.	75' 0"	22·75 m.	Gridiron Floor above Stage at Curtain Line	50' 0"	15·25 m.
Sunlight Opening above Area .	.	42' 3"	12·75 m.	Cellar Floor below Stage at Curtain Line .	16' 0"	4·75 m.
Highest Seat above Street .	.	35' 6"	10·75 m.	Stage Floor at Curtain Line below Street .	5' 9"	1·75 m.
Lowest Seat below Street .	.	9' 0"	2·75 m.			

"GARRICK" THEATRE, LONDON.

WALTER EMDEN.

BLOCK PLAN.

THE "Garrick" Theatre falls under the same class as the example with which we have just dealt, and though in this instance the architect responsible for the original conception of the block was Walter Emden, whose "Trafalgar" Theatre was one of the subjects of the preceding volume, the execution, if I am correctly informed, was, to a great extent, in the hands of C. J. Phipps, who in different directions modified the plans. As regards the position of the block and the irregularity of the site, a certain similarity exists between the "Garrick" and the "Lyric," and here, as there, the building has had to be planned in a most intricate manner in order that the available superficial area might be economically utilised. There is also a likeness in the semicircular entrance to the vestibule. In the "Garrick" Theatre there are, again, three tiers, with the area level below that of the street, and the same unfortunate "well" for the uppermost seats. The ceiling of the auditorium, however, is different, for it somewhat resembles, in its dome-like shape, that of the "Trafalgar" Theatre. In architectural rendering and in decoration I would only say that the block here under consideration is of the most nondescript character, while in equipment it has nothing that calls for notice.

"GARRICK" THEATRE, LONDON. GENERAL VIEW.

Taken as a whole, the "Garrick" Theatre, no doubt, typically represents the modern theatre of the metropolis, and, like the preceding example, undoubtedly merits some attention as an instance of particularly clever planning under most difficult circumstances. The sites of both buildings, let me say in conclusion, in no way accord with the purposes of a playhouse, and would not even be sanctioned to-day by the local authorities, as our latest regulations require a theatre to have a more extensive frontage on public thoroughfares than is the case with either of these examples. Owing to the various complications which arose during its construction, no details are available in regard to the actual time of erection, the accommodation afforded, or the cost of the structure, but the opening performance took place in 1889. I need hardly say that this establishment had its origin in a desire for theatrical speculation.

APPROXIMATE DIMENSIONS.

Width of Proscenium Opening at Curtain Line	31' 0"	9·50 m.
Height of Proscenium Opening at Curtain Line	32' 9"	10·00 m.

AUDITORIUM.

Curtain Line to Front of First Tier . .	34' 0"	10·25 m.
Curtain Line to Front of Third Tier . .	37' 0"	11·25 m.
Curtain Line to Furthest Seat . . .	50' 0"	15·25 m.
Sunlight Opening above Area . . .	44' 0"	13·50 m.
Highest Seat above Street	23' 6"	7·25 m.
Lowest Seat below Street	16' 6"	5·00 m.

STAGE.

Width inside Containing Walls . . .	50' 0"	15·25 m.
Curtain Line to Containing Back Wall .	40' 0"	12·25 m.
Gridiron Floor above Stage at Curtain Line	45' 0"	13·75 m.
Cellar Floor below Stage at Curtain Line .	19' 6"	6·00 m.
Stage Floor at Curtain Line below Street .	13' 0"	4·00 m.

"EMPIRE" VARIETY THEATRE, LONDON.

THOMAS VERITY, FRANK T. VERITY.

BLOCK PLAN.

THE purposes fulfilled by the "Empire" Variety Theatre are identical with those of its contemporary, the "Alhambra" Theatre, which was included in the first volume. I there referred to the requirements which an architect is expected to fulfil in a building of this description. As I have also indicated, the "Eden" Variety Theatre of Paris has had considerable influence on the general conception of similar establishments both on the Continent and in this country.

The "Empire" Variety Theatre practically stands on a piece of back land, having only a comparatively narrow frontage on a square, and a small side entrance from an adjoining thoroughfare, while at the rear it overlooks an insignificant street. The theatre occupies the same site on which formerly stood the historic Savile House, which was destroyed by fire in 1865. Subsequent to this conflagration the ground had been occupied by a panorama, which, however, did not prove a success, and in 1882 the late Thomas Verity was commissioned with the adaptation of that building to the purposes of a high-class music hall. As a matter of fact, an almost entire reconstruction of the premises became necessary, as only the foundations of the old panorama could be utilised. These, however, to a certain extent influenced the planning, and the outlines of the original walls are still distinctly discernible in the drawings of the new house produced here. In the period intervening between the opening of the establishment and the production of these volumes, there have been a number of material alterations in the structure and in the general equipment and decoration of the interior, partly with a view to conforming to the more stringent demands of the local authorities, and partly for the purpose of providing improved accommodation for the audience. The plans presented here are taken from the original working drawings, but the side entrance, which I have been able to embody in my illustrations, is one of the recent additions. The views of the house, I should add, are from recent photographs, and, hence, show the interior in its present form.

On entering the building one is struck by the great breadth and dignity of the auditorium, the lines of which must be considered highly satisfactory, while the general decoration is of pleasing effect. The detail of the architectural rendering, it is true, might have received more attention, but the impression, as a whole, leaves little to be desired. It is this breadth and dignity of the auditorium, combined with the spaciousness of the promenades and the convenient position of the saloons, which so materially adds to the popularity of this establishment. The "Empire" Theatre is, no doubt, the best known institution of its kind in the world, but apart from the forms of entertainment associated with the playhouse, I believe that its success is, to a great extent, due to the ingenious method of planning adopted by Thomas Verity. The various alterations and additions referred to, and the remodelling of much of the decorations, I should add, have been undertaken by Frank T. Verity, who succeeded his father as architect to the building, and

"EMPIRE" VARIETY THEATRE, LONDON.
VIEW OF AUDITORIUM.

to whom considerable credit is also due. The side entrance above mentioned is, for instance, from his plans.

The area level is here again well below that of the street, the promenade of the first tier being on a line with the pavement. The second tier is reached by a flight of stairs from the grand vestibule, and slightly above the second tier level we find the principal lounge, from which, by-the-bye, a fair view of the stage can be obtained. There is also a third tier, the seats of which are, however, largely in a "well," and the "sighting" of this part of the house is much interrupted by the row of columns which support the ceiling. Both the first and second tiers have the usual promenades, and there is also extensive standing-room on either side of the stalls. On the first tier level are two sets of boxes besides the large proscenium boxes, and their doors, I would add, open on to the promenade just referred to. The hearing qualities are above the average, but the ventilation of the auditorium might be materially improved, as smoking is, of course, permitted in an establishment of this description.

As to staircase accommodation, and the general facilities for approach and exit, I do not consider them to be of the

"EMPIRE" VARIETY THEATRE, LONDON.
VIEW OF SIDE VESTIBULE.

same high standard of efficiency evident in other portions of the structure, but this cannot well be otherwise, considering the position of the building on a site with such limited frontage. Such improvements as have been made from time to time, more particularly in the arrangement of the extra side entrance referred to, are only too necessary.

As for the general equipment of the auditorium, excepting, perhaps, the ventilation referred to, and, to a certain extent, the lighting, the requirements of the audience have been observed in every respect; but, on the other hand, the "back of the house" in no way reflects the influence of modern progress. The stage and the accommodation for the staff require almost entire remodelling, and it is strange that the economy derived from modern appliances has not been considered in connection with the stage machinery, as the constant expenditure on the many makeshifts necessarily introduced now and again for the production of various spectacular effects, appears far too wasteful, while the large staff of stage-hands seems somewhat superfluous when suitable mechanism is available as a substitute for manual labour.

Taken generally, however, there is no doubt that the "Empire" Variety Theatre not only occupies the leading position among English institutions of its kind, but can hold its own among many of the structures of greater architectural pretension to be found on the Continent. The plan may not be altogether academic in its character, and it may fail, to a certain degree, to meet some of the requirements in technical equipment to which such an establishment newly opening its doors to-day is put, but for all that it is undeniably a remarkable example of theatre construction, and the manner in which the comfort of the audience has been considered has certainly not been surpassed, even in the most recent production of any other country. It is curious to find so frequently some of the most successful work in theatre design associated with the home of the variety entertainment, both in England, and also abroad.

APPROXIMATE DIMENSIONS.

Width of Proscenium Opening at Curtain Line	32' 0"	0·75 m.
Height of Proscenium Opening at Curtain Line	35' 0"	10·50 m.

AUDITORIUM.			*STAGE.*		
Curtain Line to Front of First Tier . .	53' 0"	16·25 m.	Width inside Containing Walls . . .	67' 0"	20·50 m.
Curtain Line to Front of Third Tier . .	64' 6"	19·75 m.	Curtain Line to Containing Back Wall .	47' 0"	14·50 m.
Curtain Line to Furthest Seat . . .	80' 0"	24·50 m.	Curtain Line to Furthest Wall of Back Stage	62' 0"	19·00 m.
Sunlight Opening above Area . . .	54' 0"	16·50 m.	Gridiron Floor above Stage at Curtain Line	47' 0"	14·50 m.
Highest Seat above Street . . .	32' 9"	10·00 m.	Cellar Floor below Stage at Curtain Line .	18' 0"	5·50 m.
Lowest Seat below Street . . .	15' 3"	4·75 m.	Stage Floor at Curtain Line below Street .	12' 3"	3·75 m.

"EMPIRE" VARIETY THEATRE, LONDON. VIEW OF PROMENADE.

"OXFORD" VARIETY THEATRE, LONDON.

OSWALD C. WYLSON, CHARLES LONG.

BLOCK PLAN.

WHILST the "Empire" and "Alhambra" Theatres are specially adapted for entertainments on a large scale, including the production of great spectacular ballets, the "Oxford" Variety Theatre is to a far greater extent a music hall of the old type. The promenade, too, does not occupy the same position as in the larger establishments, since the audience pays far greater attention here to the actual performance than in the more important institutions.

The "Oxford" Variety Theatre, as it now stands, dates from 1893, when it was erected under the supervision of Oswald C. Wylson and Charles Long, an example of whose work has already been under consideration in the preceding volume. Only a very short time was available for the building operations to be carried out, and the difficulties encountered were numerous. The great irregularity of the site was due to the fact that the superficial area had from time to time been extended by the purchase of adjoining property, the original Music Hall, situated on this spot and dating from 1862, having occupied much less ground. This building, it should be mentioned, was destroyed by fire in 1868, and was rebuilt in 1869, only to experience the same fate after a brief existence of two years. In 1873 a more ambitious structure was erected, and this house was gradually altered to fulfil the increasing demands made upon it, until what had become a mere piece of structural patchwork had to be entirely demolished, to make room for the new building now before us.

As regards the plan, I can only say that the difficulties occasioned by the outline of the site have been overcome in a manner highly creditable to the architects, whilst the decoration of the interior, though perhaps somewhat heavy in its detail, is above the average of similar work in London. There is a certain dignity in the architectural feeling of the auditorium which calls for comment, and it is only to be regretted

"OXFORD" VARIETY THEATRE, LONDON. GENERAL VIEW.

that the same characteristics are not observable in the principal façade, which is by no means so successful as the other parts of the block, and has undoubtedly also suffered by the addition of two porticos.

APPROXIMATE DIMENSIONS.

Width of Proscenium Opening at Curtain Line .	. . . . .	29' 6"	9·00 m.
Height of Proscenium Opening at Curtain Line .	. . . . .	24' 6"	7·50 m.

AUDITORIUM.				*STAGE.*			
Curtain Line to Front of First Tier .	.	46' 6"	14·25 m.	Width inside Containing Walls . . .	56' 0"	17·00 m.
Curtain Line to Front of Second Tier	.	50' 6"	15·50 m.	Curtain Line to Containing Back Wall .	17' 0"	5·25 m.
Curtain Line to Furthest Seat . .	.	62' 6"	19·00 m.	Curtain Line to Furthest Wall of Back Stage	41' 0"	12·50 m.
Sunlight Opening above Area . .	.	44' 3"	13·50 m.	Gridiron Floor above Stage at Curtain Line	37' 6"	11·50 m.
Highest Seat above Street . .	.	28' 0"	8·50 m.	Cellar Floor below Stage at Curtain Line .	14' 0"	4·25 m.
Lowest Seat below Street . .	.	0' 9"	0·25 m.	Stage Floor at Curtain Line above Street .	3' 3"	1·00 m.

SHAKESPEARE MEMORIAL THEATRE
STRATFORD-ON-AVON.

W. F. UNSWORTH.

IT is remarkable that so many years were allowed to elapse after Shakespeare's death before anything like a fitting monument was erected to his memory. Even at the present time the memorials of this great master which we have in London are utterly unworthy of their purpose, both in design and execution. It is not pretended that the most magnificent monument could add anything to the position his work occupies in history, but it is highly discreditable to the metropolis that we do not pay some slight token of reverence to the greatest of English dramatists. It was not until the tercentenary of his birth that a serious suggestion was made for the erection of some permanent and worthy memorial in his native town of Stratford-on-Avon, but owing to difference of opinion as to what form such a monument should take, nothing was done in this direction until quite ten years later, when a site for the erection of a memorial theatre was presented, together with a considerable sum of money towards its cost. An influential committee was then formed for the furtherance of the scheme as well as for the raising of additional funds, and the local authorities at Stratford-on-Avon gave a great impetus to the movement by both subscribing themselves and by issuing an appeal to other public bodies in different parts of Great Britain. Nevertheless, the money thus obtained would not have been sufficient to meet the proposed expenditure, and the original donor actually found it necessary to guarantee any possible deficiency, in order that the undertaking might be proceeded with. For once in this country a competition was opened for the design of a theatre, and the plans of Dodgshun and Unsworth having been selected as the most suitable, building operations were commenced, the foundation stone being laid in April, 1877, and the inauguration of the theatre proper taking place two years later, i.e. on April 23rd, 1879. The scheme, I should at once say, comprises, in addition to the Memorial Theatre proper, a library, a picture gallery, and a room for mementos relating to the poet and his works, which were placed in a separate block known as the Museum, subsequently connected with the theatre by a gallery. This Museum was only opened in 1881. Another feature in the conception of the scheme is a tower, which marks the position of the block in the landscape, and, I might almost say, gives the whole the character of a monument. This tower also was not completed till after the opening of the theatre. As for the cost of the erection, the approximate outlay on the buildings has

SHAKESPEARE MEMORIAL THEATRE, STRATFORD-ON-AVON.
GENERAL VIEW.

been 20,000*l.*, of which nearly 11,500*l.* were expended on the theatre proper. The accommodation is for an audience of nine hundred. The situation of the block in its own grounds near the river is very picturesque, and when the gardens have been developed, the memorial will no doubt have one of the most attractive positions ever accorded to a playhouse.

In examining the plans the purpose of the block must not be forgotten, the requirements including much that referred to the necessarily economic management of an institution of this kind. Thus, one of the conditions was that the number of check-takers should be limited to two, an instruction that was very difficult to fulfil and which had some influence on the planning. Another demand was for the possible isolation of the Museum from the theatre, in order to lessen the risk of fire, while it was also deemed requisite that the main approach to the playhouse should be through the building that contained the collections. As I have said, the competition for the design was won by Unsworth and Dodgshun, but the collaboration did not extend far as Unsworth must be considered wholly responsible for the execution of the block. All concerned, however, deserve congratulation for the manner in which the undertaking was conceived and eventually carried out, and not the least to whom it is due are the contractors, on account of the excellent workmanship shown.

The Museum has its library on the ground floor, and its picture gallery and collections on the first-floor level, the latter having top-lights. The hall is carried up through both floors, and whilst the first floor is connected by a gallery to the first tier of the theatre, the approach to the area level of the playhouse is through the open, and under the shelter of this gallery. The auditorium has two tiers, and the manner in which its lines have been laid out is worthy of remark. The way in which the structure expresses its purpose on the exterior, I would add, is fully in accordance with the most recent ideas on that point, and both its picturesque grouping and the architectural rendering are extremely pleasing. The Gothic feeling in the treatment is unique in the annals of theatre construction, where, with few exceptions, the Renaissance and lighter French styles have alone been employed. I know that many would have preferred to see the theatre dealt with in a more classic manner, expressing, perhaps, the character of Shakespeare's work; but, though such a memorial theatre would no doubt be appropriate for London, it would have been lamentably out of place at Stratford-on-Avon. If anything falls short of the standard aspired to in this building, it is the interior decoration of the auditorium, which requires considerable elaboration.

As a whole, however, the memorial scheme may be said to be one of the most successful achievements of its kind, and though the playhouse, no doubt, only occupies a secondary position in relation to the main idea of providing a fitting monument to the poet, that part of the block which contains the auditorium and stage must be recognised as a *bona fide* theatre of no slight architectural pretensions.

APPROXIMATE DIMENSIONS.

Width of Proscenium Opening at Curtain Line	27' 0"	8·25 m.
Height of Proscenium Opening at Curtain Line	28' 0"	8·50 m.

AUDITORIUM.				*STAGE.*		
Curtain Line to Front of First Tier . .	37' 9"	11·50 m.	Width inside Containing Walls . . .	52' 9"	16·00 m.
Curtain Line to Front of Second Tier .	37' 9"	11·50 m.	Curtain Line to Containing Back Wall .	29' 0"	8·75 m.
Curtain Line to Furthest Seat . . .	47' 0"	14·25 m.	Curtain Line to Furthest Wall of Back Stage	41' 0"	12·50 m.
Sunlight Opening above Area . . .	43' 6"	13·25 m.	Gridiron Floor above Stage at Curtain Line	45' 6"	13·75 m.
Highest Seat above Street	32' 0"	9·75 m.	Cellar Floor below Stage at Curtain Line .	18' 0"	5·50 m.
Lowest Seat above Street	5' 0"	1·50 m.	Stage Floor at Curtain Line above Street .	8' 0"	2·50 m.

SHAKESPEARE MEMORIAL THEATRE, STRATFORD-ON-AVON.
GENERAL VIEW FROM RIVER.

"GRAND" THEATRE, LEEDS.

GEORGE CORSON.

BLOCK PLAN.

THOUGH the earliest example among the English playhouses presented in this work, the "Grand" Theatre at Leeds is by no means the least important establishment of its class to be found in the United Kingdom. Its conception comprises the somewhat unusual combination of a theatre, a concert-hall and an assembly-room, in the same block. There may be doubts as to the advisability of thus uniting in one group these various places of entertainment, together with a number of shops and offices, since the safety of the audience is certainly lessened by such an arrangement. Nevertheless, for a provincial town, the breadth of the conception is noteworthy, and, as will be observed in the plans, no little skill has been bestowed on the endeavour partially to divide the block into two separate buildings, so that the one contains the theatre only, while the other is devoted to the various halls, together with the business premises. It is only to be regretted that the main approach to the auditorium had to be constructed through that part of the block containing the shops.

"GRAND" THEATRE, LEEDS. VIEW OF AUDITORIUM.

The intention of those responsible for the "Grand" Theatre was to provide Leeds with a large and well-equipped playhouse, and after making allowance for the date of its erection, and the little attention which was paid at the time to protection against fire, I hold that the original purpose has, to a great extent, been attained in the design of this structure. In its architectural rendering also it stands above the average of buildings of its class. The Leeds Theatre, I might mention, took the place of two other establishments, which had been successively burnt down within ten months of each other. Building operations on the new block were commenced in 1875, and the inauguration took place on the 18th November, 1876. The cost of the erection was 60,000*l.*, and seating accommodation was provided in the auditorium for 2600 persons, besides standing room for an additional 600. The commission was placed in the hands of a local architect, George Corson, who designed and executed the building in collaboration with J. R. Watson.

The plans are sufficiently clear to explain themselves, and I need only add that the general lines of the auditorium are very effective. There are few features that call for special comment, but the staircase accommodation must be said to be insufficient. The façade gives the structure the character of a public building, but scarcely explains its purpose as a place of entertainment. As I have already indicated, the early date of the erection must not be overlooked if we would form a true estimate of the value of this playhouse.

APPROXIMATE DIMENSIONS.

Width of Proscenium Opening at Curtain Line	30' 3"	9·25 m.
Height of Proscenium Opening at Curtain Line	40' 0"	12·25 m.

AUDITORIUM.			*STAGE.*		
Curtain Line to Front of First Tier . .	55' 0"	16·75 m.	Width inside Containing Walls . . .	70' 9"	21·50 m.
Curtain Line to Front of Third Tier .	61' 0"	18·50 m.	Curtain Line to Containing Back Wall .	47' 6"	14·50 m.
Curtain Line to Furthest Seat . .	91' 0"	27·75 m.	Curtain Line to Furthest Wall of Back Stage	65' 0"	19·75 m.
Sunlight Opening above Area . .	55' 0"	16·75 m.	Gridiron Floor above Stage at Curtain Line	59' 0"	18·00 m.
Highest Seat above Street . .	54' 3"	16·50 m.	Cellar Floor below Stage at Curtain Line .	26' 0"	8·00 m.
Lowest Seat above Street . . .	6' 0"	1·75 m.	Stage Floor at Curtain Line above Street .	10' 0"	3·00 m.

"NEW" THEATRE, CAMBRIDGE.

ERNEST RÜNTZ.

THE concluding example of this series of theatres erected in London and the provinces is but a comparatively small building. Nevertheless, to my mind, it is one of the most important instances of recent theatre construction, since we find in it, for once, a playhouse which, though essentially a commercial establishment, and situated on a piece of back land, reveals, in every detail, evidence that the greatest possible pains have been taken to give it an architectural rendering fully in accord with its purpose. I have every reason to believe that financial considerations received, in this venture, the same marked attention as in other enterprises of the kind, but for all that the architectural treatment was not here limited to the achievements of the plastic decorator in the interests of vulgar advertisement. Both the owners and the architect should be congratulated on the result, but, more particularly, perhaps, the latter, Ernest Rüntz, who, in the face of conventional ideas, regarded the interests of architecture in its higher sense, and strove to provide both client and public with a piece of work which should in every way surpass the usual standard of the provincial playhouse. I have already remarked that, as a rule, the theatre architecture of this country is in the hands of men who are primarily financial agents, and who only give architecture, as such, quite secondary attention. The architect, in this instance, is no doubt also thoroughly familiar with the financial aspects of theatre enterprise, and has indeed already shown considerable ability in this direction, yet he has not disregarded the claims of his profession, as is generally the case with the theatre specialist. He has even been bold enough to risk the confidence of those who employed him by giving them something better than they had perhaps desired. In other words, he has treated his commission from the point of view of an architect in the best sense of the word, and on this account alone, although new to this class of work, he already holds an important position in the annals of theatre construction in this country.

"NEW" THEATRE, CAMBRIDGE. VIEW OF PROSCENIUM.

The "New" Theatre at Cambridge has to cater for the requirements of a University town, and, this has, to a certain extent, influenced the plan, more especially in the division of the various sections of the audience. Accommodation has been provided for 1400 spectators. The inaugural ceremony took place in January, 1896, after a comparatively short period of building operations; the total cost of the structure, with all decorations, and its installation for lighting, etc., being 15,500l.

The block is screened from the main thoroughfare by two buildings, and can only be approached by a passage between them leading to the main entrance and the principal vestibule. From the latter, a broad corridor leads to the stalls, whilst the first tier is reached by a staircase overlooking the vestibule. The entrance to the second tier and to the pit are kept distinct. Suitable saloons have been provided for each section of the audience, and it is noticeable that their arrangement is particularly adapted for serving rapidly. It is only too usual to find the bar fronts much too small in comparison to the accommodation offered, but in this instance there is no reason for complaint on that account. The position of the two saloons for the stalls and pit, with the lavatories leading out of them, has been especially well managed. The conspicuous position of lavatories generally, I would here say, is a fault extremely common in our playhouses, and the approach through the saloon is an improvement. As for facilities for entrance and exit and the arrangement of the staircases, they are far better than might have been expected on a site of this description. There should, however, have been two distinct stairs to the first tier. The principal characteristic of the rendering in the lobbies, refreshment rooms and passages is one of dignity and comfort, without any redundancy of decoration.

The auditorium has only two tiers, both of which are deep, but, unfortunately, the upper seats of the second tier are situated in a "well." Among the principal features are the lines of the auditorium and the arrangement of the proscenium with its boxes on either side.   The ceiling, I would add, is a flat one.   The colour study in this part of the building is excellent, and the plaster work throughout is most pleasing in detail.   The colours employed are old gold, blue, cream and white, and the feeling of the architecture is that of the Renaissance period.   A particularly satisfactory

"NEW" THEATRE, CAMBRIDGE. VIEW OF LOBBY.

effect is obtained by a frieze over the proscenium opening, giving representations of Shakespeare's characters as depicted in his plays, but the division between the proscenium boxes of the first and second tiers cannot be termed satisfactory, nor does it accord with the otherwise careful conception of the interior.   The manner in which the drapery is here arranged to partially screen the upper boxes is not in keeping with the apparent purposes of the latter. The general impression, however, throughout the auditorium is that the decoration has been used to contribute, to a great extent, to the well-being of the audience, and that all the usual methods of vulgar elaboration and unnecessary gilding have been scrupulously avoided. It is not often one can say so much of a theatre situated in the provinces.

I consider it a particularly pleasant duty to be able to say some words of praise in regard to the building by Ernest Rüntz at Cambridge, and I hold it to be only a matter of regret that so much adverse criticism has had to be offered in regard to English examples of theatre construction generally.   The "New" Theatre only too distinctly shows that, with due regard for the financial aspects of theatre enterprise, it is possible to erect a playhouse without ignoring the claims of architecture, and I trust that the lesson which this building affords will be appreciated.

APPROXIMATE DIMENSIONS.

Width of Proscenium Opening at Curtain Line	28' 6"	8·75 m.
Height of Proscenium Opening at Curtain Line	26' 6"	8·00 m.

AUDITORIUM.

Curtain Line to Front of First Tier	34' 6"	10·50 m.
Curtain Line to Front of Second Tier	37' 0"	11·25 m.
Curtain Line to Furthest Seat	60' 0"	18·25 m.
Sunlight Opening above Area	40' 3"	12·25 m.
Highest Seat above Street	37' 9"	11·50 m.
Lowest Seat below Street	3' 3"	1·00 m.

STAGE.

Width inside Containing Walls	54' 0"	16·50 m.
Curtain Line to Containing Back Wall	35' 3"	10·75 m.
Gridiron Floor above Stage at Curtain Line	53' 6"	16·25 m.
Cellar Floor below Stage at Curtain Line	10' 0"	3·00 m.
Stage Floor at Curtain Line above Street	0' 9"	0·25 m.

"NEW" THEATRE CAMBRIDGE. VIEW OF GRAND VESTIBULE.

GREECE.

NATIONAL THEATRE, ATHENS.

ERNEST ZILLER.

GREECE is usually only associated with the drama of the classical era and the great amphitheatres of that period. Nevertheless, its capital, Athens, has to-day several modern playhouses of some architectural pretensions, as well as various minor establishments, whilst Piræus has lately been given a small Summer Theatre built on the principles of the Bayreuth Opera House. The two leading institutions of Athens are the Municipal Theatre erected in 1872, affording accommodation for an audience of 1800, and the National Theatre now before us, built at the expense of the King of Greece and opened in 1895. Both are designed by Ernest Ziller, a German architect practising at Athens.

Considering the associations of this city, it would not have been unnatural to expect a building which, in its architectural rendering, would take a high place among the playhouses illustrated in these volumes, but, as a matter of fact, though there is a distinct attempt to give this block a classical appearance, the manner in which the lines have been set out, as well as the execution of the detail, cannot be said to support any claim for special consideration. It has, no doubt, as I have indicated, architectural pretensions, and the theatre occupies an important position, while the general grouping is ambitious. The difficulties, however, which the architect had to encounter, owing to the unequal levels of the site, have not been quite satisfactorily overcome, and the result is that the effect he desired has scarcely been attained.

The plan shows a very distinct division between the main section containing the auditorium with its offices, and another containing a restaurant on ground level, with a large hall above, which, though serving as a lounge in connection with the theatre, must also be regarded in the light of an assembly room, and is frequently used separately for various forms of entertainment.

The theatre proper is most economically planned, and the fact of the site not being a deep one has received full consideration with a view to the best possible utilisation of the space available. As will be seen, it is a two-tier house, in which the area is, comparatively speaking, a small one, whilst the first tier is of an average depth, and the second tier unusually spacious. The Court has been provided with a Royal Box on the left of the proscenium, having an ante-room and its own staircase. The plan is a clear one, and the staircases have been carefully thought out, though their position,

NATIONAL THEATRE, ATHENS. DETAIL OF FRONT ELEVATION.

with windows overlooking the small areas only, by no means accords with the requirements of to-day. The offices appear to be somewhat cramped, and there is a great lack of cloak-room and lavatory accommodation.

On examining the lines of the auditorium in greater detail we find that the area rises somewhat steeply, as compared with other playhouses. Next we notice that the first tier only overlaps the area to a very small extent, while the latter is divided into three sections, each of which has separate sets of doors. As in the case of one of Seeling's theatres, illustrated in this volume, there is no proscenium here, as we understand it, for the grand box of the first tier, which is reserved for royal visitors, is simply built into the auditorium irrespective of the lines of the ceiling, and the box opposite has been treated in a similar fashion. Underneath are some minor boxes, but otherwise, there are no half-open boxes in this building, such as are found elsewhere on the Continent, the whole of the seats being in continuous rows. The total accommodation provided is for about 1100. The ceiling of the auditorium is practically flat, only rising slightly towards the opening in the centre. The back of the second tier is in the form of a "well," but its arrangement is far more spacious than is commonly the case, so that the impression given is not unsatisfactory. In the architectural rendering, the classical feeling gives the auditorium a severity which does not quite accord with the purposes of a place of public entertainment, though it may be fitting for an establishment where the presentation of drama is intended to be a means of education. The idea of treating the front of the second tier on the same principle as a balustrade is exceptional, but very satisfactory in appearance. The absence of the proscenium, however, detracts much from the dignity of the framing of the stage picture.

Taken as a whole, the block merits attention more on account of the associations of the city in which it stands than for any special structural merits, and yet it affords an interesting example of its class.

APPROXIMATE DIMENSIONS.

Width of Proscenium Opening at Curtain Line	31' 0"	9·50 m.
Height of Proscenium Opening at Curtain Line	25' 6"	7·75 m.

AUDITORIUM.			*STAGE.*		
Curtain Line to Front of First Tier . .	43' 3"	13·25 m.	Width inside Containing Walls . . .	60' 6"	18·50 m.
Curtain Line to Front of Second Tier .	47' 6"	14·50 m.	Curtain Line to Containing Back Wall .	42' 6"	13·00 m.
Curtain Line to Furthest Seat . . .	75' 6"	23·00 m.	Curtain Line to Furthest Wall of Back Stage	59' 0"	18·00 m.
Sunlight Opening above Area . . .	36' 0"	11·00 m.	Gridiron Floor above Stage at Curtain Line	55' 9"	14·25 m.
Highest Seat above Street	37' 6"	11·50 m.	Cellar Floor below Stage at Curtain Line .	13' 9"	4·25 m.
Lowest Seat above Street	3' 3"	1·00 m.	Stage Floor at Curtain Line above Street .	7' 3"	2·25 m.

MUNICIPAL THEATRE, ROTTERDAM.
VIEW OF LOUNGE.

HOLLAND AND BELGIUM.

MUNICIPAL THEATRE, ROTTERDAM.

J. VERHEUL.

BLOCK PLAN.

IN the preceding volume, when the Municipal Theatre at Amsterdam was presented, I referred to it as having almost attained perfection in planning and construction, especially in the direction of the safety of the audience against fire. The Municipal Theatre at Rotterdam is by no means a despicable rival, for here, likewise, we find that the general arrangement is of considerable merit. It is strange that we should discover in Holland, one of the smallest of Continental countries, such marked instances where great attention has been given to modern requirements, whilst such countries as France and Italy leave so much to be desired in this respect.

The playhouse at Rotterdam possesses the peculiarity of having to fulfil two purposes, namely, that of an Opera House on the one hand, and that of the home of national drama on the other, each species of entertainment having a separate management. The inauguration of this establishment took place on the 15th of September, 1887, the building operations having been spread over three years. Both the design and execution of the plans were in the hands of a local architect, J. Verheul, who had to provide seating for an audience of 1250, at a total outlay of 58,000*l.*

The general lines of this structure claim attention on account of the very commendable clearness of the plan, and it will also be seen that the vestibule, halls and stairs are of ample dimensions. The auditorium has three tiers, and, though the manner in which both the tiers and the ceiling are supported by columns is detrimental to the "sighting" from many of the seats, the accommodation, as a whole, is by no means unsatisfactory. Besides the large proscenium boxes, there are half-open boxes on either side of the area, as well as round the entire first tier and at the back of the second. In the latter case they have been so constructed as to allow one or two rows of seats being placed in front of them. The manner in which the seats of the area are reached from two main gangways leading direct out of the vestibule contrasts markedly with the ideas of Heinrich Seeling, who generally contrives to give each sequence of rows its own entrances from the sides. In the general equipment of the building a number of recent improvements are visible, though these cannot lay claim to the same high standard as is apparent in the Amsterdam Theatre.

In regard to the architectural rendering of this block, little need be said as to either the exterior or the interior, though the appearance of the building as a whole is pleasing. If I may say so, the Rotterdam Theatre is a thoroughly practical playhouse of an essentially symmetrical plan, but without any particular architectural pretension.

APPROXIMATE DIMENSIONS.

Width of Proscenium Opening at Curtain Line	36' 0"	11·00 m.
Height of Proscenium Opening at Curtain Line	37' 6"	11·50 m.

AUDITORIUM.			*STAGE.*		
Curtain Line to Front of First Tier . .	59' 9"	18·25 m.	Width inside Containing Walls . . .	82' 0"	25·00 m.
Curtain Line to Front of Third Tier . .	62' 3"	19·00 m.	Curtain Line to Containing Back Wall .	56' 6"	17·25 m.
Curtain Line to Furthest Seat . . .	78' 9"	24·00 m.	Curtain Line to Furthest Wall of Back Stage	63' 9"	19·50 m.
Sunlight Opening above Area . . .	52' 6"	16·00 m.	Gridiron Floor above Stage at Curtain Line	62' 3"	19·00 m.
Highest Seat above Street . . .	50' 9"	15·50 m.	Cellar Floor below Stage at Curtain Line .	16' 3"	5·00 m.
Lowest Seat above Street . . .	9' 9"	3·00 m.	Stage Floor at Curtain Line above Street .	12' 3"	3·75 m.

ROUMANIA.

NATIONAL THEATRE, BUCHAREST.

G. STERIAN.

BLOCK PLAN.

THE National Theatre at Bucharest can scarcely be considered an entirely new building, for, as a matter of fact, it is an old National playhouse remodelled. The new work, however, has assumed such proportions that but little of the original theatre remains, except, perhaps, the main containing walls, which to a certain extent have governed the general arrangement. The building operations are in the hands of George Sterian, an architect of considerable local standing, and will see completion next year.

No doubt one of the most notable features of this block is its grouping on a particularly difficult site, for, as may be seen from the illustrations, the ground which it occupies falls to so steep a gradient that various makeshifts had to be resorted to, such as the arrangement of a large terrace on one side, in order to obtain a practical plan. It is on account of these differences of level that, for instance, a somewhat unusual device had to be contrived for the entrance and exit of the audience, for it will be observed that, while the main carriage approach and the grand vestibule are situated on what I will term the terrace level, there is a special side door in the basement for foot passengers, with a further vestibule beneath the auditorium proper.

It is noticeable that this building is an example of the so-called "central" system of planning, with a grand staircase in the middle and minor stairs on either side. The latter, I should perhaps at once say, accord in their arrangement with the modern requirements of isolation. There appear also to be ample facilities for exit on one side of the area level, as the passage to this part has no less than three doors into the open. Unfortunately, however, the difficulties of the site have apparently prevented a similar treatment on the other side, for which the exits are by no means sufficient.

There is little in the arrangement of the auditorium or in other parts of the building that calls for comment, except, perhaps, that the staircase produces an exceedingly good impression, and the manner in which it is overlooked from the balconies in the second tier is very pleasing. The equipment, when complete, will conform to recent demands, both in the matter of warming and ventilation as well as in minor appliances, and the scenery has its separate storehouse.

Of the details of the decoration in the interior little can as yet be said, but to judge from the careful ornamentation shown in the drawings of the exterior, there is no doubt that a high standard will be reached in this part. Taken as a whole, the building is a notable example of theatre construction in a city that is seldom associated with architecture in the higher sense, and we should not forget the peculiar circumstances which have governed its erection.

APPROXIMATE DIMENSIONS.

Width of Proscenium Opening at Curtain Line ᴮ⸝ᴸ .	33' 5"	10·75 m.
Height of Proscenium Opening at Curtain Line .	36' 0"	11·00 m.

AUDITORIUM.				*STAGE.*		
Curtain Line to Front of First Tier .	52' 2"	16·00 m.	Width inside Containing Walls . . .	65' 6"	20·00 m.
Curtain Line to Front of Second Tier	59' 0"	18·00 m.	Curtain Line to Containing Back Wall .	52' 9"	17·00 m.
Curtain Line to Furthest Seat . .	68' 9"	21·00 m.	Gridiron Floor above Stage at Curtain Line	72' 3"	22·00 m.
Sunlight Opening above Area . .	54' 0"	16·50 m.	Cellar Floor below Stage at Curtain Line .	19' 9"	6·00 m
Highest Seat above Terrace . .	46' 0"	14·00 m.	Stage Floor at Curtain Line above Terrace	5' 0"	1·50 m.
Lowest Seat above Terrace . .	1' 6"	0·50 m.			

SWITZERLAND

MUNICIPAL THEATRE, GENEVA.

J. E. GOSS.

WE are not accustomed to associate Switzerland with the production of dramatic entertainments of any great value, though, as a matter of fact, many of the towns in that country possess theatres of some pretensions. It is true that the capital, Berne, has a playhouse of only secondary importance, but what Berne at present lacks will be found amply supplied by Geneva and Zürich, both of which have modern establishments. Of these two the example at Zürich is the most recent, having been opened in 1891, whereas the theatre at Geneva was completed in 1879.

I encountered some difficulty in selecting the position which these two Swiss examples should occupy in this volume, for there is no doubt that the building at Zürich as plainly shows Teutonic influence as the establishment at Geneva exhibits much that is common to Latin countries. Their situation, of course, somewhat accounts for this, Zürich belonging essentially to so-called "German" Switzerland, whilst Geneva may be called the capital of the French cantons. The architects, too, are equally distinguishable, in that the author of the Geneva building had a training on Parisian lines, and no doubt considered the Paris Opera House as his model, whilst the Zürich establishment was the work of the Austrian specialists, Fellner and Helmer. The latter had no restrictions put upon them as regards local requirements, and hence, naturally, designed their building practically on the same lines as those of the playhouses in their own country. On consideration, however, I deemed it right to place these two examples among buildings exhibiting Teutonic influence, as it seemed inadvisable to divide Switzerland into two parts for the purposes of a book of this description. I was the more inclined to adopt this course, as an examination of the plans will show that the Geneva building is not so markedly a typical French playhouse as one would imagine from its exterior. The absence of the great supporting columns, which are characteristic of a French auditorium, and the manner in which the rows of seats

MUNICIPAL THEATRE, GENEVA. GENERAL VIEW.

are placed in front of the half-open boxes of the first and second tiers, do not speak of Latin influence, nor does the open third tier. Another feature of the French playhouse is that its area reaches back with a sharp gradient to the front of the first tier as in the case of the Paris Opera House, and this characteristic again is absent at Geneva. Altogether, one might almost say that the example is a compromise between the two distinct types of planning which I have illustrated. In its architectural rendering, more particularly in the exterior, the building is no doubt thoroughly French in feeling, but, otherwise, Teutonic influence is strikingly observable throughout the block.

The Municipal Theatre at Geneva replaced an old structure which had long been the only playhouse in that town, and which, as far back as 1861, had been declared inadequate for its purposes. There appears to have been a lack of funds for the new establishment, for it was not until the Municipality had received a considerable legacy from the Duke of Brunswick that the building could be commenced. As I have said, the inauguration took place in 1879, or, to be exact, on the 2nd of October of that year. Building operations were spread over five years, and the total expenditure incurred reached nearly 100,000*l.* The seating capacity of the auditorium, I should add, is for 1200, whilst there is standing room for an additional hundred. The architect of the building was J. E. Goss, who held a commission from the Municipality.

With regard to the plan, it may be considered a symmetrical one, as far as entrances, lobbies and staircases are concerned. One of the features of the arrangement is the manner in which the first tier is approached by two flights of main stairs on either side of the inner hall. The second tier stairs do not accord with the ideas of to-day, owing to their having no windows, and the "winders" on their lower flights, as well as their approach from the main hall, are scarcely satisfactory. As for the entrances and exits from the seats on the area level, it would have been advisable if some means of gaining the open had been provided besides those through the hall, for, as will be seen, not only the spectators in the area, but also those on both the first and second tiers have to pass through one vestibule on entering and leaving the house. It was quite unnecessary that the cloak-room accommodation should have been so planned as to prevent there being doors from the side passages directly into the streets.

As to the lines of the auditorium, I would only remark that the effect obtained is a very pleasing one, and the way in which the rows of seats have been placed in front of the half-open boxes, as was also the case at Rotterdam, is particularly convenient. The decorations are in good taste, without being ostentatious. The equipment, however, scarcely accords with recent demands. As to the exterior, the illustrations fully express the character of the design, and I would only say that the manner in which the freestone has been worked adds much to the appearance of the building. If anything, parts of the exterior, perhaps, show too marked an assimilation of some of the features of the Paris Opera House, as, for instance, in the treatment of the roofs. Taken as a whole, however, the Municipal Theatre at Geneva must be considered to rank among the leading structures which were erected in the seventies.

APPROXIMATE DIMENSIONS.

Width of Proscenium Opening at Curtain Line	39' 3"	12·00 m.
Height of Proscenium Opening at Curtain Line	39' 3"	12·00 m.

AUDITORIUM.			*STAGE.*		
Curtain Line to Front of First Tier . .	53' 3"	16·25 m.	Width inside Containing Walls . . .	78' 9"	24·00 m.
Curtain Line to Front of Third Tier . .	59' 0"	18·00 m.	Curtain Line to Containing Back Wall .	50' 9"	15·50 m.
Curtain Line to Furthest Seat . . .	65' 6"	20·00 m.	Gridiron Floor above Stage at Curtain Line	77' 0"	23·50 m.
Sunlight Opening above Area . . .	52' 6"	16·00 m.	Cellar Floor below Stage at Curtain Line .	30' 3"	9·25 m.
Highest Seat above Street . . .	55' 0"	14·00 m.	Stage Floor at Curtain Line above Street .	13' 0"	4·00 m.
Lowest Seat above Street . . .	9' 0"	2·75 m.			

MUNICIPAL THEATRE, ZÜRICH. VIEW OF AUDITORIUM.

MUNICIPAL THEATRE, ZÜRICH

FERDINAND FELLNER, HERMANN HELMER.

BLOCK PLAN.

THE example with which I close the series of playhouses illustrated in this volume again testifies to the very excellent work of the Austrian theatre specialists, Fellner and Helmer. The great skill of the designers is, as usual, shown in the clearness of plan, with the brilliant arrangement of the main vestibule and staircases, and, further, by the practical manner in which the auditorium has been set out. We find again also, on the one hand, their customary and very pleasing decorations of the interior; but, on the other, I regret to say, the commonplace rendering of the exterior which so frequently marks the productions of these architects. That the building under examination is almost a repetition, or rather, a modification of one of their regular types of theatre planning goes without saying; nevertheless, it will be observed that this example contains several points greatly differing from other buildings executed by the same firm and illustrated in these volumes. In this case we have, for instance, in the absence of the extension of the area level below the first tier, a special variation of their so-called "three-tier" type. The area in this building rises with a steep gradient to the level of that tier, a point no doubt borrowed from French architecture. This variation, I should perhaps at once say, appears disadvantageous to the plan generally, for, to my mind, it detracts somewhat from the clearness which otherwise so markedly distinguishes the general conception.

The Municipal Theatre at Zürich is an institution managed in a similar way to that in which the Frankfort Opera House is conducted, for it is owned by subscribers, and managed under the auspices of the Municipality, which has given a free lease of the ground as well as a grant of money towards the execution of the scheme. The present building replaces an old theatre destroyed by fire in 1890, and the necessary funds were, to a large extent, raised a few weeks after that catastrophe. There was no competition in the usual sense of the term, though designs by various Swiss architects were submitted. The commission was eventually given to the Vienna specialists, regardless of the claims of local members of the profession. In June, 1890, the works were commenced, and in spite of serious difficulties with the foundations, and from the severe weather, the opening performance took place in October, 1891, or, after a lapse of some fifteen months. The accommodation provided includes seats for an audience of 1238, and there is also some additional standing room.

After having presented several of Fellner and Helmer's examples, it seems almost unnecessary to speak at any length of the characteristics of this building, except, perhaps, again to draw attention to the excellence of the staircases and cloakroom arrangements, and also, perhaps, to the breadth and dignity obtained in the auditorium, with the spacious accommodation afforded for the uppermost tier, without placing the seats in a "well." The depth of the proscenium calls for comment, as do also the general facilities for exit from the stalls.

In equipment, the block reaches a high standard, more particularly through the

MUNICIPAL THEATRE, ZÜRICH. GENERAL VIEW.

adoption of fire-resisting construction, and the application of light ironwork to the roof. Considerable attention has also been paid to ventilation and warming, as well as to the installation for lighting. In the stage machinery, modern methods and appliances have been introduced, though manual labour has not been replaced by any motive power. The architectural rendering of the auditorium exhibits the characteristic treatment associated with all the designs of the Austrian firm, but, if I may make one criticism, it is that the decorations in this establishment are too elaborate for a Zürich audience. The style adopted does not harmonise with the essentially democratic garb of those who frequent the building.   The exterior, though showing more satisfactory grouping than any other examples by Fellner and Helmer, is, to repeat, marked by their comparative indifference to the treatment of this part of their work, which is particularly observable in the details.

In bringing this volume to a conclusion with two theatres in Swiss towns, I cannot but remark on the similarity of purpose and the many identical requirements which prevail in the playhouses of all countries, whether the influences under which they are built be Anglo-Saxon, Latin or Teutonic.   It appears to me that dramatic entertainments throughout Europe are really too cosmopolitan in character to necessitate many of the arbitrary distinctions made at present in theatre design, and hence that there should be a greater assimilation in the planning and construction of modern playhouses generally.

APPROXIMATE DIMENSIONS.

Width of Proscenium Opening at Curtain Line	37' 6"	11·50 m.
Height of Proscenium Opening at Curtain Line	29' 6"	9·00 m.

AUDITORIUM.			*STAGE.*		
Curtain Line to Front of First Tier . .	63' 9"	19·50 m.	Width inside Containing Walls . . .	67' 0"	20·50 m.
Curtain Line to Front of Third Tier . .	62' 3"	19·00 m.	Curtain Line to Containing Back Wall .	46' 0"	14·00 m.
Curtain Line to Furthest Seat . . .	85' 3"	26·00 m.	Curtain Line to Furthest Wall of Back Stage	73' 9"	22·50 m.
Sunlight Opening above Area . . .	42' 6"	13·00 m.	Gridiron Floor above Stage at Curtain Line	57' 3"	17·50 m.
Highest Seat above Street	40' 9"	12·50 m.	Cellar Floor below Stage at Curtain Line .	12' 3"	3·75 m.
Lowest Seat above Street	5' 0"	1·50 m.	Stage Floor at Curtain Line above Street .	8' 0"	2·50 m.

MUNICIPAL THEATRE, ZÜRICH.   VIEW OF PROSCENIUM.

END OF VOLUME II.

PLATES.

NOTE.

National Opéra Comique, Paris.   For *Revised Elevation* see *Plates*.

NATIONAL OPERA COMIQUE, PARIS.   General View.
(From the Original Competition Drawing.)

Vorder Ansicht.

Edwin O. Sachs ed.:

10   0   10   20   30   40   50   100

Feet.

FRONT ELEVATION.

Façade Principale.

NATIONAL OPERA HOUSE. PARIS.

Charles Garnier.

10   0   5   10   20

Mètres.

J. Dressing Room,
    (Ankleideraum. Loge des Artistes)

K. Ballet Room,
    (Tanz. Saal. Foyer de la Danse)

L. Music Room,
    (Musik Saal. Foyer du Chant.)

M. Chorus Room,
    (Gesang Zimmer. Foyer des Choristes)

N. Chorus,
    (Sänger, Choristes.)

O. Court,
    (Hof, Cour.)

P. Wardrobe Room,
    (Kleiderkammer, Costumes)

Q. Wig Room,
    (Perückenkammer, Perruques.)

R. Stores,
    (Magazin, Dépôt.)

A. Grand Staircase,
    (Haupt Treppenhaus, Grand Escalier)

B. Lounge,
    (Erfrischungssaal, Foyer)

C. Loggia,
    (Offene Halle, Loggia)

D. Ante Room,
    (Vorzimmer, Salon.)

E. Smoking Room,
    (Rauchsaal, Fumoir)

F. Promenade,
    (Wandelgang, Promenade)

G. Saloon,
    (Erfrischungsraum. Restaurant.)

H. Lobby,
    (Vorraum, Dégagement.)

I. Service,
    (Dienst. Service)

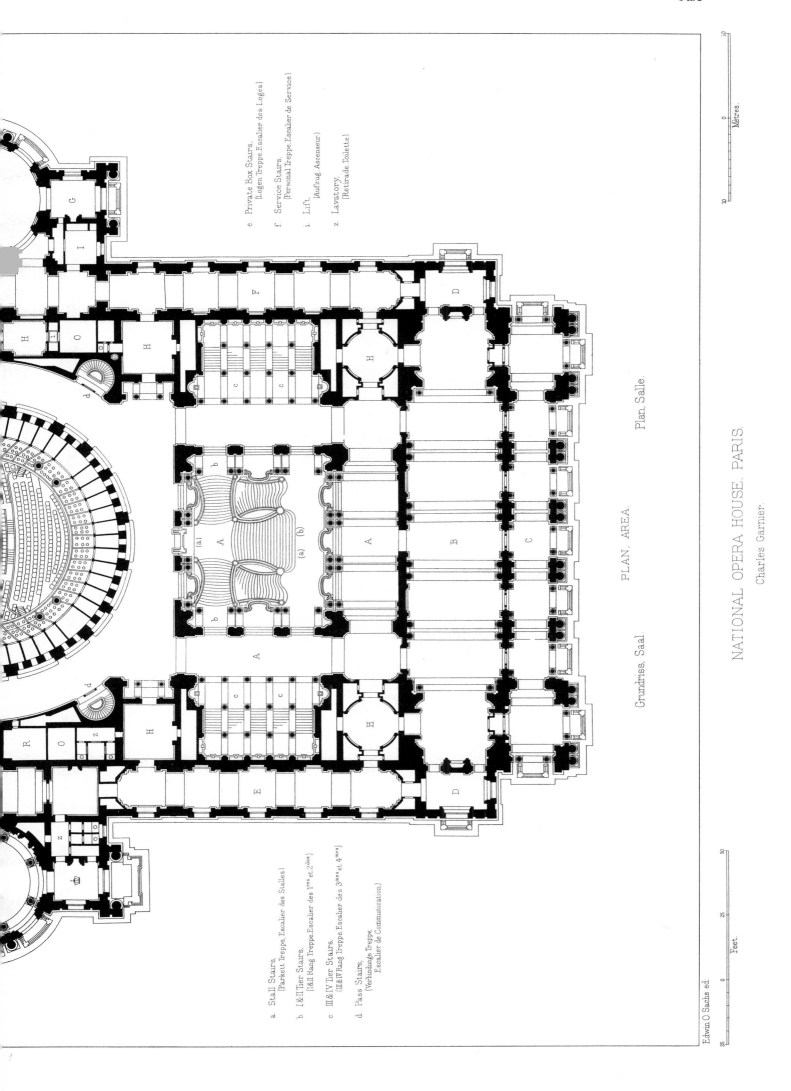

e. Private Box Stairs.
   (Logen Treppe. Escalier des Loges.)

f. Service Stairs.
   (Personal Treppe. Escalier de Service.)

i. Lift.
   (Aufzug. Ascenseur.)

z. Lavatory.
   (Retirade. Toilette.)

a. Stall Stairs.
   (Parkett Treppe. Escalier des Stalles.)

b. I & II Tier Stairs.
   (I & II Rang Treppe. Escalier des 1res et 2des.)

c. III & IV Tier Stairs.
   (III & IV Rang Treppe. Escalier des 3mes et 4mes.)

d. Pass Stairs.
   (Verbindungs Treppe.
   Escalier de Communication.)

Grundriss, Saal.   PLAN, AREA.   Plan, Salle.

NATIONAL OPERA HOUSE. PARIS

Charles Garnier.

Edwin O Sachs ed

Feet.

Mètres.

A Grand Staircase.
  (Haupt Treppenhaus, Grand Escalier)

B Lounge.
  (Erfrischungssaal, Foyer)

C Loggia.
  (Offene Halle, Loggia)

D Ante Room.
  (Vorzimmer, Salon)

E Library.
  (Bibliothek, Bibliotheque)

F Treasury.
  (Haupt Kasse, Bureau des Comptes)

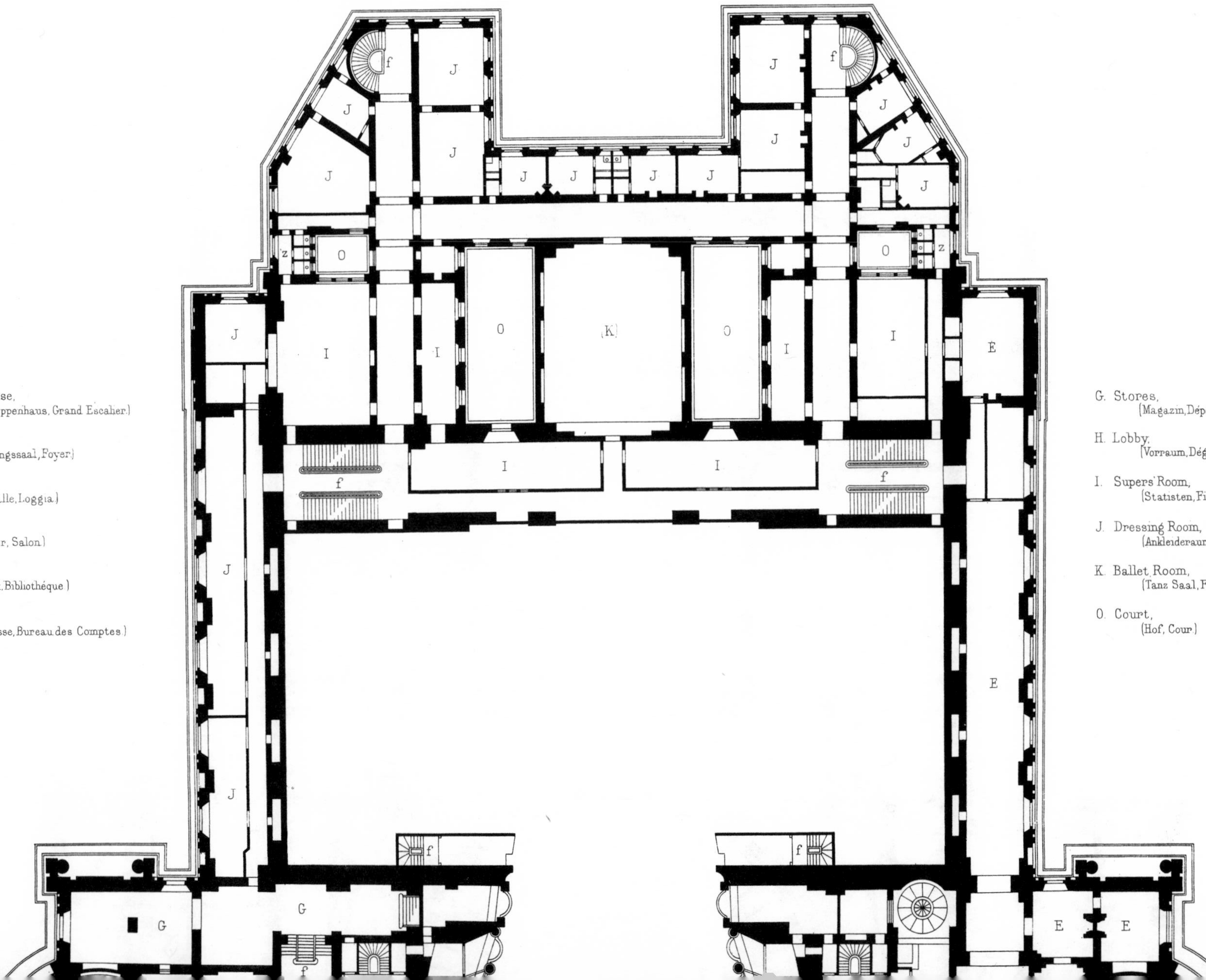

G Stores.
  (Magazin, Dépôt)

H Lobby.
  (Vorraum, Dégagement)

I Supers Room.
  (Statisten, Figuranis)

J Dressing Room.
  (Ankleideraum, Loge des Artistes)

K Ballet Room.
  (Tanz Saal, Foyer de la Dance)

O Court.
  (Hof, Cour)

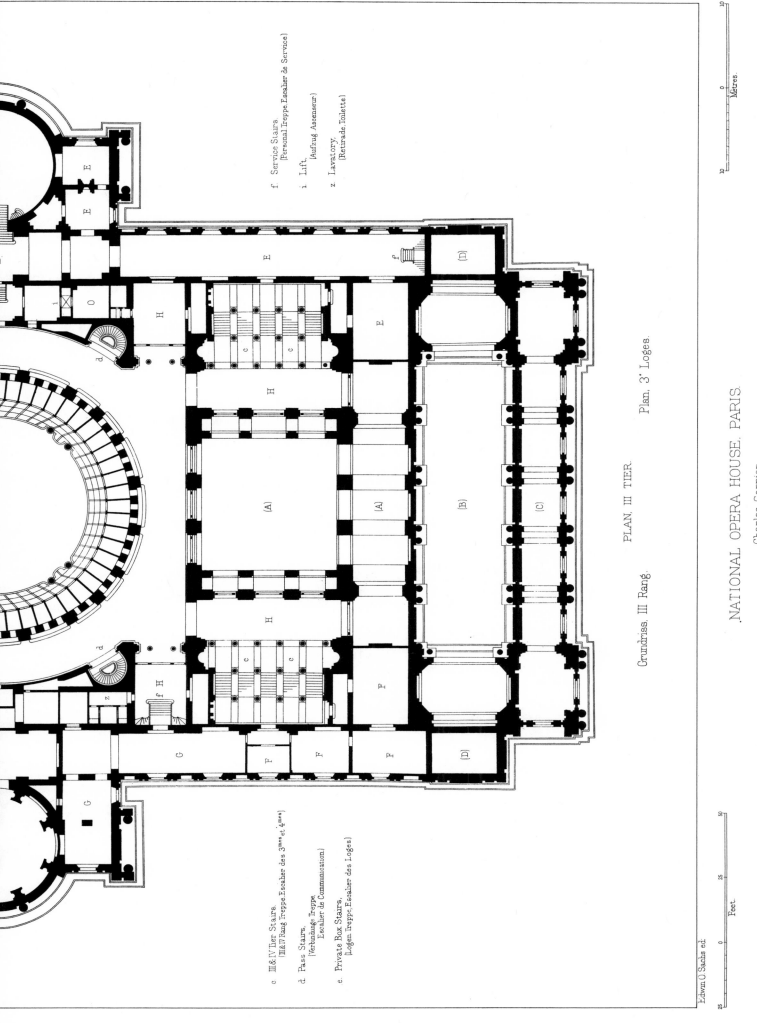

f Service Stairs.
   (Personal Treppe.Escalier de Service)

i Lift.
   (Aufzug.Ascenseur)

z Lavatory.
   (Retirade.Toilette)

c III & IV Tier Stairs.
   (III&IV Rang Treppe.Escalier des 3mes et 4mes)

d Pass Stairs,
   (Verbindungs Treppe,
   Escalier de Communication)

e Private Box Stairs,
   (Logen Treppe,Escalier des Loges)

PLAN. III TIER.   Plan, 3' Loges.

Grundriss. III Rang.

NATIONAL OPERA HOUSE. PARIS.

Charles Garnier.

Edwin O.Sachs ed.

Feet.

Mètres.

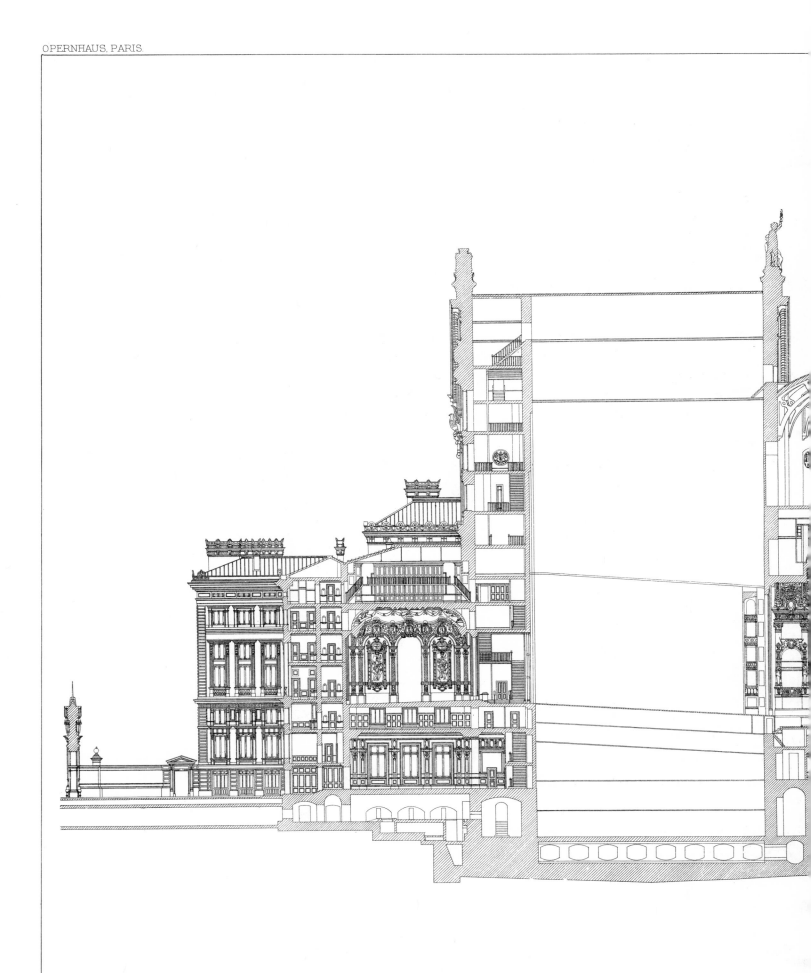

Laengsschnitt.

Edwin O. Sachs ed:

10 0 10 20 30 40 50 100

Feet.

LONGITUDINAL SECTION.

Coupe Longitudinale.

NATIONAL OPERA HOUSE, PARIS.

Charles Garnier.

Mètres.

FRONT ELEVATION DETAILS.

Vorder Ansicht, Einzelheiten.   Façade Principale, Détails.

Edwin O. Sachs ed:

Feet.

Mètres.

NATIONAL OPERA HOUSE, PARIS.

Charles Garnier.

Zuschauerraum, Einzelheiten.   AUDITORIUM, DETAILS.   Salle, Détails.

Edwin O Sachs ed.

Feet.

Mètres.

NATIONAL OPERA HOUSE. PARIS.

Charles Garnier.

AUDITORIUM CEILING.

Plafond de la Salle.

Decke des Zuschauerraums.

NATIONAL OPERA HOUSE. PARIS.

Charles Garnier.

Feet.

Mètres.

Edwin O Sachs ed

LOUNGE, DETAILS.

Erfrischungssaal, Einzelheiten.

Foyer, Détails.

Edwin O. Sachs ed.

Feet.

NATIONAL OPERA HOUSE, PARIS.

Métres.

Charles Garnier.

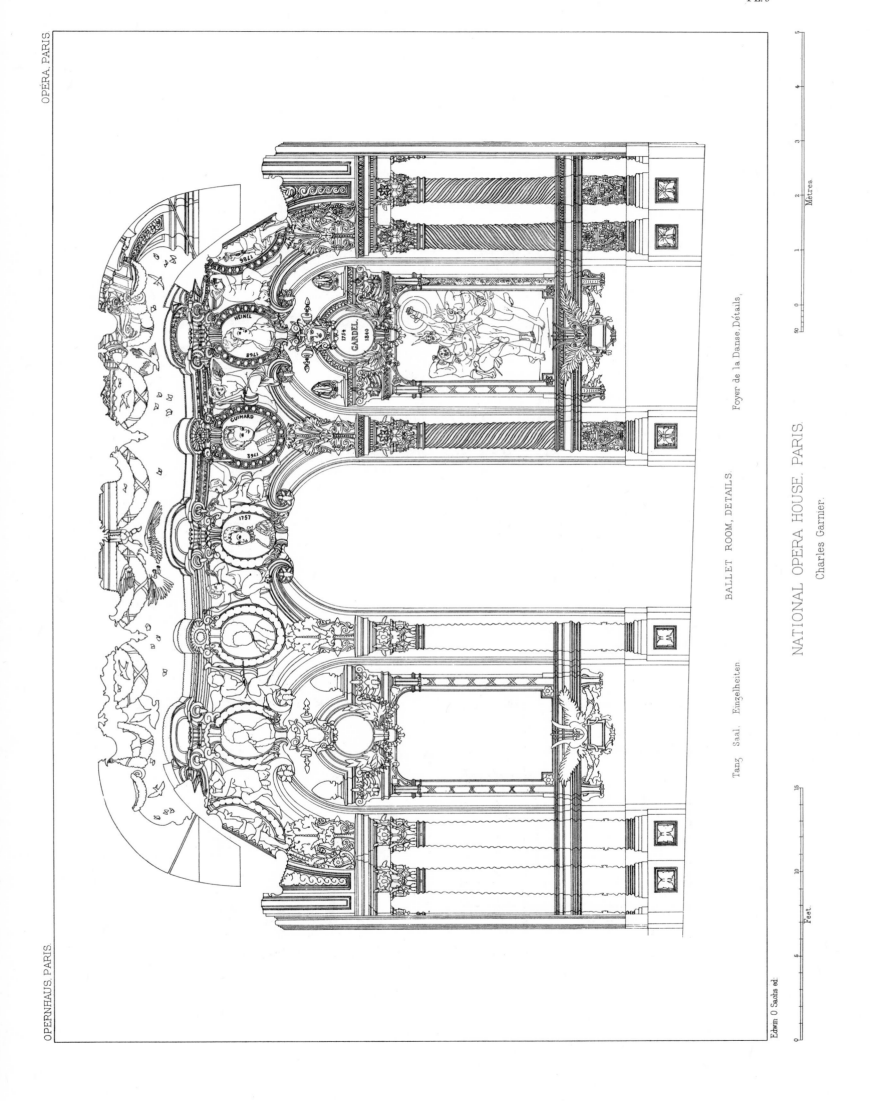

BALLET ROOM, DETAILS

Foyer de la Danse. Détails.

Tanz Saal. Einzelheiten

NATIONAL OPERA HOUSE. PARIS

Charles Garnier.

Edwm O Sachs ed.

Feet.

Metres.

Vorder Ansicht.   FRONT ELEVATION.   Façade Principale.   PL. 10

A. Grand Vestibule. (Vorhalle, Grand Vestibule.)   D. Hall, Wartehalle, Vestibule d'Attente.)   F. Police, (Polizei, Sergents de Ville.)
B. Lobby, (Vorraum, Degagement.)   E. Stage-door Keeper, (Pförtner, Concierge du Theâtre.)   G. Office, (Geschäftsraum, Bureau.)
C. Vestibule, (Vorhalle, Vestibule.)   H. Stores, (Magazin, Dépôt.)

a. Stall Stairs, (Parkett Treppe, Escalier des Stalles.)   c. II, III, IV, Tier Stairs, (II, III, IV, Rang Treppe, Escalier des 2des 3mes 4mes)   p. Box Office, (Kasse, Caisse.)
b. I Tier Stairs, (I Rang Treppe, Escalier des 1res)   d. Service Stairs, (Personal Treppe, Escalier de Service.)   w. Bar, (Anrichtetisch, Buffet.)

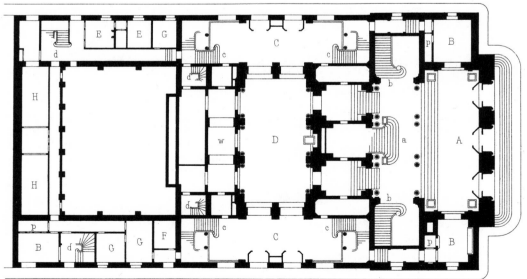

PLAN, GROUND LEVEL.

Grundriss. Erd Geschoss.   Plan. Rez de Chaussée.   PL. 11

Edwin O. Sachs ed.

NATIONAL "OPÉRA COMIQUE", PARIS.

Louis Bernier.

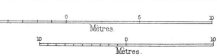

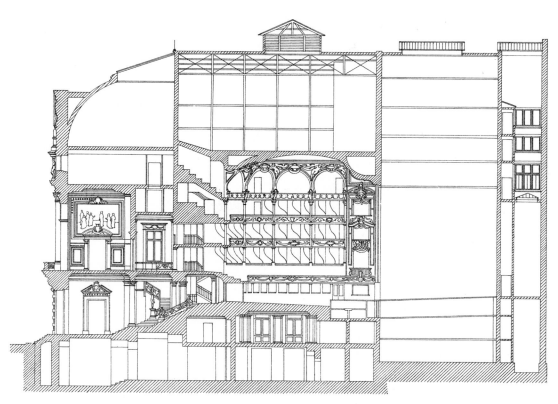

Laengsschnitt. LONGITUDINAL SECTION. Coupe Longitudinale. PL. 14

A. Grand Vestibule, (Vorhalle, Grand Vestibule.)
B. Lobby, (Vorraum, Degagement.)
C. Lounge, (Erfrischungssaal, Foyer.)

D. Saloon, (Erfrischungsraum, Restaurant.)
E. Dressing Room, (Ankleideraum, Loge des Artistes.)
F. General Management, (Verwaltung, L'Administration.)

G. Green Room, (Unterhaltungsraum, Foyer des Artistes.)
H. Scene Store, (Coulissen Magazin, Dépôt des Décors.)
I. Store, (Magazin, Dépôt.)

a. Stall Stairs, (Parkett Treppe, Escalier des Stalles.)
b. I Tier Stairs, (I Rang Treppe, Escalier des I res.)

c. II, III, IV Tier Stairs, (II, III, IV Rang Treppe, Escalier des 2des 3mes 4mes.)
d. Service Stairs, (Personal Treppe, Escalier de Service.)

w. Bar, (Anrichtetisch, Buffet.)
z. Lavatory, (Retirade, Toilette.)

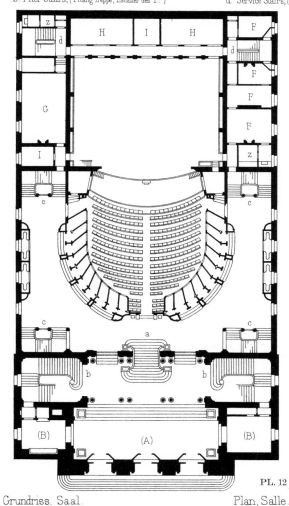

Grundriss, Saal.   Plan, Salle.
PLAN, AREA.   PL. 12

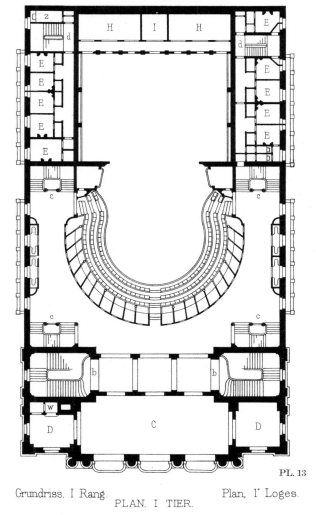

Grundriss, I Rang.   Plan, I er Loges.
PLAN, I TIER.   PL. 13

Edwin O. Sachs ed:

NATIONAL "OPÉRA COMIQUE", PARIS.
Louis Bernier.

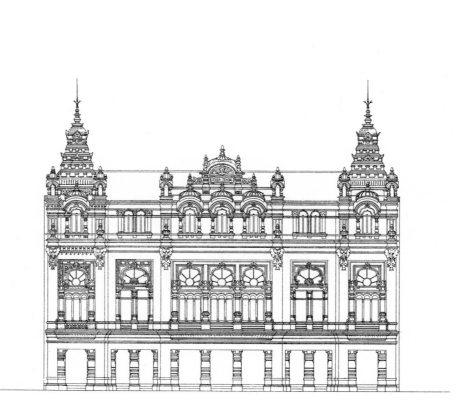

FRONT ELEVATION.   PL. 15

Vorder Ansicht.   Façade Principale.

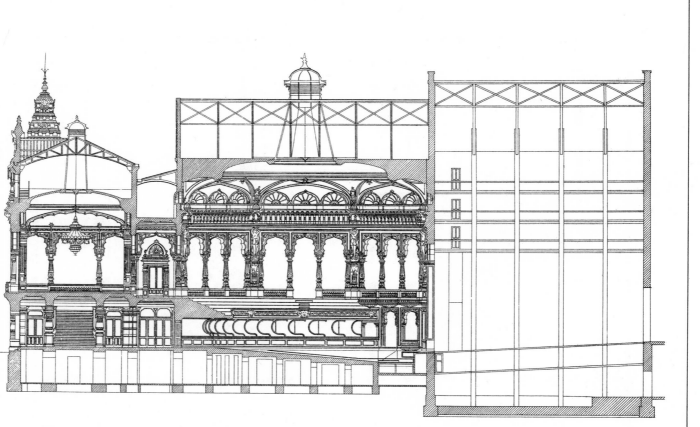

LONGITUDINAL SECTION.   PL. 18

Laengsschnitt.   Coupe Longitudinale.

Edwin O. Sachs ed:

10 5 0   10   20   30   40   50
Feet.

10   5   0   10
Mètres.

"EDEN" VARIETY THEATRE, PARIS.

W. Klein, A. Duclos.

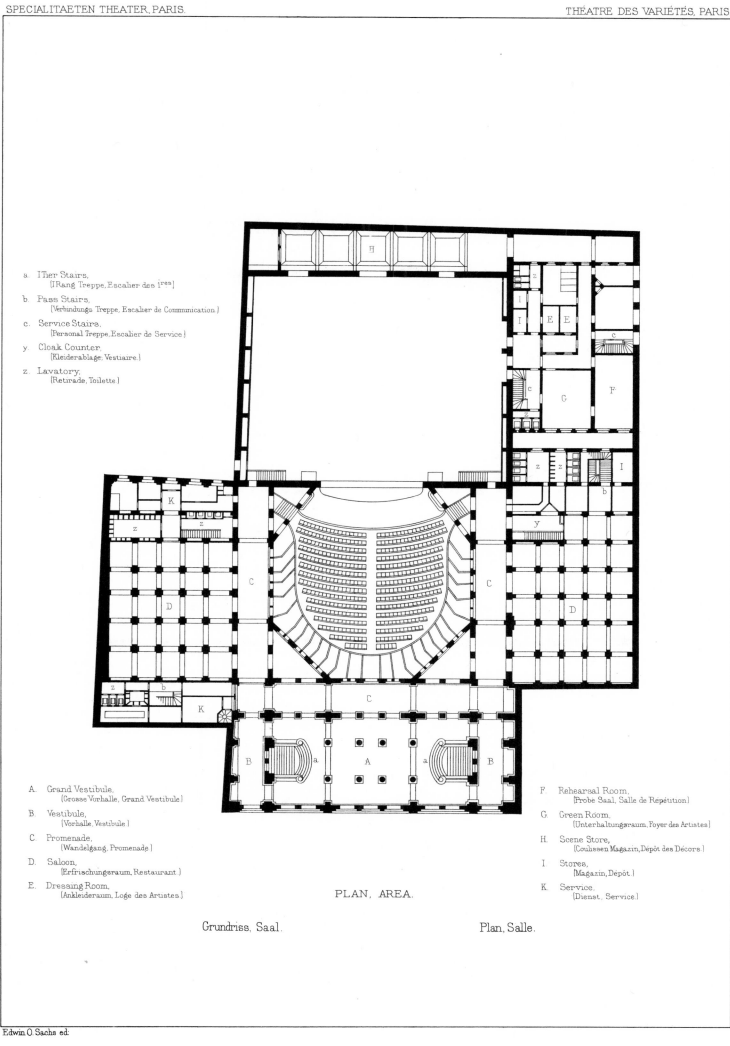

a. ITier Stairs,
   (IRang Treppe, Escalier des I^res)

b. Pass Stairs,
   (Verbindungs Treppe, Escalier de Communication.)

c. Service Stairs,
   (Personal Treppe, Escalier de Service.)

y. Cloak Counter,
   (Kleiderablage, Vestiaire.)

z. Lavatory,
   (Retirade, Toilette.)

A. Grand Vestibule,
   (Grosse Vorhalle, Grand Vestibule.)

B. Vestibule,
   (Vorhalle, Vestibule.)

C. Promenade,
   (Wandelgang, Promenade.)

D. Saloon,
   (Erfrischungsraum, Restaurant.)

E. Dressing Room,
   (Ankleideraum, Loge des Artistes.)

F. Rehearsal Room,
   (Probe Saal, Salle de Répétition.)

G. Green Room,
   (Unterhaltungsraum, Foyer des Artistes.)

H. Scene Store,
   (Coulissen Magazin, Dépôt des Décors.)

I. Stores,
   (Magazin, Dépôt.)

K. Service,
   (Dienst, Service.)

PLAN, AREA.

Grundriss, Saal.   Plan, Salle.

Edwin O. Sachs ed:

Feet.   "EDEN" VARIETY THEATRE, PARIS.   Mètres.
                                              W. Klein, A. Duclos.

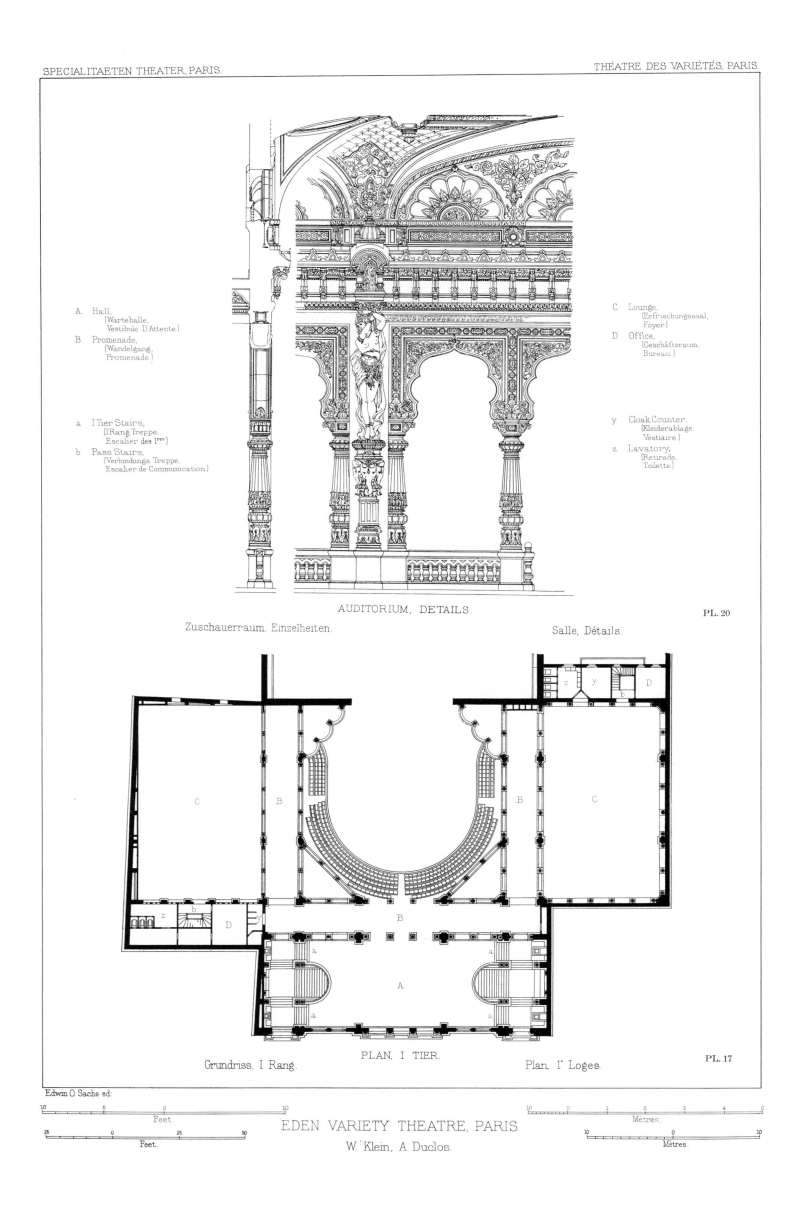

A. Hall,
    (Wartehalle,
    Vestibule D'Attente.)
B. Promenade,
    (Wandelgang,
    Promenade.)

a. I Tier Stairs,
    (I Rang Treppe,
    Escalier des 1res.)
b. Pass Stairs,
    (Verbindungs Treppe,
    Escalier de Communication.)

C. Lounge,
    (Erfrischungssaal,
    Foyer.)
D. Office,
    (Geschäftsraum,
    Bureau.)

y   Cloak Counter,
    (Kleiderablage,
    Vestiaire.)
z   Lavatory,
    (Retirade,
    Toilette.)

AUDITORIUM, DETAILS.   PL. 20

Zuschauerraum, Einzelheiten.   Salle, Détails.

PLAN, I TIER.

Grundriss, I Rang.   Plan, 1er Loges.   PL. 17

Feet.   Mètres.

Feet.   Mètres.

EDEN VARIETY THEATRE, PARIS.
W. Klein, A. Duclos.

EDEN-THEATRE

FRONT ELEVATION, CENTRAL FEATURE.

Vorder Ansicht, Mittel Partie.

Façade Principale, Partie Centrale.

Edwin O. Sachs ed:

5 4 3 2 1 0   5   10
Feet.

1   0   1   2   3   4
Mètres.

"EDEN" VARIETY THEATRE, PARIS.

W. Klein, A. Duclos.

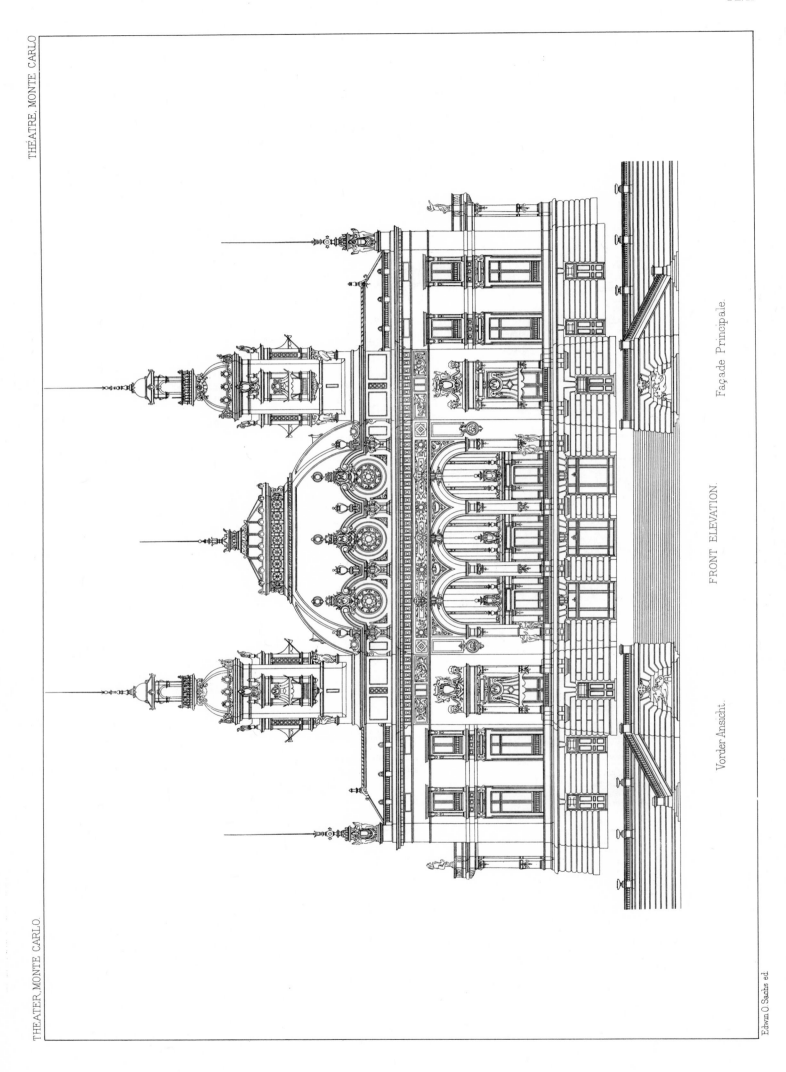

Vorder Ansicht.

FRONT ELEVATION.

Façade Principale.

"CASINO" THEATRE, MONTE CARLO.

Charles Garnier

Mètres

Feet.

Laengsschnitt.   LONGITUDINAL SECTION.   Coupe Longitudinale.   PL. 23

A. Main Entrance,
   (Haupteingang, Grande Entrée.)
B. Vestibule,
   (Vorhalle, Vestibule.)
C. Lobby,
   (Vorraum, Dégagement.)

D. Entrance from Casino,
   (Eingang vom Casino, Entrée du Casino.)
E. Green Room,
   (Unterhaltungsraum, Foyer des Artistes.)
F. Balcony,
   (Balkon, Balcon.)

a. I Tier Stairs,
   (1 Rang Treppe, Escalier des Ires.)
b. Service Stairs,
   (Personal Treppe, Escalier de Service.)
z. Lavatory,
   (Retirade, Toilette.)

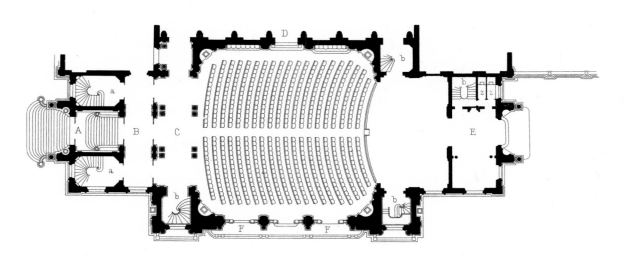

PLAN, AREA.   PL. 22

Grundriss, Saal.   Plan, Salle.

Edwin O. Sachs ed.

25   0   25   50
Feet.

"CASINO" THEATRE, MONTE CARLO

10   0   10
Mètres.

Charles Garnier.

AUDITORIUM, DETAILS.

Zuschauerraum, Einzelheiten.

Salle, Details.

Feet.

Mêtres.

"CASINO" THEATRE, MONTE CARLO.

Charles Garnier.

ANNO 1878

Zuschauerraum, Einzelheiten.

AUDITORIUM, DETAILS.

Salle, Details.

"CASINO" THEATRE. MONTE CARLO.

Charles Garnier.

Métres.

Feet.

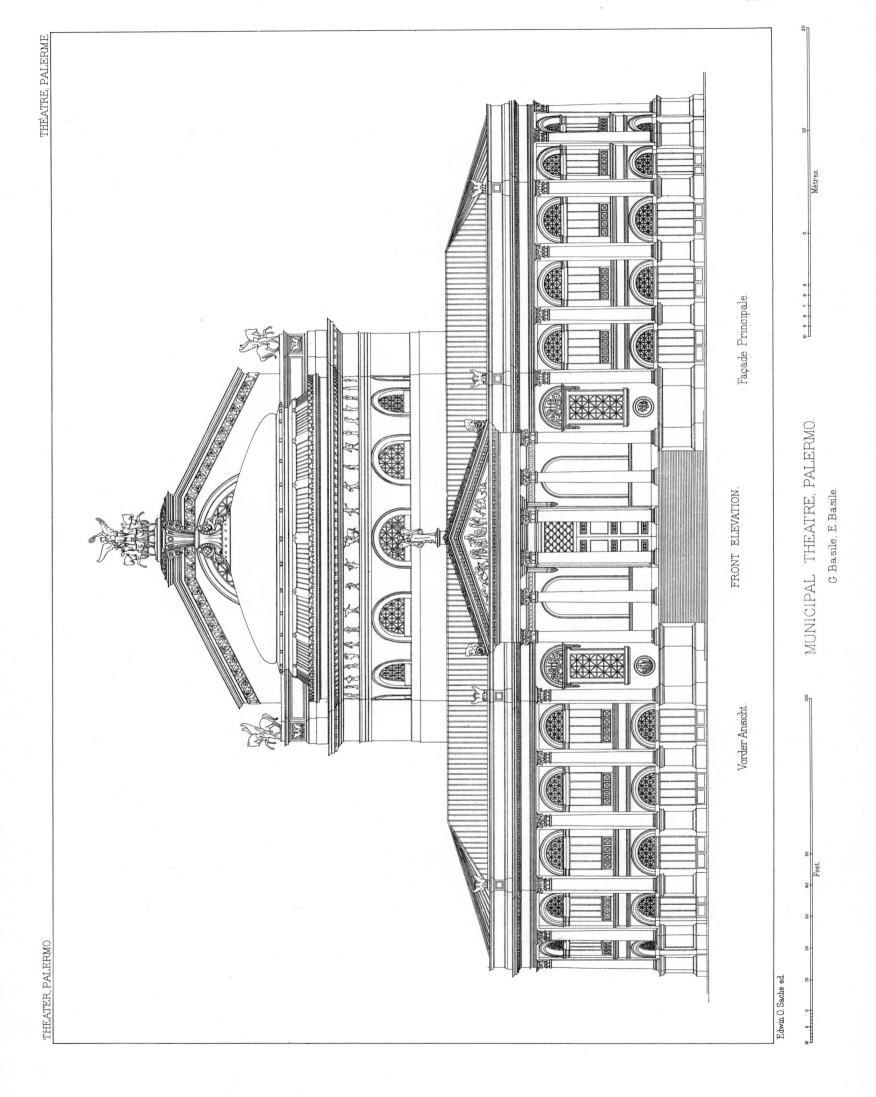

Vorder Ansicht.

FRONT ELEVATION.

Façade Principale.

MUNICIPAL THEATRE, PALERMO.

G. Basile. E. Basile.

Edwin O. Sachs ed.

Feet.

Mètres.

A Main Entrance.
   (Haupt. Eingang, Grande Entrée)

B Grand Vestibule,
   (Grosse Vorhalle, Grand Vestibule)

C Lobby.
   (Vorraum, Dégagement)

D Vestibule.
   (Vorhalle, Vestibule)

E Promenade.
   (Wandelgang, Promenade)

F Smoking Room.
   (Rauchsaal, Fumoir)

G Saloon.
   (Erfrischungsraum, Restaurant)

H Club Vestibule.
   (Vorhalle des Vereines, Vestibule du Cercle)

I Police.
   (Polizei, Sergents de Ville)

K Lobby IV & V Tier.
   (Vorhalle IV & V Rang, Vestibule 4mes et 5mes)

L Stage Lobby.
   (Bühnen Vorhalle, Vestibule du Théâtre)

M Fire Service.
   (Feuerwehr, Service des Pompiers)

N Scene Store.
   (Coulissen Magazin, Dépôt des Décors)

O Engineer.
   (Maschinenmeister, Ingénieur)

P Store.
   (Magazin, Dépôt)

Q Scene Slide.
   (Coulissen Rampe, Entrée des Décors)

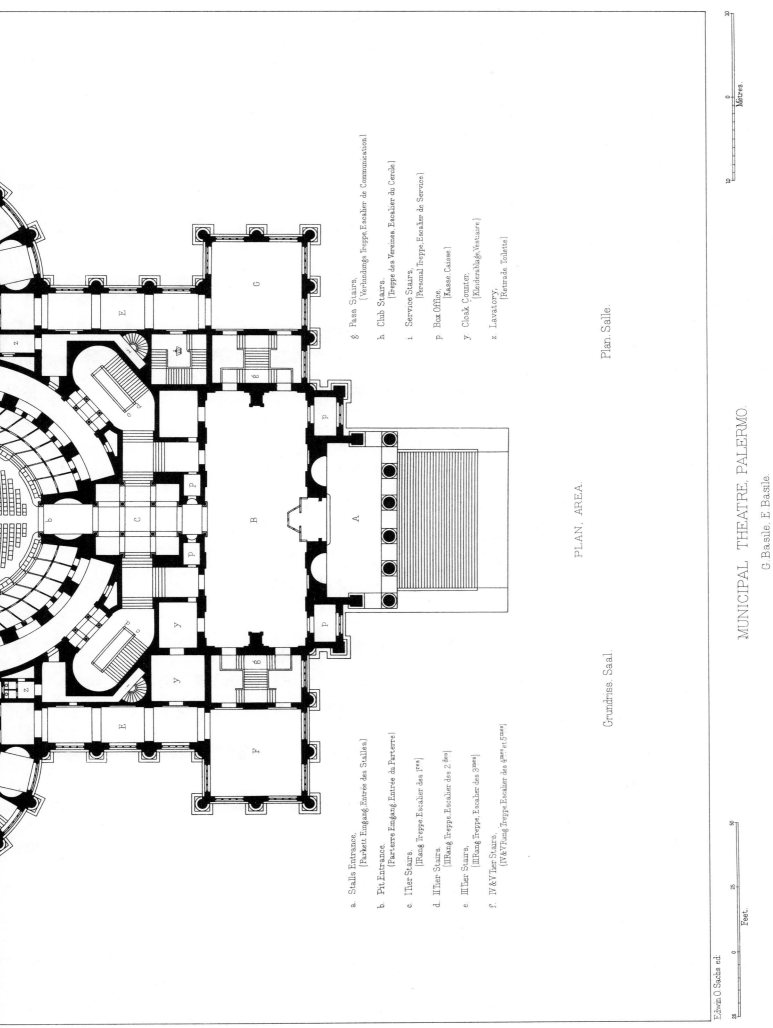

a. Stalls Entrance,
(Parkett Eingang, Entrée des Stalles.)

b. Pit Entrance,
(Parterre Eingang, Entrée du Parterre.)

c. I Tier Stairs,
(I Rang Treppe, Escalier des 1res.)

d. II Tier Stairs,
(II Rang Treppe, Escalier des 2des.)

e. III Tier Stairs,
(III Rang Treppe, Escalier des 3mes.)

f. IV & V Tier Stairs,
(IV&V Rang Treppe, Escalier des 4mes. et 5mes.)

g. Pass Stairs,
(Verbindungs Treppe, Escalier de Communication.)

h. Club Stairs,
(Treppe des Vereines, Escalier du Cercle.)

i. Service Stairs,
(Personal Treppe, Escalier de Service.)

p. Box Office,
(Kasse, Caisse.)

y. Cloak Counter,
(Kleiderablage, Vestiaire.)

z. Lavatory,
(Retirade, Toilette.)

PLAN, AREA.

Grundriss, Saal.

Plan, Salle.

MUNICIPAL THEATRE, PALERMO.

G. Basile, E. Basile.

Edwin O Sachs ed.

Feet.

Metres.

B. Grand Vestibule,
(Grosse Vorhalle, Grand Vestibule.)

C. Lounge,
(Erfrischungssaal, Foyer.)

D. Club Hall,
(Halle des Klubs, Vestibule du Cercle.)

E. Promenade,
(Wandelgang, Promenade.)

F. Saloon,
(Erfrischungsraum, Restaurant.)

G. Club Room,
(Klubzimmer, Salon du Cercle.)

H. Green Room,
(Unterhaltungsraum, Foyer des Artistes.)

I. Dressing Room,
(Ankleideraum, Loge des Artistes.)

J. Club Box,
(Klubloge, Loge du Cercle.)

K. Super's Room,
(Statisten, Comparses.)

L. Ballet Room,
(Tanz Saal, Foyer de la Dance.)

M. Wardrobe Room,
(Kleiderkammer, Costumes.)

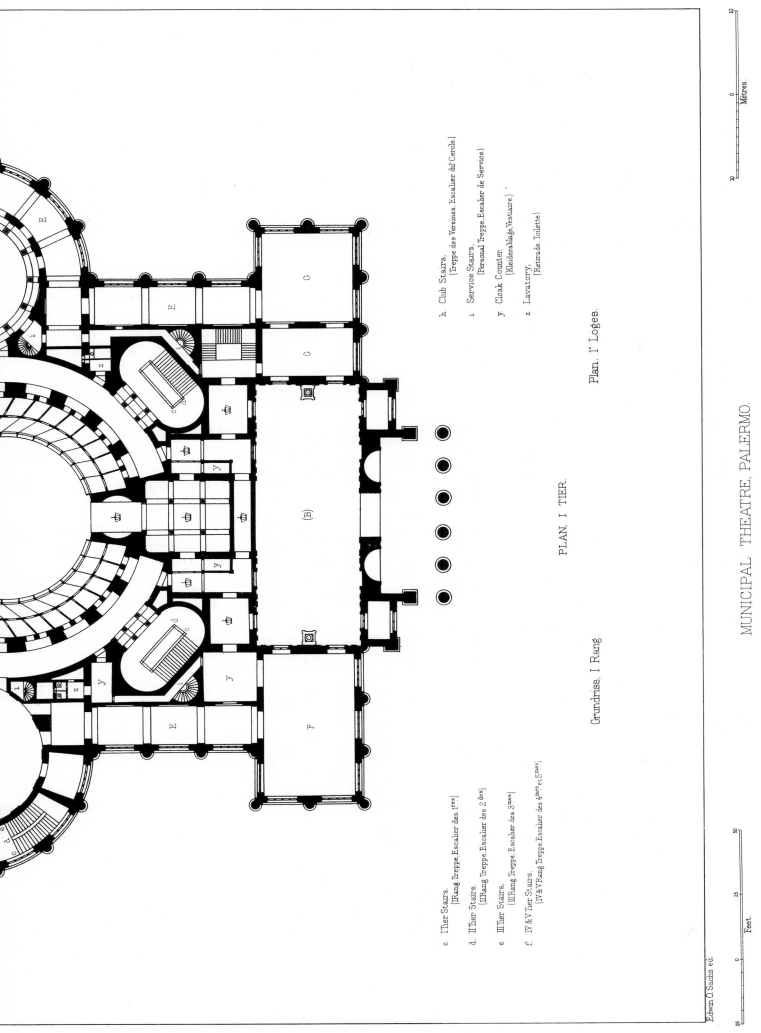

c. ITier Stairs,
(IRang Treppe, Escalier des Ires.)

d. IITier Stairs,
(II Rang Treppe, Escalier des 2 des.)

e. IIITier Stairs,
(III Rang Treppe, Escalier des 3mes.)

f. IV & VTier Stairs,
(IV & VRang Treppe, Escalier des 4 mes et 5 mes.)

h. Club Stairs,
(Treppe des Vereines, Escalier du Cercle.)

i. Service Stairs,
(Personal Treppe, Escalier de Service.)

y. Cloak Counter,
(Kleiderablage, Vestiaire.)

z. Lavatory,
(Retirade, Toilette.)

PLAN. I TIER.

Grundriss. I Rang

Plan. 1er Loges.

MUNICIPAL THEATRE, PALERMO.

G. Basile, E. Basile.

Feet.

Mètres.

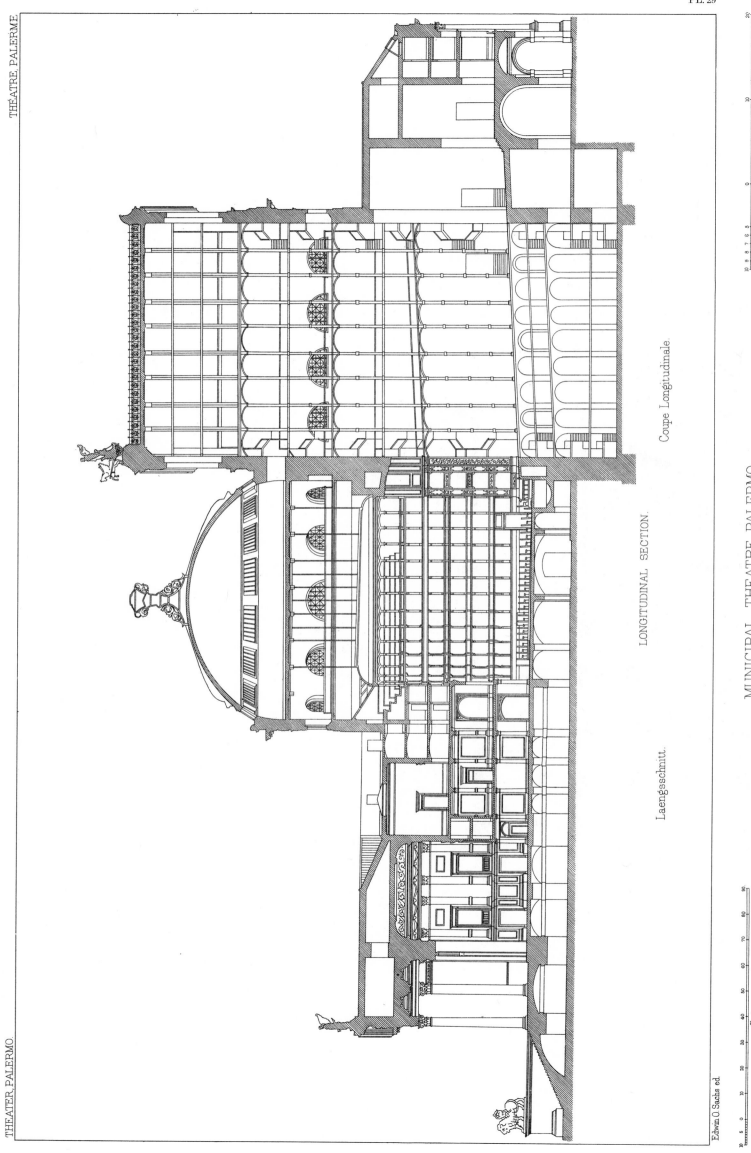

THEATER, PALERMO

Edwin O. Sachs ed.

Coupe Longitudinale.

LONGITUDINAL SECTION.

Laengsschnitt.

MUNICIPAL THEATRE, PALERMO.

G. Basile, E. Basile.

Métres.

Feet.

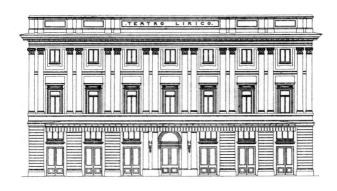

FRONT ELEVATION.

Vorder Ansicht.   Façade Principale.   PL. 30

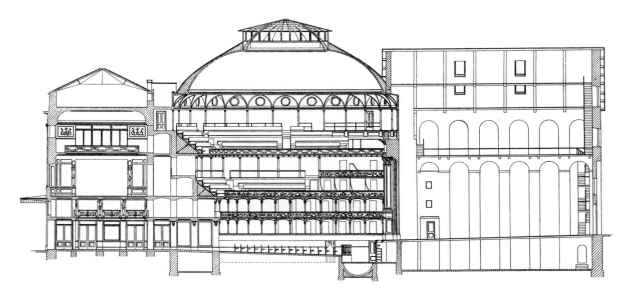

LONGITUDINAL SECTION.   PL. 33

Laengsschnitt.   Coupe Longitudinale.

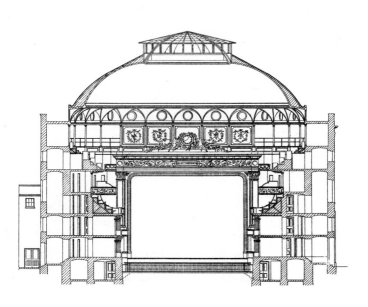

TRANSVERSE SECTION.   PL. 34

Querschnitt.   Coupe Transversale.

Edwin O. Sachs ed:

25   0   25   50
Feet.

"LIRICO" THEATRE, MILAN.

Achille Sfondrini.

10   0   10
Mètres.

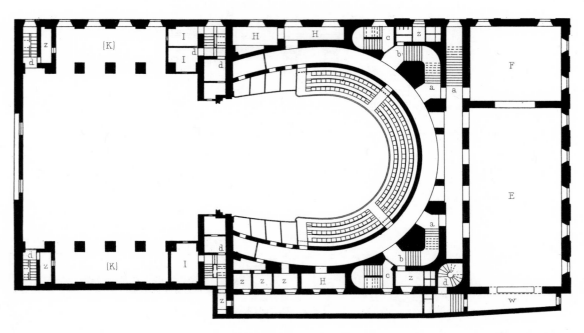

Grundriss, I Rang.   PLAN, I TIER.   Plan, Ier Loges.

PL. 32

A. Main Entrance,
      (Haupt Eingang, Grande Entrée.)
B. Grand Vestibule,
      (Grosse Vorhalle, Grand Vestibule.)
C. Lobby,
      (Vorraum, Dégagement.)
D. II Tier Lobby,
      (Vorhalle II Rang, Vestibule des 2des.)

a. I Tier Stairs,
      (I Rang Treppe, Escalier des 1res.)
b. II Tier Stairs,
      (II Rang Treppe, Escalier des 2des.)
c. III Tier Stairs,
      (III Rang Treppe, Escalier des 3mes.)

E. Lounge,
      (Erfrischungssaal, Foyer.)
F. Saloon,
      (Erfrischungsraum, Restaurant.)
G. General Management,
      (Verwaltung, L'Administration.)

d. Service Stairs,
      (Personal Treppe, Escalier de Service.)
p. Box Office,
      (Kasse, Caisse.)
s. Stage Door,
      (Bühnen Eingang, Entrée du Théâtre.)

H. Store,
      (Magazin, Dépôt.)
I. Dressing Room,
      (Ankleideraum, Loge des Artistes.)
K. Scene Store,
      (Coulissen Magazin, Dépôt des Décors.)
L. Restaurant,
      (Bierhalle, Brasserie.)

w. Bar,
      (Anrichtetisch, Buffet.)
y. Cloak Counter,
      (Kleiderablage, Vestiaire.)
z. Lavatory,
      (Retirade, Toilette.)

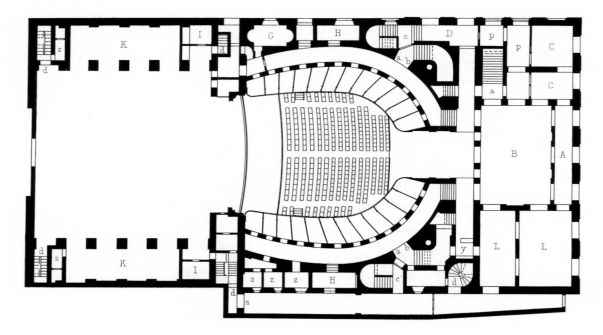

Grundriss, Saal.   PLAN, AREA.   Plan, Salle.

PL. 31

Edwin O. Sachs ed.

Feet.   "LIRICO" THEATRE, MILAN.   Mètres.

Achille Sfondrini.

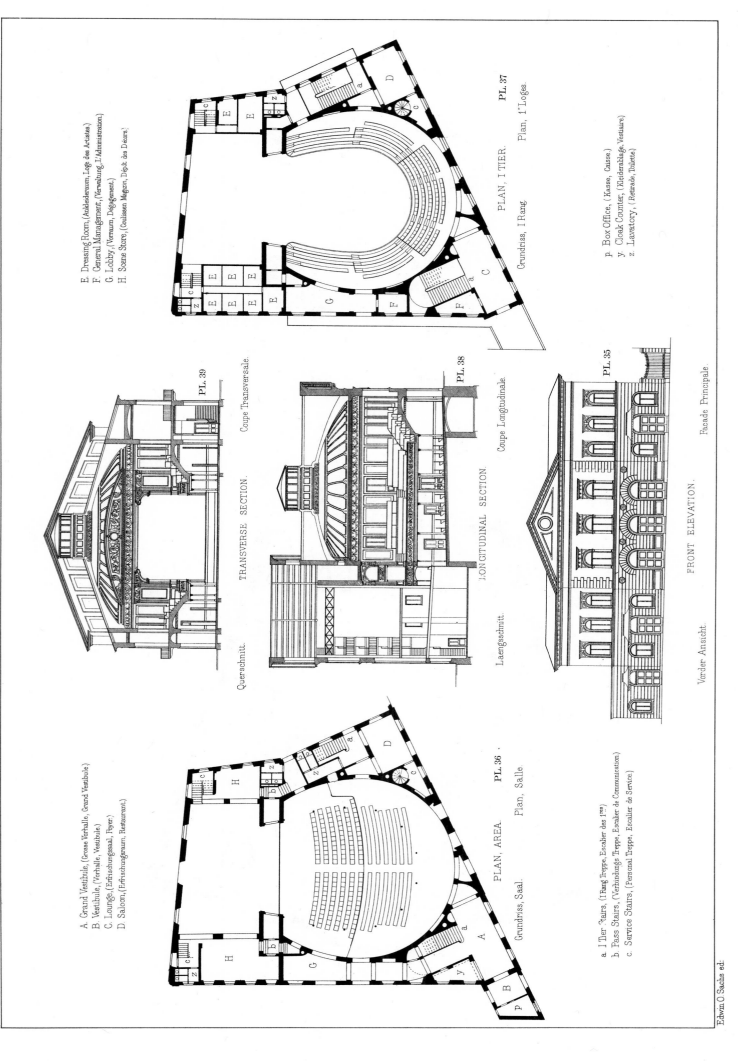

E. Dressing Room, (Ankleideraum, Loge des Artistes.)
F. General Management, (Verwaltung, l'Administration.)
G. Lobby, (Vorraum, Dégagement.)
H. Scene Store, (Coulissen Magazin, Dépôt des Décors.)

PLAN, I TIER.   PL. 37

Grundriss, I Rang.   Plan, I Loges.

p. Box Office, (Kasse, Caisse.)
y. Cloak Counter, (Kleiderablage, Vestiaire.)
z. Lavatory, (Retirade, Toilette.)

Coupe Transversale.   PL. 39

TRANSVERSE SECTION.

Querschnitt.

Coupe Longitudinale.

LONGITUDINAL SECTION.   PL. 38

Laengsschnitt.

PL. 35

FRONT ELEVATION.

Vorder Ansicht.   Facade Principale.

A. Grand Vestibule, (Grosse Vorhalle, Grand Vestibule.)
B. Vestibule, (Vorhalle, Vestibule.)
C. Lounge, (Erfrischungssaal, Foyer.)
D. Saloon, (Erfrischungsraum, Restaurant.)

PLAN, AREA.   PL. 36

Grundriss, Saal.   Plan, Salle.

a. I Tier Stairs, (I Rang Treppe, Escalier des 1res.)
b. Pass Stairs, (Verbindungs Treppe, Escalier de Communication.)
c. Service Stairs, (Personal Treppe, Escalier de Service.)

PEOPLE'S THEATRE TURIN.

Camillo Riccio

Edwin O Sachs ed:

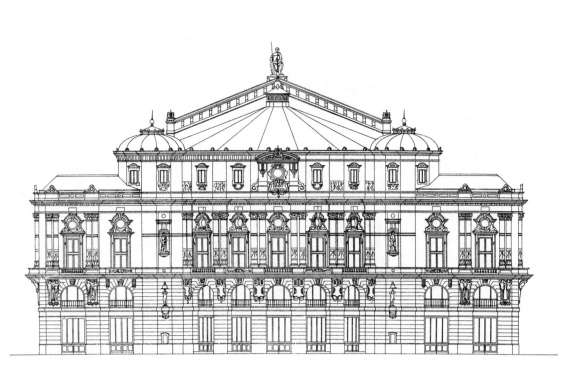

FRONT ELEVATION.

PL. 40

Vorder Ansicht.

Façade Principale.

A. Lounge,
(Erfrischungssaal, Foyer.)
B. Promenade,
(Wandelgang, Promenade.)

C. Scene Store,
(Coulissen Magazin, Dépôt des Décors.)
D. Stores,
(Magazin, Dépôt.)

E. Dressing Room,
(Ankleideraum, Loge des Artistes.)

a. Stalls Stairs,
(Parkett Treppe,
Escalier des Stalles.)
b. I Tier Stairs,
(I Rang Treppe,
Escalier des 1res.)
c. II & III Tier Stairs,
(II & III Rang Treppe,
Escalier des 2mes et 3mes.)
d. Pass Stairs,
(Verbindungs Treppe,
Escalier de Communication.)

e. Service Stairs,
(Personal Treppe,
Escalier de Service.)
i. Lift,
(Aufzug,
Ascenseur.)
y. Cloak Counter,
(Kleiderablage,
Vestiaire.)
z. Lavatory,
(Retirade,
Toilette.)

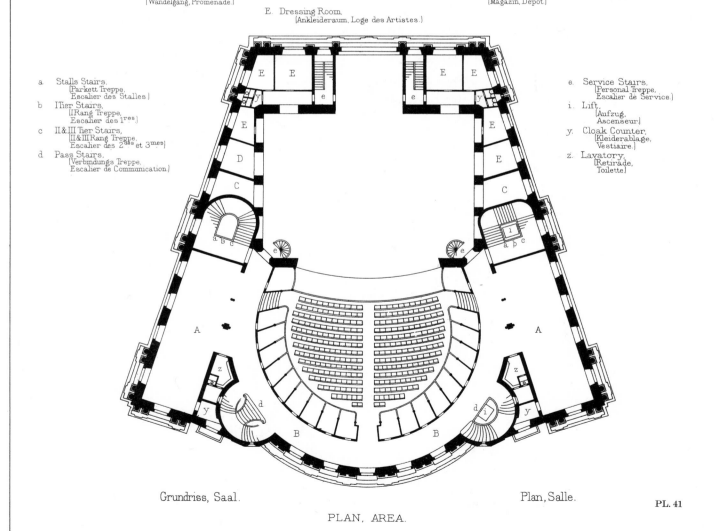

Grundriss, Saal.

Plan, Salle.

PL. 41

PLAN, AREA.

Edwin O. Sachs ed.

MUNICIPAL THEATRE, BILBAO.

Joaquin Rucoba.

25   0   25   50
Feet.

10   0   10
Mètres.

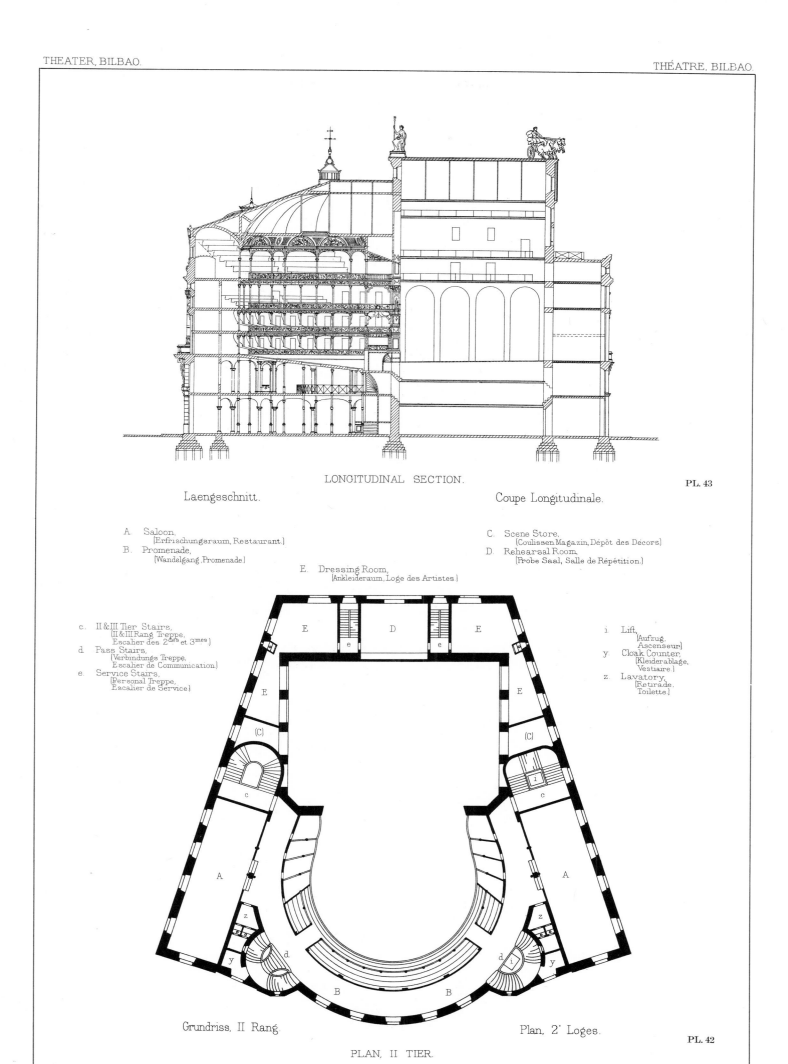

LONGITUDINAL SECTION.

PL. 43

Laengsschnitt.

Coupe Longitudinale.

A   Saloon,
    (Erfrischungsraum, Restaurant.)
B   Promenade,
    (Wandelgang, Promenade.)

C   Scene Store,
    (Coulissen Magazin, Dépôt des Décors.)
D   Rehearsal Room,
    (Probe Saal, Salle de Répétition.)

E   Dressing Room,
    (Ankleideraum, Loge des Artistes.)

c.   II & III Tier Stairs,
    (II & III Rang Treppe,
    Escalier des 2des et 3mes.)
d.   Pass Stairs,
    (Verbindungs Treppe,
    Escalier de Communication.)
e.   Service Stairs,
    (Personal Treppe,
    Escalier de Service.)

i   Lift,
    (Aufzug,
    Ascenseur.)
y   Cloak Counter,
    (Kleiderablage,
    Vestiaire.)
z   Lavatory,
    (Retirade,
    Toilette.)

Grundriss, II Rang.

Plan, 2' Loges.

PL. 42

PLAN, II TIER.

Edwin O. Sachs ed:

Feet.

MUNICIPAL THEATRE, BILBAO.

Joaquin Rucoba.

Mètres.

THÉATRE ROYAL, VIENNE.

HOFOPERNHAUS, WIEN.

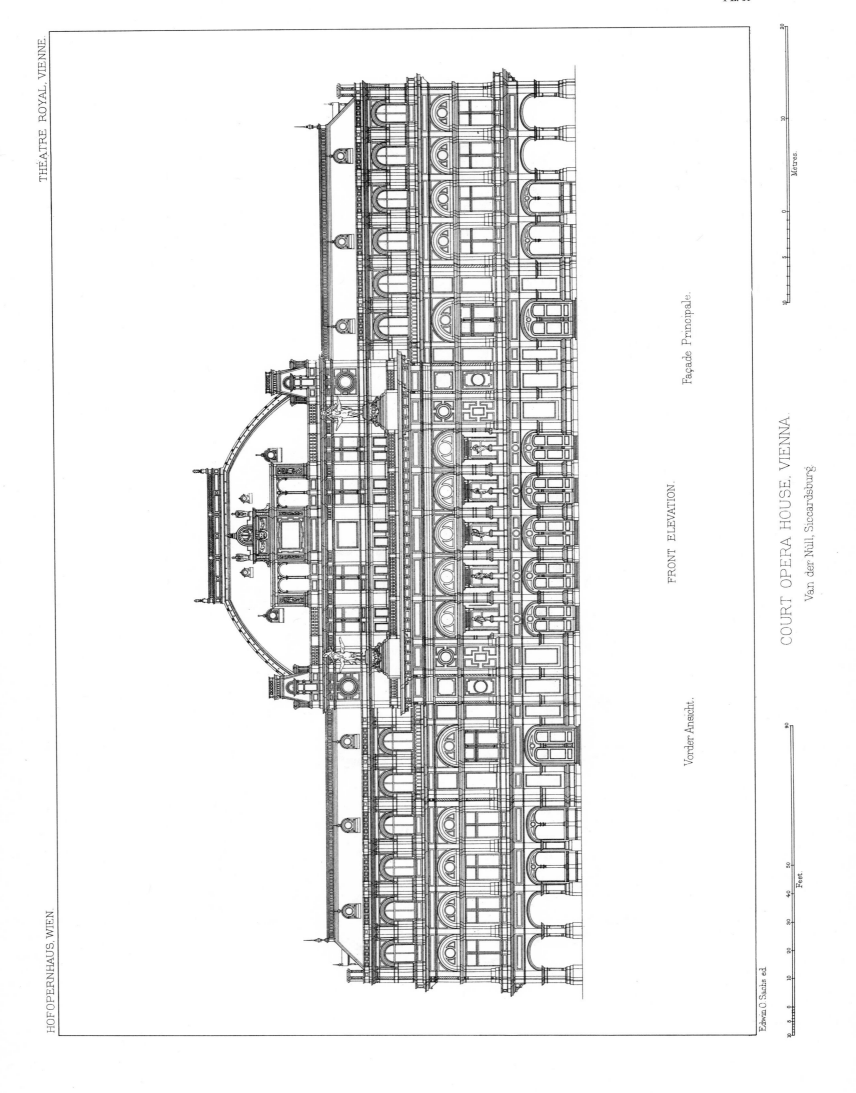

FRONT ELEVATION.

Façade Principale.

Vorder Ansicht.

COURT OPERA HOUSE, VIENNA.

Van der Nüll, Siccardsburg

Edwin O. Sachs ed.

Feet.

Metres.

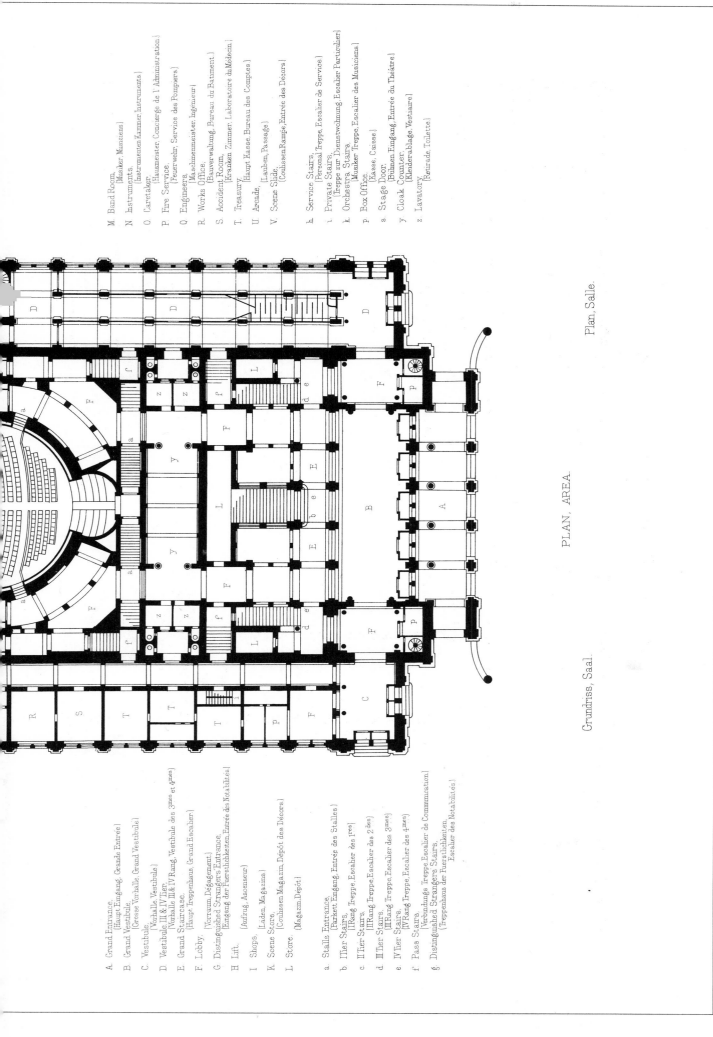

A. Grand Entrance, (Haupt.Eingang, Grande Entrée)
B. Grand Vestibule, (Grosse Vorhalle, Grand Vestibule)
C. Vestibule, (Vorhalle, Vestibule)
D. Vestibule, III & IV Tier, (Vorhalle, III & IV Rang, Vestibule des 3mes et 4mes)
E. Grand Staircase, (Haupt Treppenhaus, Grand Escalier)
F. Lobby, (Vorraum, Dégagement)
G. Distinguished Strangers Entrance, (Eingang der Fuerstlichkeiten, Entrée des Notabilités)
H. Lift, (Aufzug, Ascenseur)
I. Shops, (Laden, Magazins)
K. Scene Store, (Coulissen Magazin, Dépôt des Décors)
L. Store, (Magazin Depôt)
a. Stalls Entrance, (Parkett Eingang, Entrée des Stalles)
b. I Tier Stairs, (I Rang Treppe, Escalier des 1res)
c. II Tier Stairs, (II Rang Treppe, Escalier des 2 des)
d. III Tier Stairs, (III Rang Treppe, Escalier des 3mes)
e. IV Tier Stairs, (IV Rang Treppe, Escalier des 4 mes)
f. Pass Stairs, (Verbindungs Treppe, Escalier de Communication)
g. Distinguished Strangers Stairs, (Treppenhaus der Fuerstlichkeiten, Escalier des Notabilités)

M. Band Room, (Musiker, Musiciens)
N. Instruments, (Instrumenten Kammer, Instruments)
O. Caretaker, (Hausmeister, Concierge de l'Administration)
P. Fire Service, (Feuerwehr, Service des Pompiers)
Q. Engineers, (Maschinenmeister, Ingénieur)
R. Works Office, (Bauverwaltung, Bureau du Batiment)
S. Accident Room, (Kranken Zimmer, Laboratoire du Médecin)
T. Treasury, (Haupt Kasse, Bureau des Comptes)
U. Arcade, (Lauben, Passage)
V. Scene Slide, (Coulissen Rampe, Entrée des Décors)
h. Service Stairs, (Personal Treppe, Escalier de Service)
i. Private Stairs, (Treppe zur Dienstwohnung, Escalier Particulier)
k. Orchestra, Stairs, (Musiker Treppe, Escalier des Musiciens)
p. Box Office, (Kasse, Caisse)
s. Stage Door, (Bühnen Eingang, Entrée du Théâtre)
y. Cloak Counter, (Kleiderablage, Vestiaire)
z. Lavatory, (Retirade, Toilette)

PLAN, AREA.

Grundriss, Saal.

Plan, Salle.

COURT OPERA HOUSE, VIENNA.

Van der Nüll Siccardsburg

Edwin O. Sachs ed.

Feet.

Mètres.

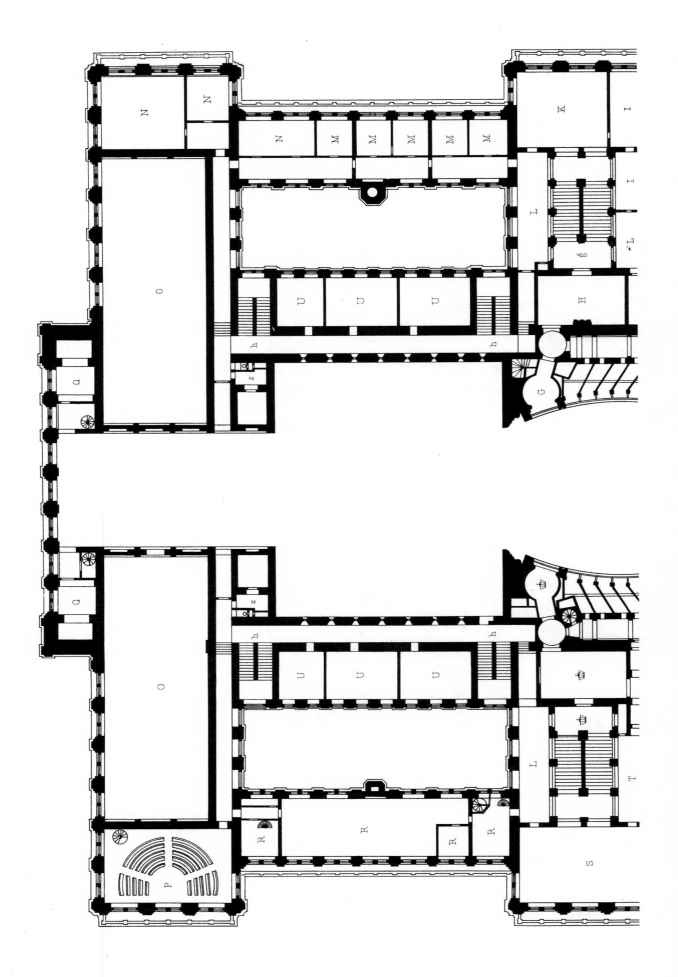

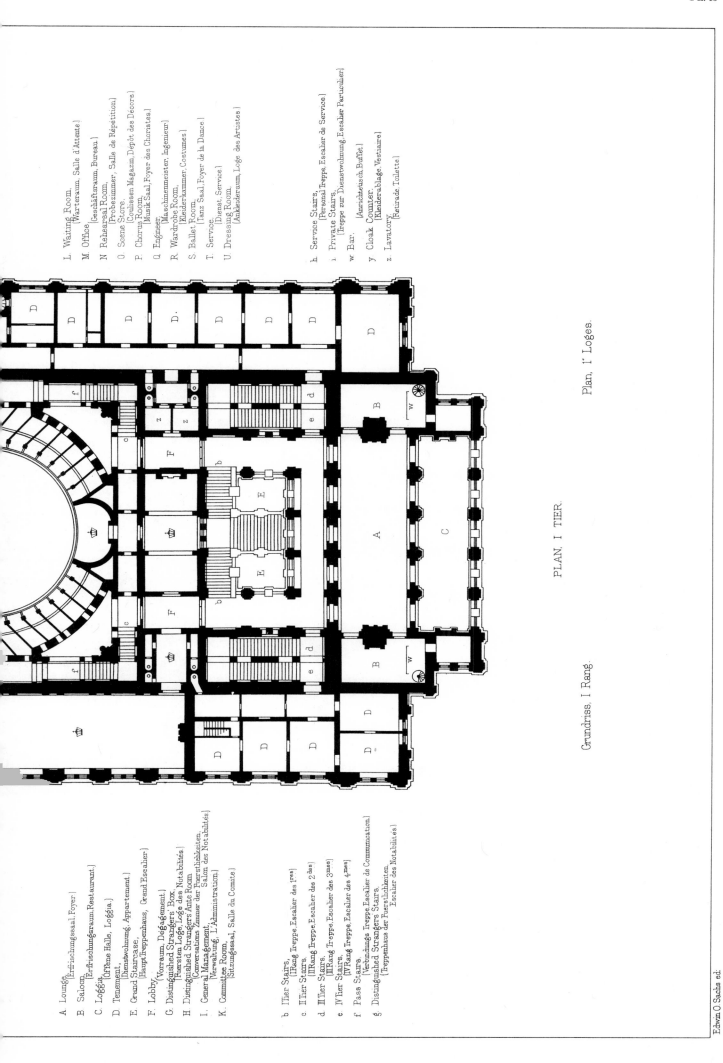

A Lounge, [Erfrischungssaal.Foyer]
B Saloon, [Erfrischungsraum.Restaurant.]
C Loggia, [Offene Halle, Loggia.]
D Tenement, [Dienstwohnung, Appartement.]
E Grand Staircase, [Haupttreppenhaus, Grand Escalier]
F Lobby, [Vorraum, Dégagement.]
G Distinguished Strangers' Box, [Fuersten Loge, Loge des Notabilités]
H Distinguished Strangers' Ante Room, [Conversations Zimmer der Fuerstlichkeiten. Salon des Notabilités]
I General Management, [Verwaltung, L'Administration]
K Committee Room, [Sitzungssaal, Salle du Comité]

b I Tier Stairs, [I Rang Treppe, Escalier des 1res]
c II Tier Stairs, [II Rang Treppe, Escalier des 2des]
d III Tier Stairs, [III Rang Treppe, Escalier des 3mes]
e IV Tier Stairs, [IV Rang Treppe, Escalier des 4mes]
f Pass Stairs, [Verbindungs Treppe, Escalier de Communication.]
g Distinguished Strangers Stairs, [Treppenhaus der Fuerstlichkeiten, Escalier des Notabilités]

L Waiting Room, [Warteraum, Salle d'Attente]
M Office, [Geschäftsraum, Bureau]
N Rehearsal Room, [Probezimmer, Salle de Répétition]
O Scene Store, [Coulissen Magazin, Dépôt des Décors.]
P Chorus Room, [Musik Saal, Foyer des Choristes.]
Q Engineer, [Maschinenmeister, Ingénieur]
R Wardrobe Room, [Kleiderkammer, Costumes]
S Ballet Room, [Tanz Saal, Foyer de la Dance]
T Service, [Dienst, Service]
U Dressing Room, [Ankleideraum, Loge des Artistes]

h Service Stairs, [Personal Treppe, Escalier de Service]
i Private Stairs, [Treppe zur Dienstwohnung, Escalier Particulier]
w Bar, [Anrichetisch, Buffet.]
y Cloak Counter, [Kleiderablage, Vestiaire]
z Lavatory, [Retirade, Toilette]

PLAN, I TIER.

Grundriss, I Rang.

Plan, 1er Loges.

COURT OPERA HOUSE, VIENNA.

Van der Nüll. Siccardsburg

Edwin O. Sachs ed.

Feet.

Mètres.

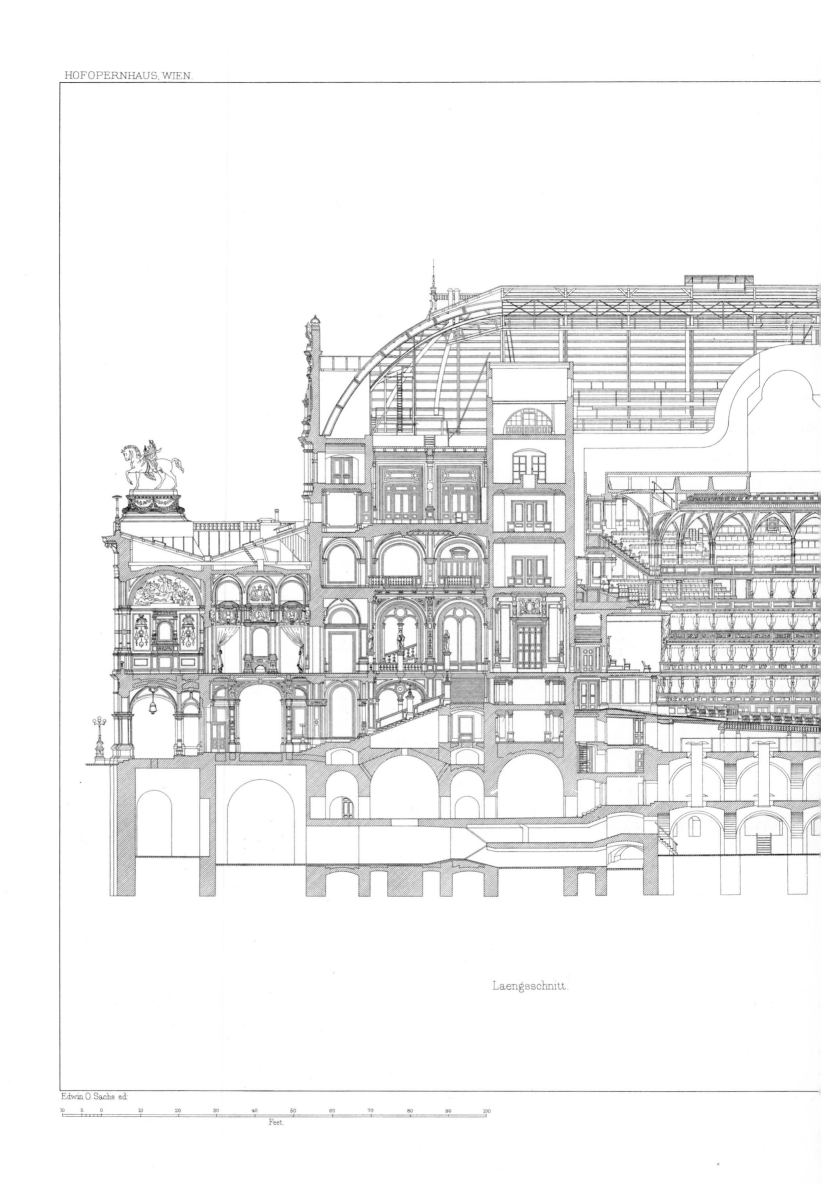

Laengsschnitt.

Edwin O Sachs ed:

10 5 0   10   20   30   40   50   60   70   80   90   100

Feet.

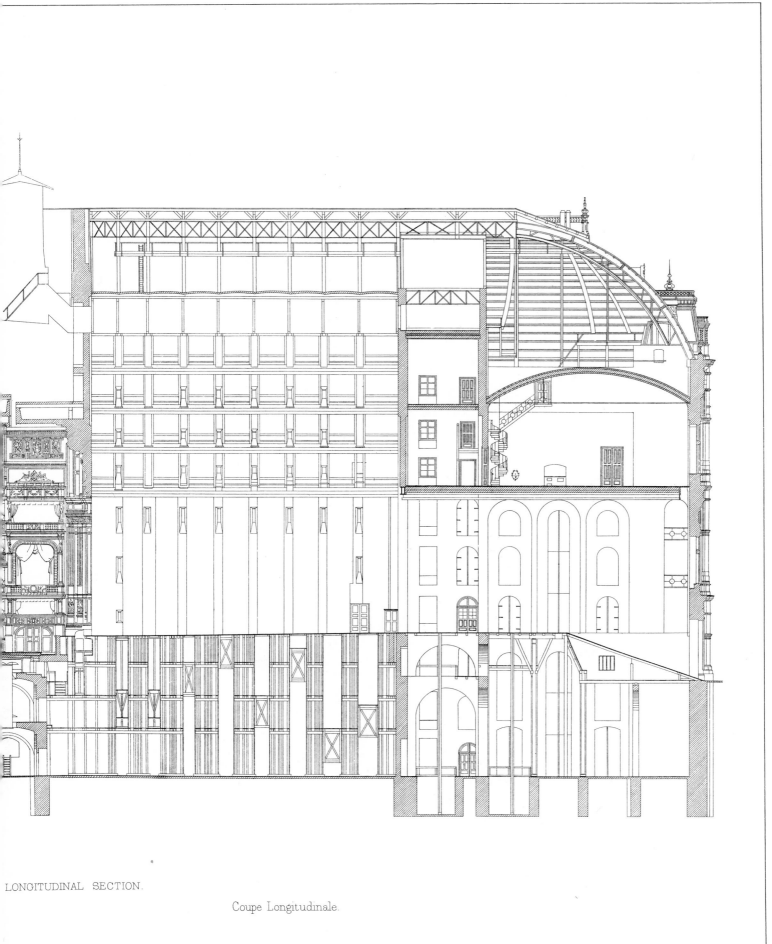

LONGITUDINAL SECTION.

Coupe Longitudinale.

Photo-Lithographed & Printed by James Akerman, 6, Queen Square. W.C.

5 4 3 2 1 0   5   10   15   20   25   30

Mètres.

COURT OPERA HOUSE, VIENNA.

Van der Nüll, Siccardsburg

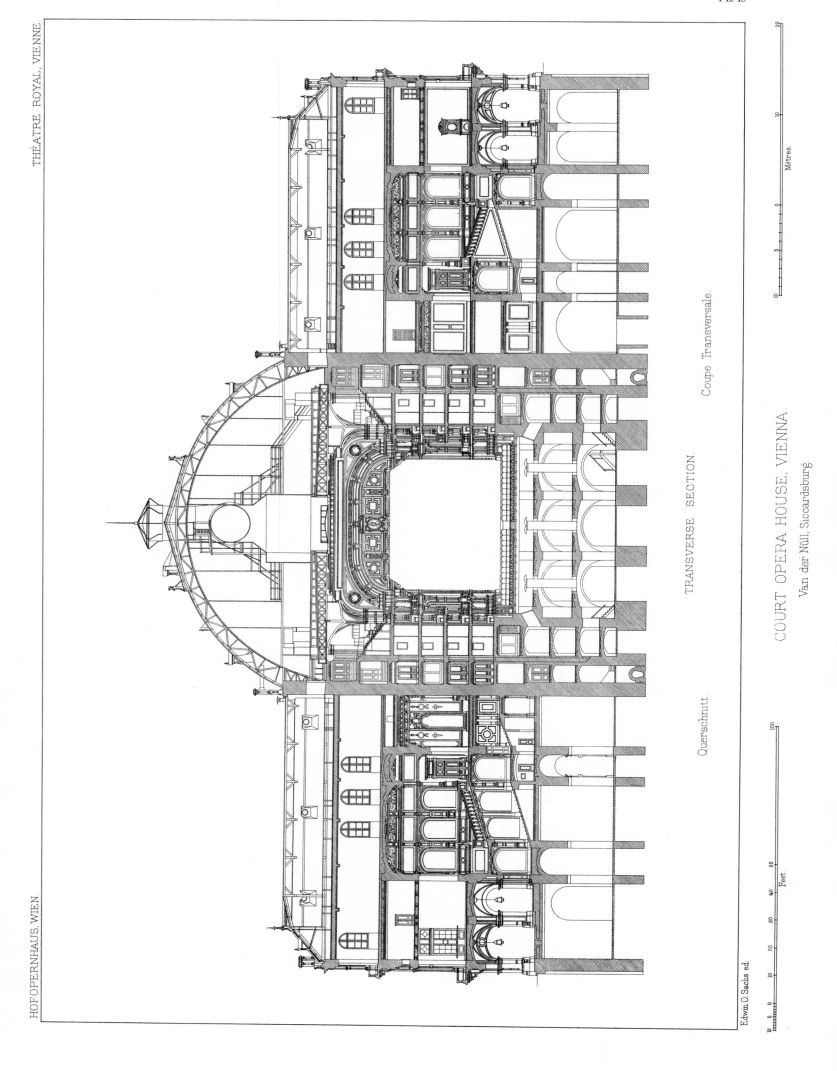

THÉATRE ROYAL, VIENNE.

HOF OPERNHAUS. WIEN

Querschnitt.

TRANSVERSE SECTION

Coupe Transversale.

COURT OPERA HOUSE. VIENNA.

Van der Nüll, Siccardsburg

Edwn. O. Sachs ed

Feet.

Métres.

FRONT ELEVATION, DETAILS.

Vorder Ansicht, Einzelheiten   Façade, Principale, Détails.

Edwin O. Sachs ed:

Feet.

COURT OPERA HOUSE, VIENNA.
Van der Null. Siccardsburg.

Mètres.

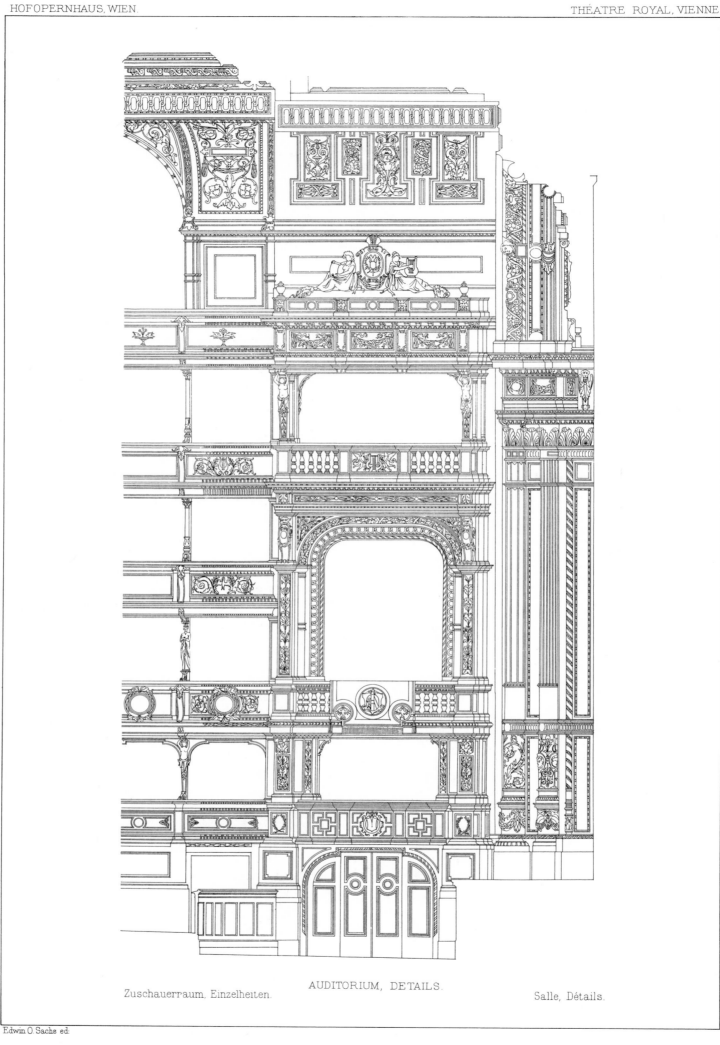

AUDITORIUM, DETAILS.

Zuschauerraum, Einzelheiten.

Salle, Détails.

Edwin O.Sachs ed:

Feet.

Mètres.

COURT OPERA HOUSE, VIENNA.

Van der Nüll, Siccardsburg.

GRAND STAIRCASE, DETAILS.

Haupt Treppenhaus. Einzelheiten,　　　　　　　　Grand Escalier, Details.

Edwin O. Sachs ed:

Feet.

COURT OPERA HOUSE, VIENNA.

Van der Null. Siccardsburg.

Metres

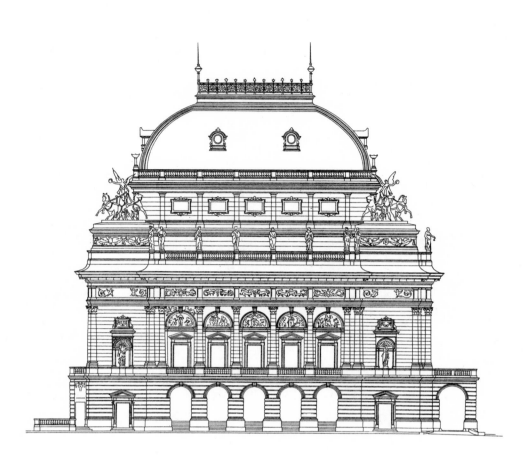

Vorder Ansicht.   FRONT ELEVATION.   Façade Principale.   PL. 52

A. Saloon,
  (Erfrischungsraum, Restaurant.)
B. Lobby,
  (Vorraum, Dégagement.)

C. Treasury,
  (Hauptkasse, Bureau des Comptes.)
D. Store,
  (Magazin, Dépôt.)

c. III & IV Tier Stairs,
  (III & IV Rang Treppe, Escalier des 3mes & 4mes.)
d. Pass Stairs,
  (Verbindungs Treppe, Escalier de Communication.)

w. Bar,
  (Anrichtetisch, Buffet.)
y. Cloak Counter,
  (Kleiderablage, Vestiaire.)
z. Lavatory,
  (Retirade, Toilette.)

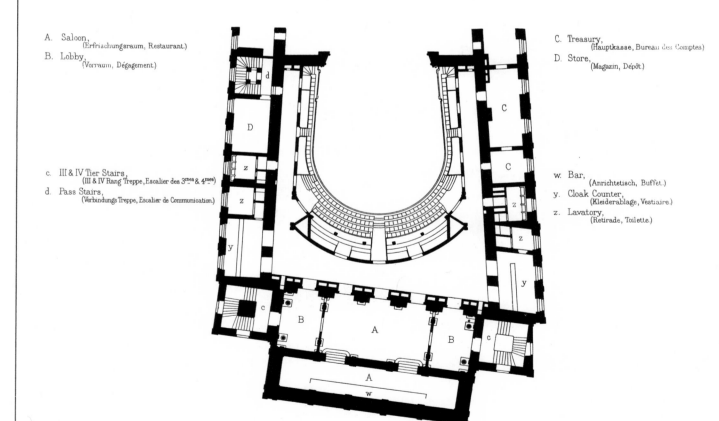

Grundriss, III Rang.   PLAN, III TIER.   Plan, 3e Loges.   PL. 55

Edwin O. Sachs ed.

0 5 10 20 30 40 50 80
Feet.

25 0 25 50
Feet.

CZECH NATIONAL THEATRE, PRAGUE.
Joseph Zítek, Joseph Schulz.

0 5 10 15 20 25
Mètres.

10 0 10
Mètres.

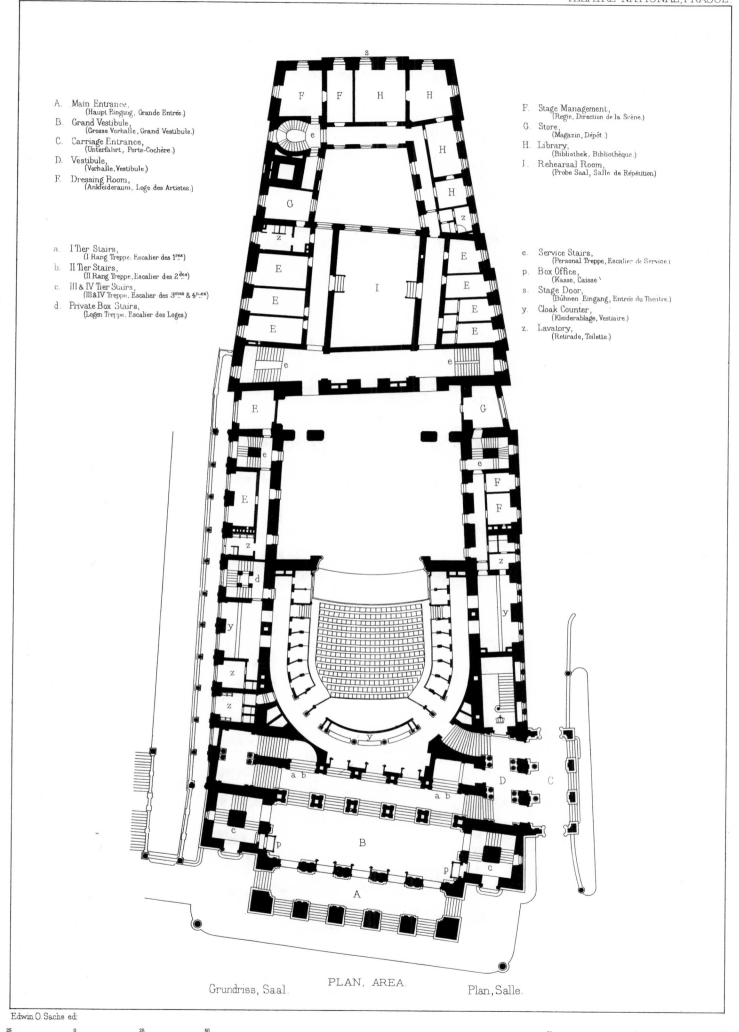

A. Main Entrance,
    (Haupt Eingang, Grande Entrée.)
B. Grand Vestibule,
    (Grosse Vorhalle, Grand Vestibule.)
C. Carriage Entrance,
    (Unterfahrt, Porte-Cochère.)
D. Vestibule,
    (Vorhalle, Vestibule.)
E. Dressing Room,
    (Ankleideraum, Loge des Artistes.)

a. I Tier Stairs,
    (I Rang Treppe, Escalier des 1res.)
b. II Tier Stairs,
    (II Rang Treppe, Escalier des 2des.)
c. III & IV Tier Stairs,
    (III & IV Treppe, Escalier des 3mes & 4mes.)
d. Private Box Stairs,
    (Logen Treppe, Escalier des Loges.)

F. Stage Management,
    (Regie, Direction de la Scène.)
G. Store,
    (Magazin, Dépôt.)
H. Library,
    (Bibliothek, Bibliothèque.)
I. Rehearsal Room,
    (Probe Saal, Salle de Répétition.)

e. Service Stairs,
    (Personal Treppe, Escalier de Service.)
p. Box Office,
    (Kasse, Caisse.)
s. Stage Door,
    (Bühnen Eingang, Entrée du Théatre.)
y. Cloak Counter,
    (Kleiderablage, Vestiaire.)
z. Lavatory,
    (Retirade, Toilette.)

PLAN, AREA.

Grundriss, Saal.   Plan, Salle.

Edwin O. Sachs ed:

25   0   25   50
                Feet.

CZECH NATIONAL THEATRE, PRAGUE.

Joseph Zitek   Joseph Schulz.

10   0   10
                Mètres.

A. Lounge,
(Erfrischungssaal, Foyer.)
B. Loggia,
(Offene Halle, Loggia.)
C. Balcony,
(Balkon, Balcon.)
D. Office,
(Geschäftsraum, Bureau.)

E. Engineer,
(Maschinenmeister, Ingénieur.)
F. Ballet Room,
(Tanz Saal, Foyer de la danse.)
G. Chorus Room,
(Musik Saal, Foyer des Choristes.)
H. General Management,
(Verwaltung, L'Administration.)

a. I Tier Stairs,
(I Rang Treppe, Escalier des 1res.)
b. II Tier Stairs,
(II Rang Treppe, Escalier des 2des.)
c. III & IV Tier Stairs,
(III & IV Rang Treppe, Escalier des 3mes & IVmes.)
d. Private Box Stairs,
(Logen Treppe, Escalier des Loges.)

e. Service Stairs,
(Personal Treppe, Escalier de Service.)
w. Bar,
(Anrichtetisch, Buffet.)
y. Cloak Counter,
(Kleiderablage, Vestiaire.)
z. Lavatory,
(Retirade, Toilette.)

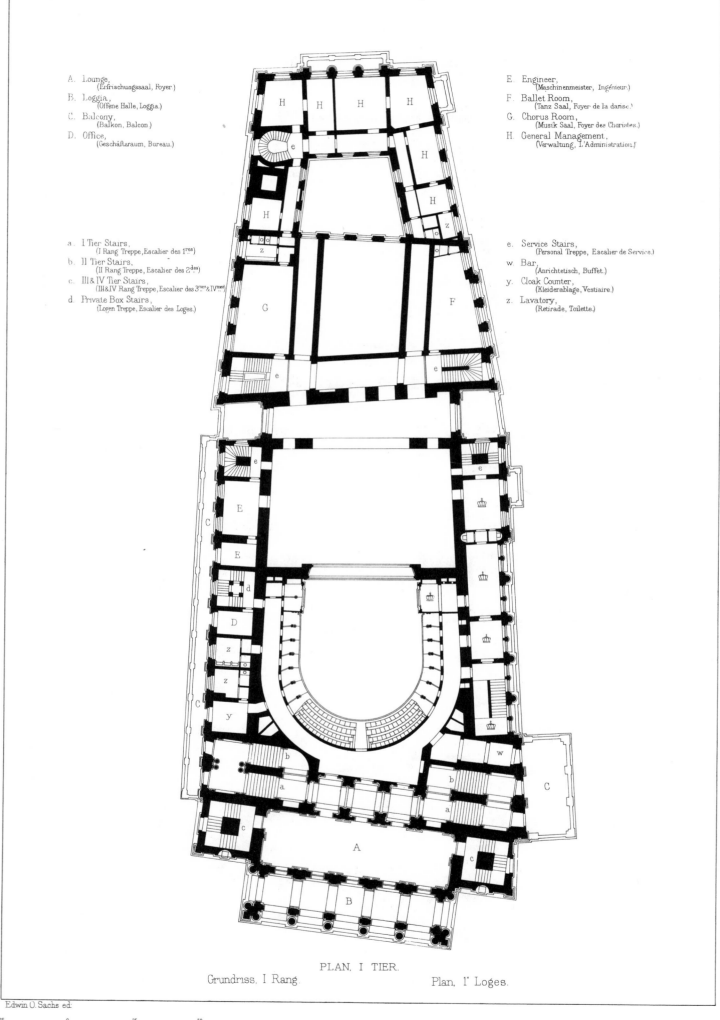

PLAN, I TIER.

Grundriss, I Rang.   Plan, 1er Loges.

25   0   25   50
Feet.

CZECH NATIONAL THEATRE, PRAGUE.
Joseph Zitek   Joseph Schulz

10   0   10
Mètres.

PL. 56

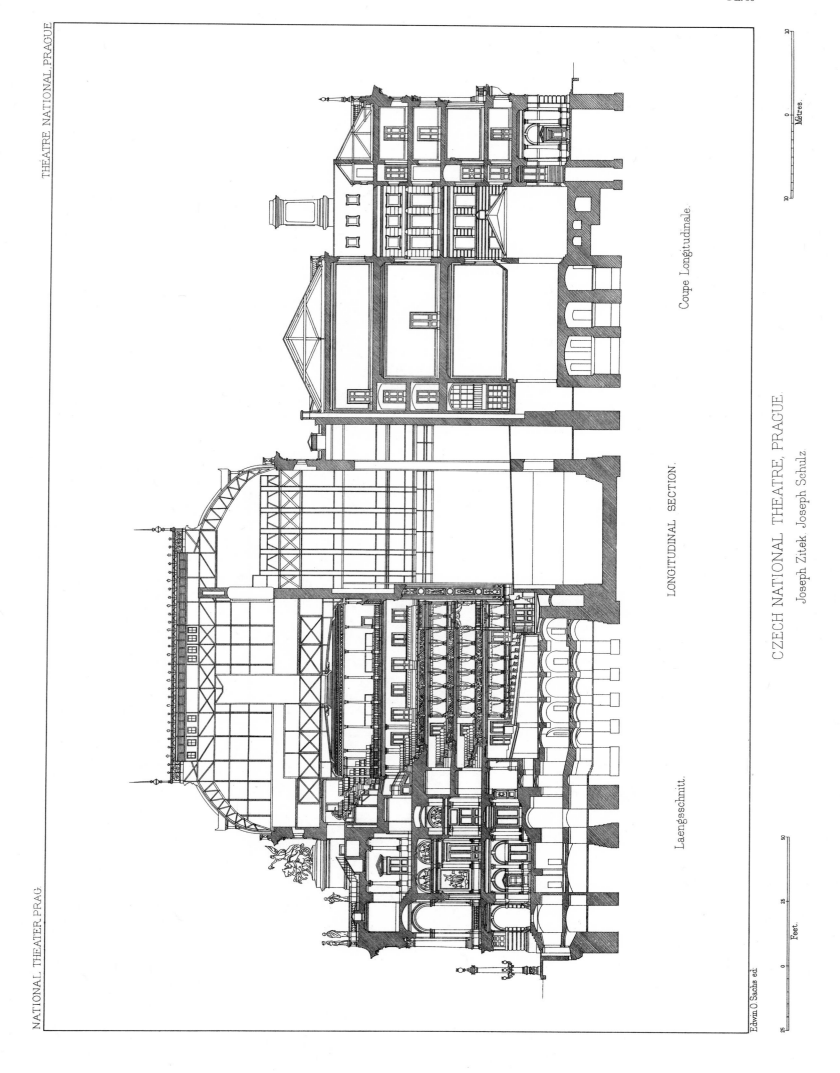

Coupe Longitudinale.

LONGITUDINAL SECTION.

Laengsschnitt.

CZECH NATIONAL THEATRE, PRAGUE.

Joseph Zitek   Joseph Schulz

Edwin O Sachs ed.

Feet.

Mètres.

FRONT ELEVATION, DETAILS.

Vorder Ansicht, Einzelheiten.

Façade Principale, Détails.

Edwin O Sachs ed:

CZECH NATIONAL THEATRE, PRAGUE

Joseph Zitek Joseph Schulz.

Feet

Metres.

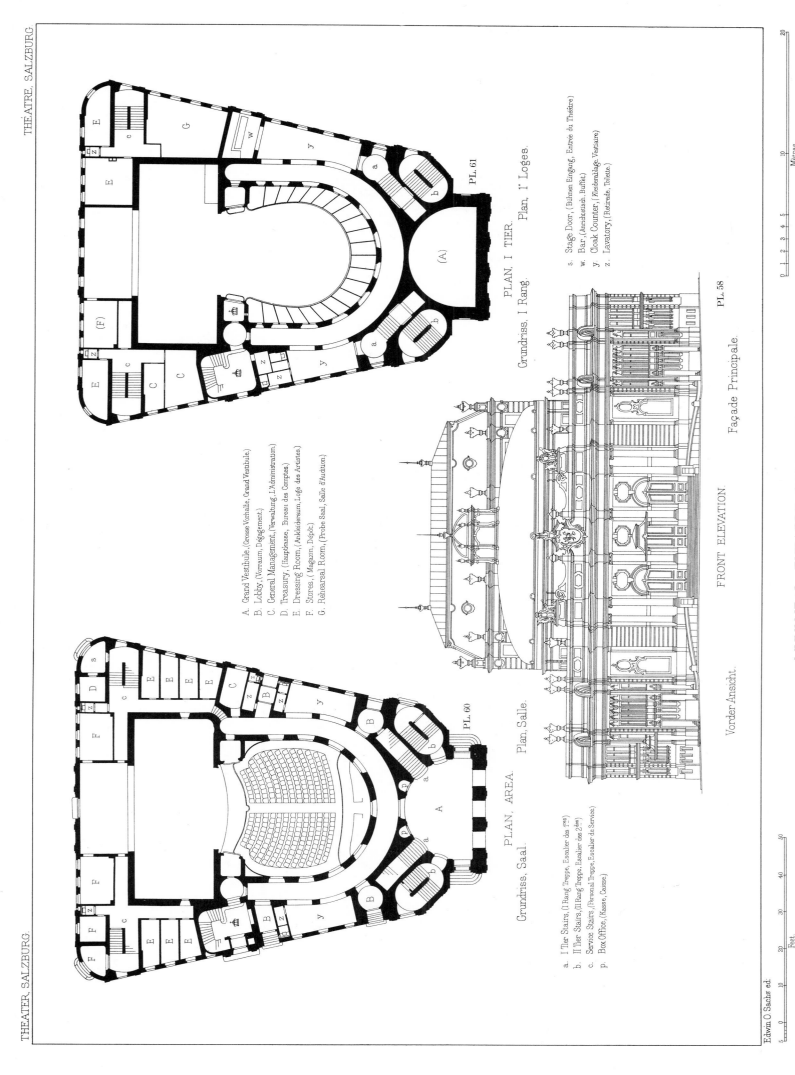

PL. 61

PLAN, I TIER.

Grundriss, I Rang.　Plan, I° Loges.

PL. 60

PLAN, AREA.

Grundriss, Saal.　Plan, Salle.

PL. 58

FRONT ELEVATION.

Vorder Ansicht.　Façade Principale.

A. Grand Vestibule, (Grosse Vorhalle, Grand Vestibule.)
B. Lobby, (Vorraum, Dégagement.)
C. General Management, (Verwaltung, L'Administration.)
D. Treasury, (Hauptkasse, Bureau des Comptes.)
E. Dressing Room, (Ankleideraum, Loge des Artistes.)
F. Stores, (Magazin, Dépôt.)
G. Rehearsal Room, (Probe Saal, Salle d'Auditum.)

s. Stage Door, (Bühnen Eingang, Entrée du Théâtre.)
w. Bar, (Anrichtensch. Buffet.)
y. Cloak Counter, (Kleiderablage, Vestiaire.)
z. Lavatory, (Retirade, Toilete.)

a. I Tier Stairs, (I Rang Treppe, Escalier des I°es.)
b. II Tier Stairs, (II Rang Treppe, Escalier des 2°es.)
c. Service Stairs, (Personal Treppe, Escalier de Service.)
p. Box Office, (Kasse, Caisse.)

MUNICIPAL THEATRE, SALZBURG.

Ferdinand Fellner, Hermann Helmer.

Edwin O Sachs ed.

Feet.

Feet.

Métres.

Métres.

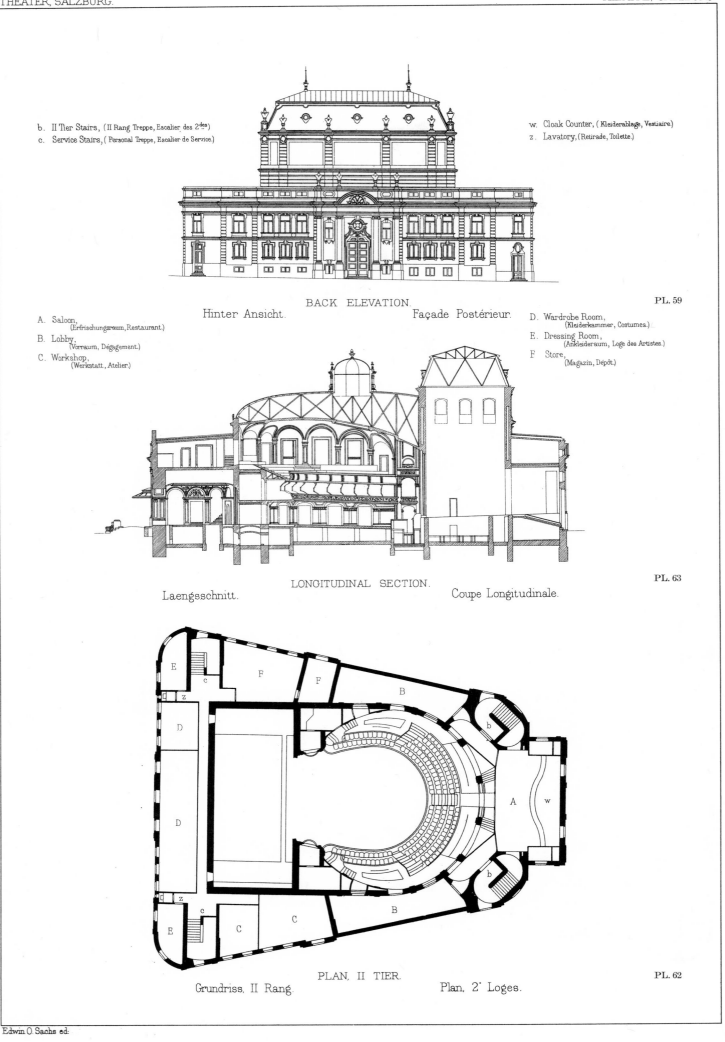

b. II Tier Stairs, (II Rang Treppe, Escalier des 2des)

c. Service Stairs, (Personal Treppe, Escalier de Service.)

w. Cloak Counter, (Kleiderablage, Vestiaire.)

z. Lavatory, (Retirade, Toilette.)

BACK ELEVATION.

Hinter Ansicht.   Façade Postérieur.

PL. 59

A. Saloon,
   (Erfrischungsraum, Restaurant.)

B. Lobby,
   (Vorraum, Dégagement.)

C. Workshop,
   (Werkstatt, Atelier.)

D. Wardrobe Room,
   (Kleiderkammer, Costumes.)

E. Dressing Room,
   (Ankleideraum, Loge des Artistes.)

F. Store,
   (Magazin, Dépôt.)

LONGITUDINAL SECTION.

Laengsschnitt.   Coupe Longitudinale.

PL. 63

PLAN, II TIER.

Grundriss, II Rang.   Plan, 2e Loges.

PL. 62

Edwin O. Sachs ed:

Feet.

MUNICIPAL THEATRE, SALZBURG.

Ferdinand Fellner, Hermann Helmer.

Mètres.

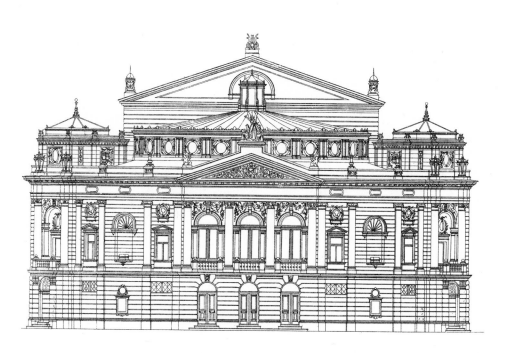

FRONT ELEVATION.   PL. 64

Vorder Ansicht.   Façade Principale.

A. Grand Vestibule, (Grosse Vorhalle, Grand Vestibule.)   D. Ante Room, (Vorzimmer, Salon.)   F. Stores, (Magazin, Dépôt.)
B. Lobby, II Tier, (Vorhalle, II Rang; Vestibule des 2des) E. Dressing Room, (Ankleideraum, Loge des Artistes.) G. Treasury, (Hauptkasse, Bureau des Comptes.)
C. Lounge, (Erfrischungssaal, Foyer.)   H. Stage Management, (Regie, Direction de la Scène.)

a. I Tier Stairs, (I Rang Treppe, Escalier des 1res.)   c. Service Stairs, (Personal Treppe, Escalier de Service.) y. Cloak Counter, (Kleiderablage, Vestiaire.)
b. II Tier Stairs, (II Rang Treppe, Escalier des 2des.)   p. Box Office, (Kasse, Caisse.)   z. Lavatory, (Retirade, Toilette.)

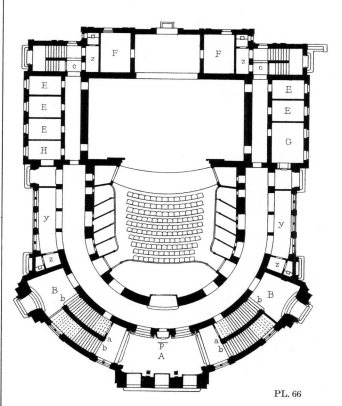

PL. 66

Grundriss, Saal.   Plan, Salle.

PLAN, AREA.

Grundriss, I Rang.   Plan, 1´ Loges.

PLAN, I TIER.

PL. 67

Edwin O. Sachs ed.

Feet.

Feet.

Mètres.

Mètres.

MUNICIPAL THEATRE, LAIBACH.

Vlad. Hrásky.

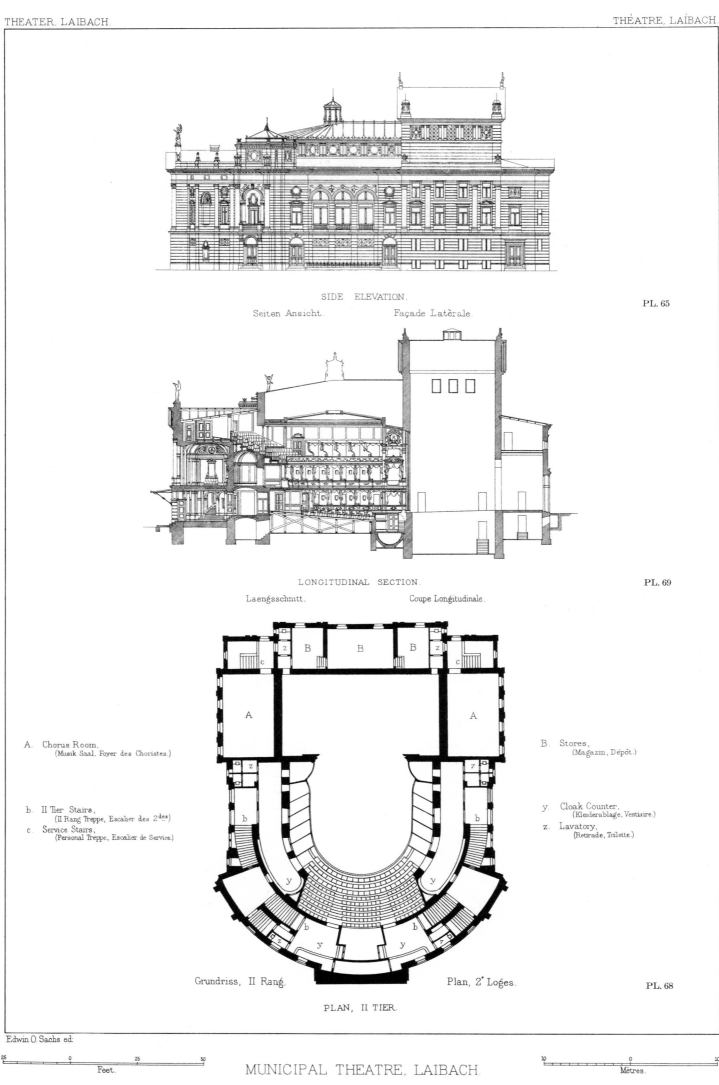

SIDE ELEVATION.

Seiten Ansicht. Façade Latèrale.

PL. 65

LONGITUDINAL SECTION.

Laengsschnitt. Coupe Longitudinale.

PL. 69

A. Chorus Room,
    (Musik Saal, Foyer des Choristes.)

b. II Tier Stairs,
    (II Rang Treppe, Escalier des 2des)
c. Service Stairs,
    (Personal Treppe, Escalier de Service.)

B. Stores,
    (Magazin, Dépôt.)

y. Cloak Counter,
    (Kleiderablage, Vestiaire.)
z. Lavatory,
    (Retirade, Toilette.)

Grundriss, II Rang. Plan, 2ᵉ Loges.

PL. 68

PLAN, II TIER.

Edwin O. Sachs ed:

25 0 25 50
Feet.

10 0 10
Mètres.

MUNICIPAL THEATRE, LAIBACH.

Vlad. Hrásky.

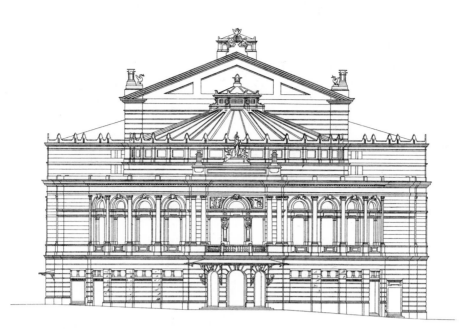

Vorder Ansicht.　　　　　FRONT ELEVATION　　　Façade Principale.　　　　PL. 70

A. Main Entrance, (Haupt Eingang, Grande Entrée.)　　D. Lobby I Tier, (Vorhalle I Rang, Vestibule des I^{res}.)　　F. Green Room, (Unterhaltungsraum, Foyer des Artistes.)

B. Main Vestibule, (Grosse Vorhalle, Grand Vestibule.)　　E. Lobby II Tier, (Vorhalle II Rang, Vestibule des 2des.)　　G. Stores, (Magazin, Dépôt.)

C. Hall, (Wartehalle, Vestibule d'Attente.)　　　　　　　　　　　　　　　　　　　　　　　　　　H. Yard, (Hof, Cour.)

a. I Tier Stairs, (I Rang Treppe, Escalier des I^{res}.)　　b. II Tier Stairs, (II Rang Treppe, Escalier des 2des.)　　c. Service Stairs, (Personal Treppe, Escalier de Service.)

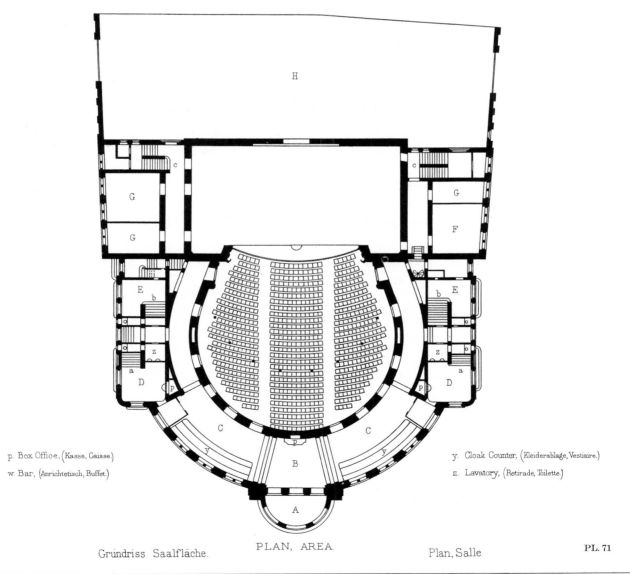

p. Box Office, (Kasse, Caisse.)　　　　　　　　　　　　　　　　　　y. Cloak Counter, (Kleiderablage, Vestiaire.)

w. Bar, (Anrichtetisch, Buffet.)　　　　　　　　　　　　　　　　　　z. Lavatory, (Retirade, Toilette.)

Grundriss Saalfläche.　　　　　PLAN, AREA.　　　　　Plan, Salle.　　　　PL. 71

Edwin O. Sachs ed:

Feet.　　　　　　　　　　　　"RAIMUND" THEATRE, VIENNA.　　　　　　　　Mètres.

Franz Roth.

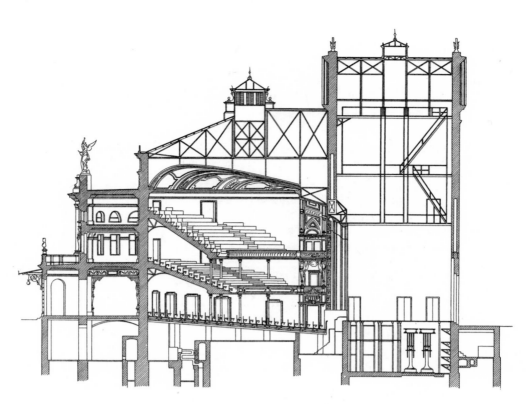

Laengsschnitt.   LONGITUDINAL SECTION.   Coupe Longitudinale.   PL. 74

A. Lounge, (Erfrischungssaal, Foyer.)   C. Accident Room, (Kranken Zimmer, Laboratoire du Médecin.)   E. Dressing Room, (Ankleideraum, Loge des Artistes.)
B. Balcony, (Balkon, Balcon.)   D. General Management, (Verwaltung, L'Administration.)   G. Treasury, (Haupt Kasse, Bureau des Comptes.)

a. I Tier Stairs, (I Rang Treppe, Escalier des I.res)   c. Service Stairs, (Personal Treppe, Escalier de Service.)   y. Cloak Counter, (Kleiderablage, Vestiaire.)
b. II Tier Stairs, (II Rang Treppe, Escalier des 2.des) w. Bar, (Anrichtetisch, Buffet.)   z. Lavatory, (Retirade, Toilette.)

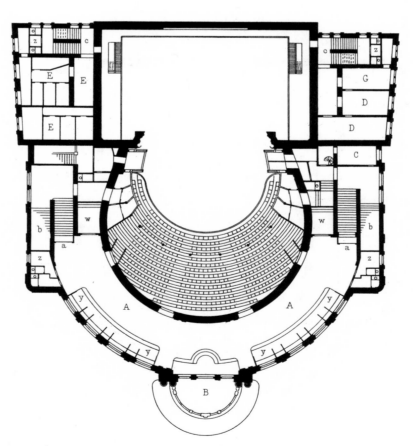

PLAN, I TIER.
Grundriss, I Rang.   Plan, I. Loges.   PL. 72

Edwin O. Sachs ed:

25   0   25   50   "RAIMUND" THEATRE, VIENNA.   10   0   10
Feet.   Franz Roth.   Mètres.

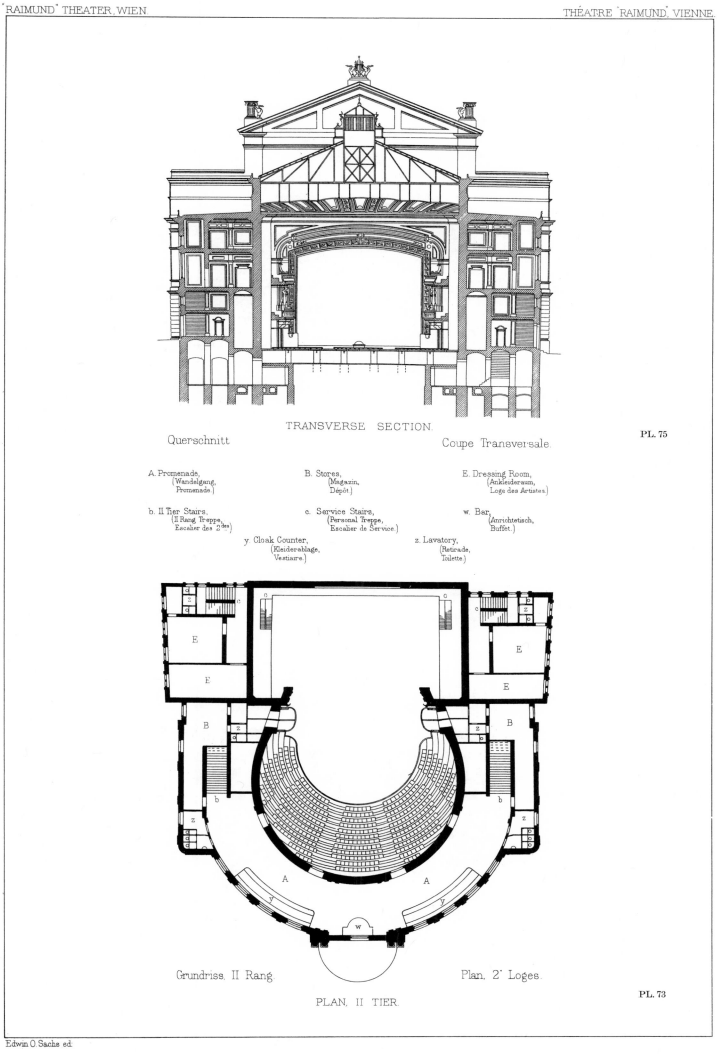

TRANSVERSE SECTION.

Querschnitt   Coupe Transversale.

PL. 75

A. Promenade,   B. Stores,   E. Dressing Room,
   (Wandelgang,   (Magazin,   (Ankleideraum,
    Promenade.)   Dépôt.)   Loge des Artistes.)

b. II Tier Stairs,   c. Service Stairs,   w. Bar,
   (II Rang Treppe,   (Personal Treppe,   (Anrichtetisch,
    Escalier des 2des)   Escalier de Service.)   Buffet.)

        y. Cloak Counter,   z. Lavatory,
           (Kleiderablage,   (Retirade,
            Vestiaire.)   Toilette.)

Grundriss, II Rang.   Plan, 2º Loges.

PLAN, II TIER.

PL. 73

Edwin O. Sachs ed:

25   0   25   50
Feet.

"RAIMUND" THEATRE, VIENNA.

Franz Roth

10   0   10
Mètres.

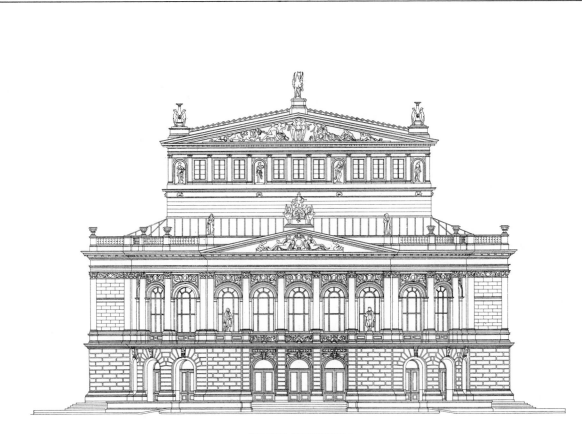

FRONT ELEVATION.   PL. 76

Vorder Ansicht.   Façade Principale.

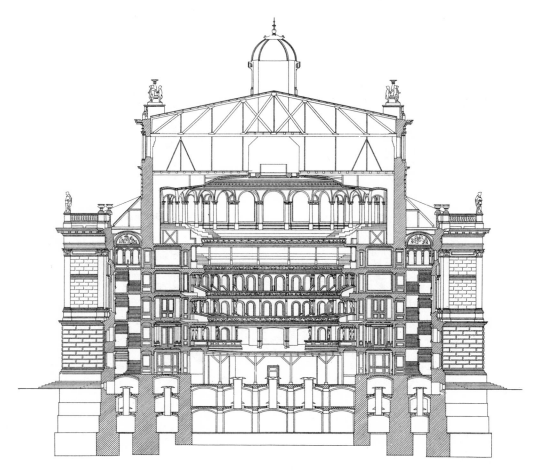

TRANSVERSE SECTION.   PL. 80

Querschnitt.   Coupe Transversale.

MUNICIPAL OPERA HOUSE, FRANKFORT

Lucae, Becker Giesenberg.

A. Main Entrance,
    (Haupt Eingang, Grande Entrée.)
B. Grand Vestibule,
    (Grosse Vorhalle, Grand Vestibule.)
C. Vestibule,
    (Vorhalle, Vestibule.)
D. Grand Staircase,
    (Haupt Treppe, Grand Escalier.)
E. Lobby,
    (Vorraum, Dégagement.)
F. General Management,
    (Verwaltung, L'Administration.)

G. Green Room,
    (Unterhaltungsraum, Foyer des Artistes.)
H. Library,
    (Bibliothek, Bibliotheque.)
I. Dressing Room,
    (Ankleideraum, Loge des Artistes.)
K. Store,
    (Magazin, Dépôt.)
L. Engineer,
    (Maschinenmeister, Ingénieur.)
M. Accident Room,
    (Kranken Zimmer, Laboratoire du Médecin.)

a. Stalls Entrance,
    (Parkett Eingang, Entrée des Loges.)
b. Pit Stairs,
    (Parterre Treppe, Escalier du Parterre.)
c. I Tier Stairs,
    (I Rang Treppe, Escalier des 1res.)
d. II Tier Stairs,
    (II Rang Treppe, Escalier des 2des.)
e. III Tier Stairs,
    (III Rang Treppe, Escalier des 3res.)
f. IV Tier Stairs,
    (IV Rang Treppe, Escalier des 4mes.)

g. Pass Stairs,
    (Verbindungs Treppe, Escalier de Communication.)
h. Service Stairs,
    (Personal Treppe, Escalier de Service.)
p. Box Office,
    (Kasse, Caisse.)
y. Cloak Counter,
    (Kleiderablage, Vestiaire.)
z. Lavatory,
    (Retirade, Toilette.)

PLAN, AREA.

Grundriss, Saal.   Plan, Salle.

25   0   25   50   MUNICIPAL OPERA HOUSE, FRANKFORT.   10   0   10
        Feet.   Mètres.

Lucae, Becker, Giesenberg.

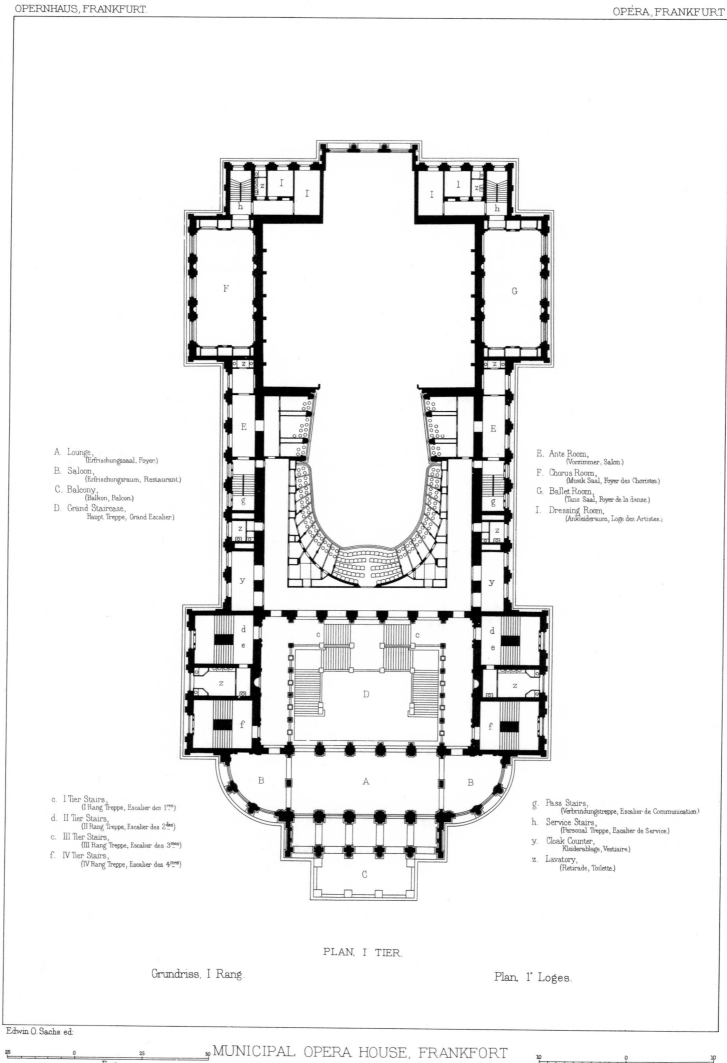

A. Lounge,
   (Erfrischungssaal, Foyer.)
B. Saloon,
   (Erfrischungsraum, Restaurant.)
C. Balcony,
   (Balkon, Balcon.)
D. Grand Staircase,
   (Haupt. Treppe, Grand Escalier.)

E. Ante Room,
   (Vorzimmer, Salon.)
F. Chorus Room,
   (Musik Saal, Foyer des Choristes.)
G. Ballet Room,
   (Tanz Saal, Foyer de la danse.)
I. Dressing Room,
   (Ankleideraum, Loge des Artistes.)

c. I Tier Stairs,
   (I Rang Treppe, Escalier des 1res.)
d. II Tier Stairs,
   (II Rang Treppe, Escalier des 2des.)
e. III Tier Stairs,
   (III Rang Treppe, Escalier des 3mes.)
f. IV Tier Stairs,
   (IV Rang Treppe, Escalier des 4mes.)

g. Pass Stairs,
   (Verbindungstreppe, Escalier de Communication.)
h. Service Stairs,
   (Personal Treppe, Escalier de Service.)
y. Cloak Counter,
   (Kleiderablage, Vestiaire.)
z. Lavatory,
   (Retirade, Toilette.)

PLAN, I TIER.

Grundriss, I Rang.   Plan, I' Loges.

Edwin O. Sachs ed:

25   0   25   50
Feet.

MUNICIPAL OPERA HOUSE, FRANKFORT
Lucae, Becker, Giesenberg

10   0   10
Mètres.

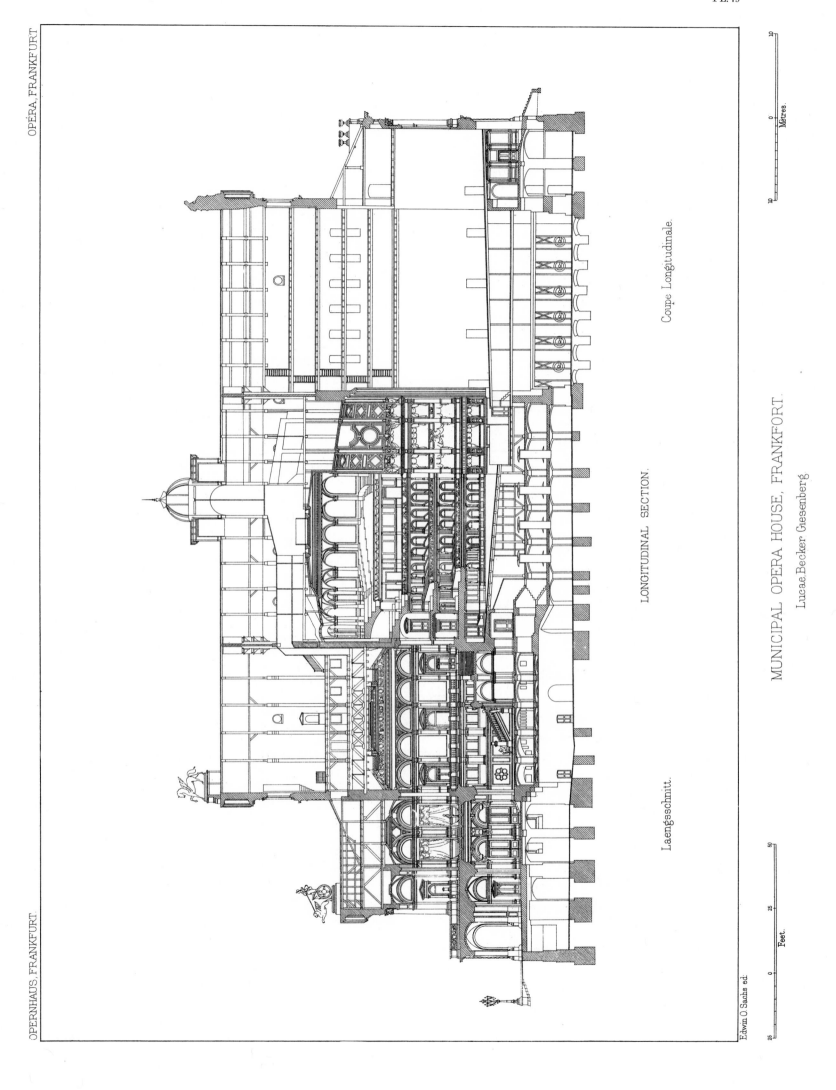

Edwin O. Sachs ed.

Laengsschnitt.

LONGITUDINAL SECTION.

Coupe Longitudinale.

MUNICIPAL OPERA HOUSE, FRANKFORT.

Lucae, Becker Giesenberg

Feet.

Mètres.

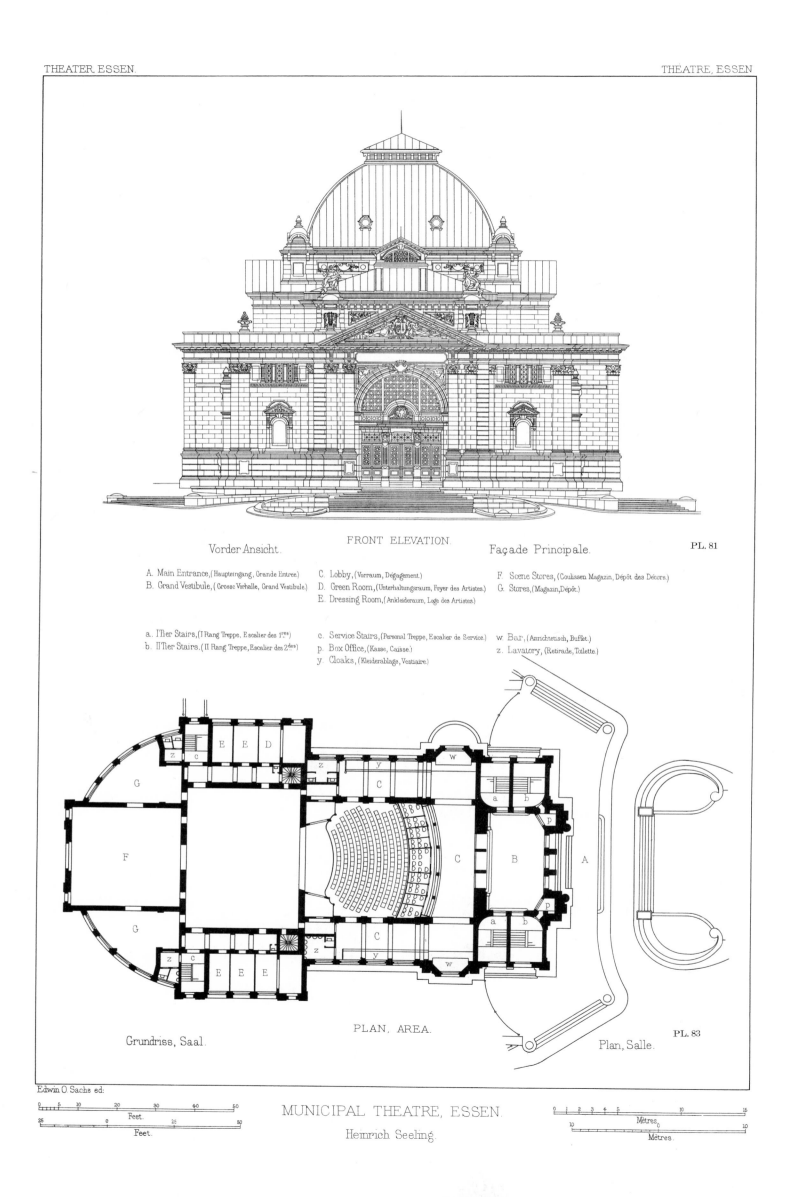

Vorder Ansicht.   FRONT ELEVATION.   Façade Principale.   PL. 81

A. Main Entrance, (Haupteingang, Grande Entree.)   C. Lobby, (Vorraum, Dégagement.)   F. Scene Stores, (Coulissen Magazin, Dépôt des Décors.)
B. Grand Vestibule, (Grosse Vorhalle, Grand Vestibule.)   D. Green Room, (Unterhaltungsraum, Foyer des Artistes.)   G. Stores, (Magazin, Dépôt.)
                                   E. Dressing Room, (Ankleideraum, Loge des Artistes.)

a. I Tier Stairs, (I Rang Treppe, Escalier des 1ces.)   c. Service Stairs, (Personal Treppe, Escalier de Service.)   w. Bar, (Anrichtetisch, Buffet.)
b. II Tier Stairs, (II Rang Treppe, Escalier des 2des.)   p. Box Office, (Kasse, Caisse.)   z. Lavatory, (Retirade, Toilette.)
                                   y. Cloaks, (Kleiderablage, Vestiaire.)

Grundriss, Saal.   PLAN, AREA.   PL. 83
                             Plan, Salle.

Edwin O Sachs ed:

Feet.   MUNICIPAL THEATRE, ESSEN.   Mètres.
Feet.   Heinrich Seeling.   Mètres.

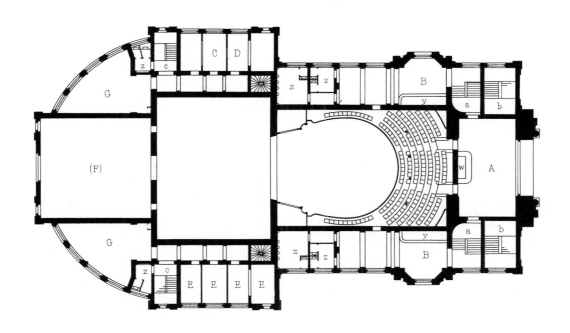

PLAN. I TIER.

Grundriss. I Rang.   Plan. 1˚ Loges.

PL. 84

A. Lounge, (Erfrischungssaal, Foyer.)
B. Lobby, (Vorraum, Dégagement.)
C. Stage Management, (Regie, Direction de la Scène.)

D. General Management, (Verwaltung, L'Administration.)
E. Dressing Room, (Ankleideraum, Loge des Artistes.)
F. Scene Store, (Coulissen Magazin, Dépôt des Décors.)
G. Stores, (Magazin, Dépôt.)

H. Wardrobe Room, (Kleiderkammer, Costumes.)
I. Supers Room, (Statisten, Comparses.)
K. Rehearsal Room, (Probe Saal, Salle de Répétition.)

a. I Tier Stairs, (I Rang Treppe, Escalier des 1˚ˢ)
b. II Tier Stairs, (II Rang Treppe, Escalier des 2˚ᵉˢ)

c. Service Stairs, (Personal Treppe, Escalier de Service.)
w. Bar, (Anrichtetisch, Buffet.)

y. Cloak Counter, (Kleiderablage, Vestiaire.)
z. Lavatory, (Retirade, Toilette.)

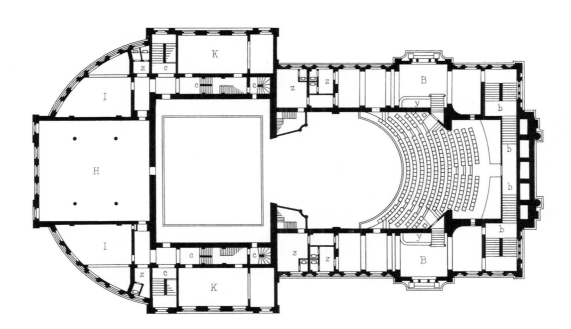

PLAN. II TIER.

Grundriss. II Rang.   Plan. 2˚ Loges.

PL. 85

MUNICIPAL THEATRE, ESSEN.

Heinrich Seeling

Feet.

Mètres.

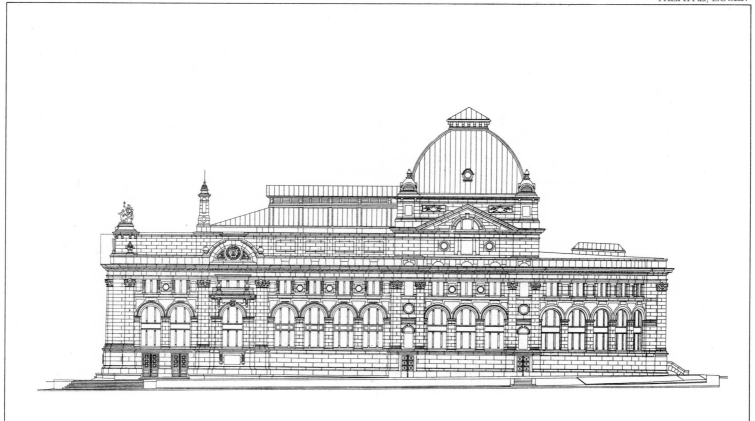

SIDE ELEVATION.

PL. 82

Seiten Ansicht.

Façade Latérale.

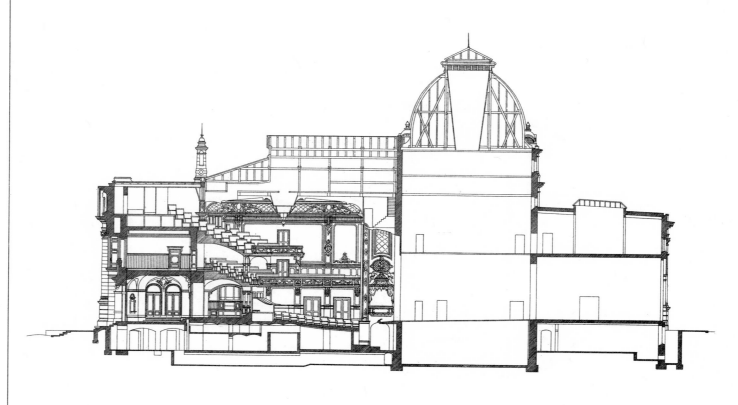

LONGITUDINAL SECTION.

PL. 86

Laengsschnitt.

Coupe Longitudinale.

Edwin O. Sachs ed.

Feet.

MUNICIPAL THEATRE, ESSEN.

Heinrich Seeling.

Mètres.

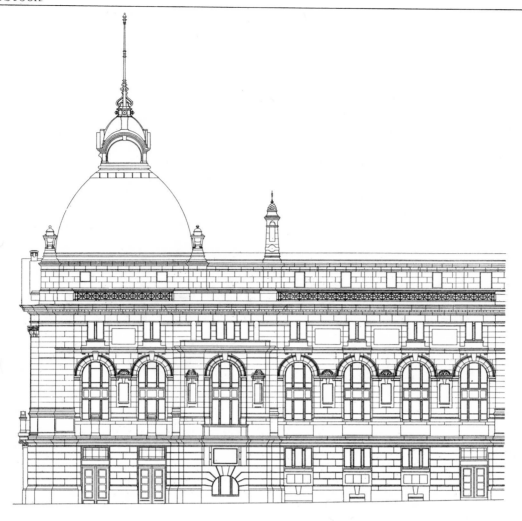

SIDE ELEVATION. DETAILS.   PL. 87

Seiten Ansicht. Einzelheiten.   Façade Latérale. Details.

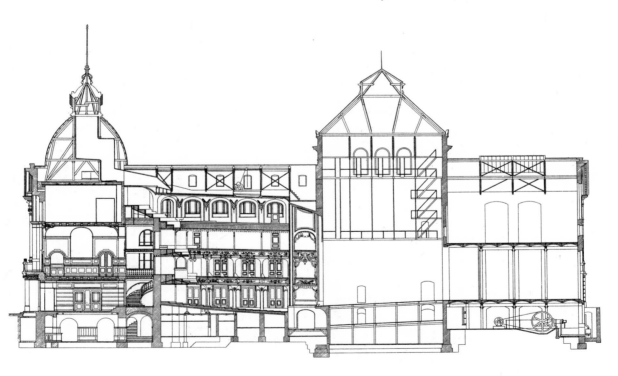

LONGITUDINAL SECTION.   PL. 90

Laengsschnitt.   Coupe Longitudinale.

Edwin O. Sachs ed.

25   0   25   50
Feet.

MUNICIPAL THEATRE, ROSTOCK.

Heinrich Seeling.

10   0   10
Mètres.

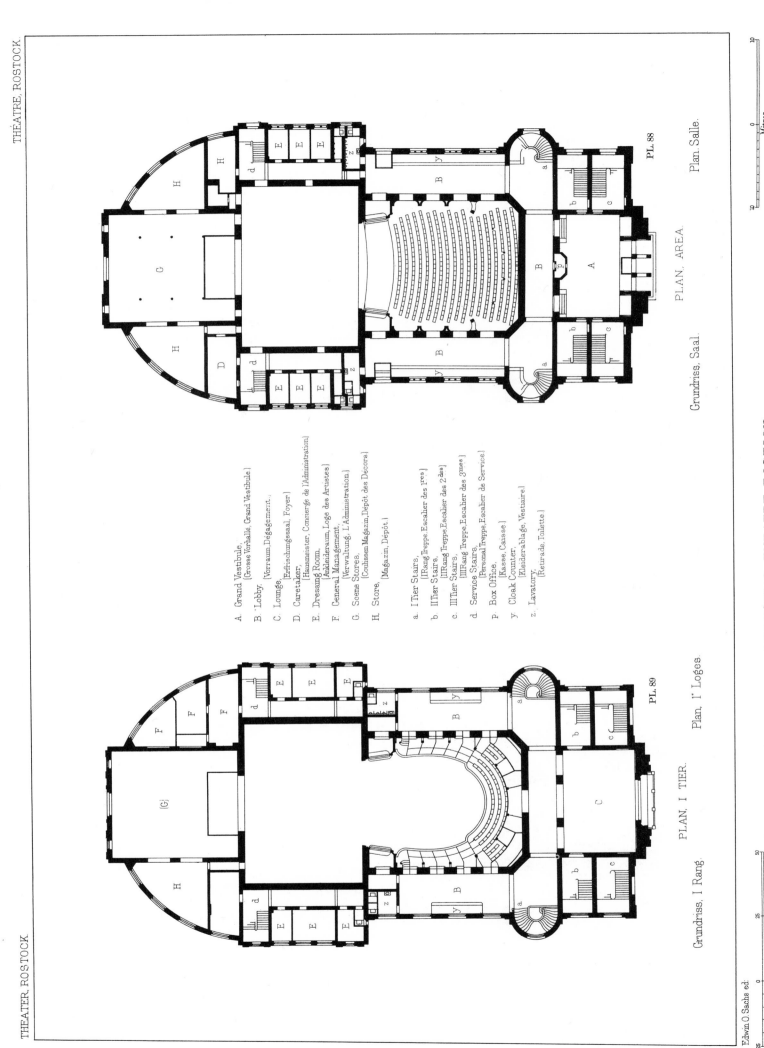

PL. 88

PLAN, AREA.

Plan. Salle.

Grundriss, Saal.

A. Grand Vestibule, (Grosse Vorhalle, Grand Vestibule.)
B. Lobby. (Vorraum, Dégagement.)
C. Lounge, (Erfrischungssaal, Foyer.)
D. Caretaker, (Hausmeister, Conciergé de l'Administration.)
E. Dressing Room, (Ankleideraum, Loge des Artistes.)
F. General Management, (Verwaltung, L'Administration.)
G. Scene Stores, (Coulissen Magazin, Dépôt des Décors.)
H. Store, (Magazin, Dépôt.)

a. I Tier Stairs, (I Rang Treppe, Escalier des 1res.)
b. II Tier Stairs, (II Rang Treppe, Escalier des 2des.)
c. III Tier Stairs, (III Rang Treppe, Escalier des 3mes.)
d. Service Stairs, (Personal Treppe, Escalier de Service.)
p. Box Office, (Kasse, Caisse.)
y. Cloak Counter, (Kleiderablage, Vestiaire.)
z. Lavatory, (Retirade, Toilette.)

PL. 89

Plan. I Loges

PLAN, I TIER.

Grundriss, I Rang.

MUNICIPAL THEATRE, ROSTOCK.

Heinrich Seeling

Edwin O. Sachs ed.

Feet.

Mètres.

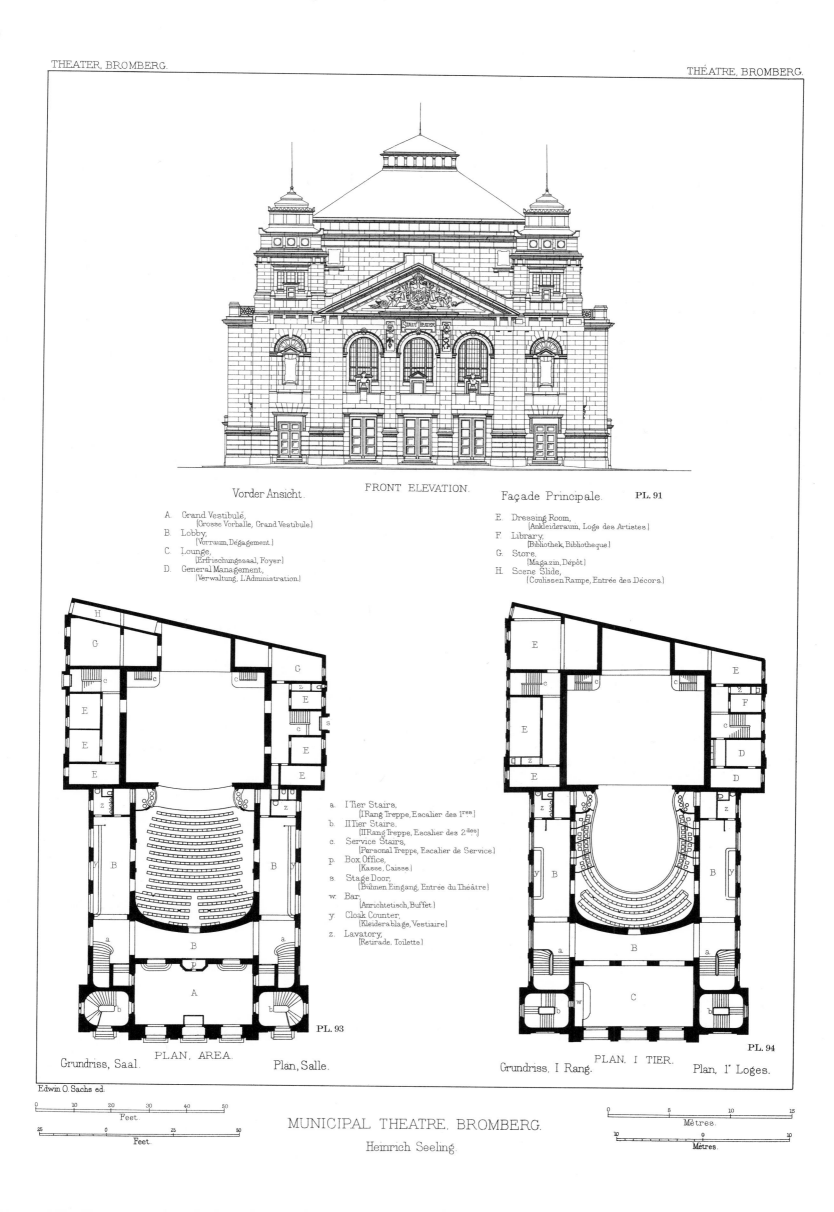

Vorder Ansicht.   FRONT ELEVATION.   Façade Principale.   PL. 91

A.   Grand Vestibule,
         (Grosse Vorhalle, Grand Vestibule.)
B.   Lobby,
         (Vorraum, Dégagement.)
C.   Lounge,
         (Erfrischungssaal, Foyer.)
D.   General Management,
         (Verwaltung, L'Administration.)

E.   Dressing Room,
         (Ankleideraum, Loge des Artistes.)
F.   Library,
         (Bibliothek, Bibliotheque.)
G.   Store,
         (Magazin, Dépôt.)
H.   Scene Slide,
         (Coulissen Rampe, Entrée des Décors.)

a.   I Tier Stairs,
         (I Rang Treppe, Escalier des 1res.)
b.   II Tier Stairs,
         (II Rang Treppe, Escalier des 2des.)
c.   Service Stairs,
         (Personal Treppe, Escalier de Service.)
p.   Box Office,
         (Kasse, Caisse.)
s.   Stage Door,
         (Bühnen Eingang, Entrée du Théâtre.)
w.   Bar,
         (Anrichtetisch, Buffet.)
y.   Cloak Counter,
         (Kleiderablage, Vestiaire.)
z.   Lavatory,
         (Retirade, Toilette.)

PL. 93   PL. 94

Grundriss, Saal.   PLAN, AREA.   Plan, Salle.   Grundriss, I Rang.   PLAN, I TIER.   Plan, 1er Loges.

Edwin O. Sachs ed.

Feet.

Feet.

MUNICIPAL THEATRE, BROMBERG.

Heinrich Seeling.

Mètres.

Mètres.

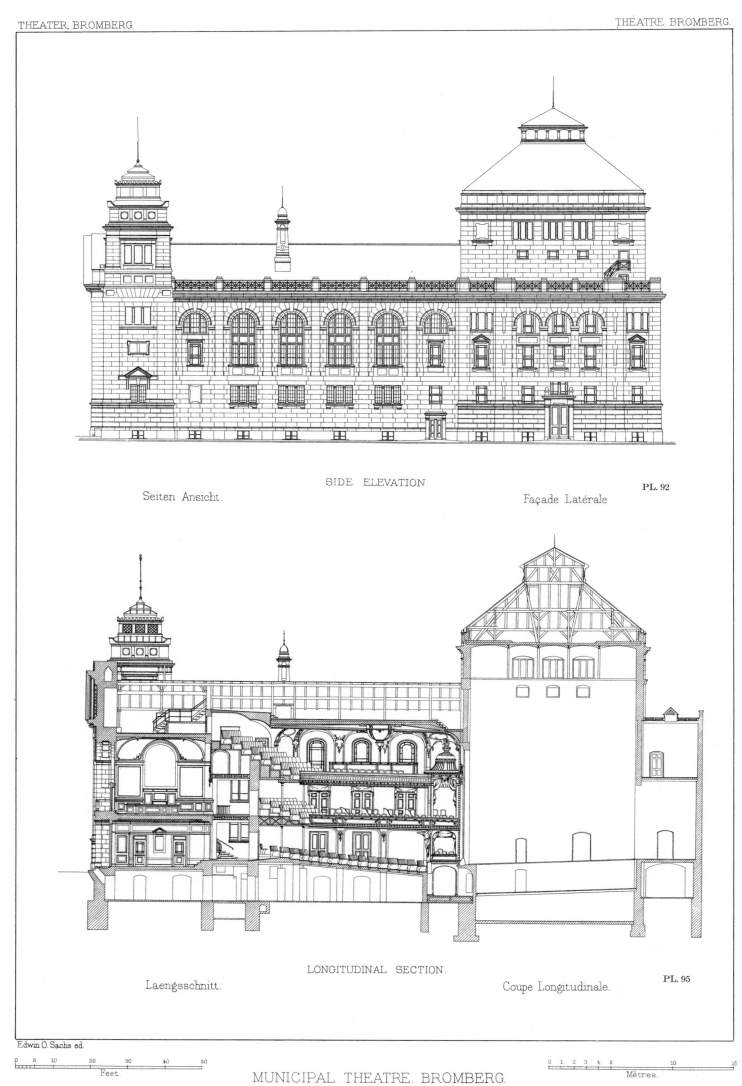

SIDE ELEVATION.

Seiten Ansicht.　　　　　　　　　　　　　　　　　　　　Façade Latérale　　　　　　　　PL. 92

LONGITUDINAL SECTION.

Laengsschnitt.　　　　　　　　　　　　　　　　　　　　Coupe Longitudinale.　　　　　　PL. 95

Edwin O. Sachs ed.

0　5　10　　20　　30　　40　　50
Feet.

0 1 2 3 4 5　　　10　　　　15
Mêtres.

MUNICIPAL THEATRE. BROMBERG.

Heinrich Seeling.

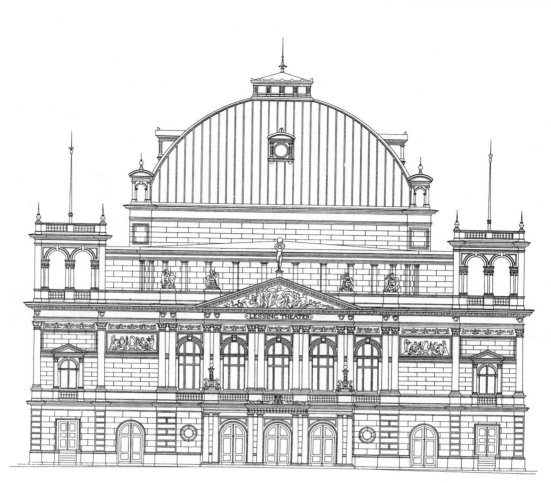

Vorder Ansicht.   FRONT ELEVATION.   Façade Principale.   PL. 96

A. Main Entrance,
   (Haupt Eingang, Grande Entrée.)
B. Grand Vestibule,
   (Grosse Vorhalle, Grand Vestibule.)

a. I Tier Stairs,
   (I Rang Treppe, Escalier des 1res.)
b. II Tier Stairs,
   (II Rang Treppe, Escalier des 2des.)

C. Caretaker,
   (Hausmeister, Concierge de L'Administration.)
D. Scene Store,
   (Coulissen Magazin, Dépôt des Décors.)

c. Service Stairs,
   (Personal Treppe, Escalier de Service.)
p. Box Office,
   (Kasse, Caisse.)

E. Dressing Room,
   (Ankleideraum, Loge des Artistes.)
F. Green Room,
   (Unterhaltungsraum, Foyer des Artistes.)

y. Cloak Counter,
   (Kleiderablage, Vestiaire.)
z. Lavatory,
   (Retirade, Toilette.)

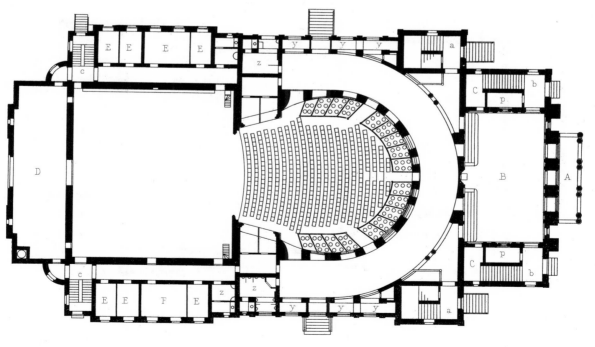

Grundriss, Saal.   PLAN, AREA.   Plan, Salle.   PL. 97

Edwin O. Sachs ed:

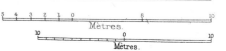

Feet
Feet.

Mètres.
Mètres.

"LESSING" THEATRE, BERLIN.

Von der Hude.

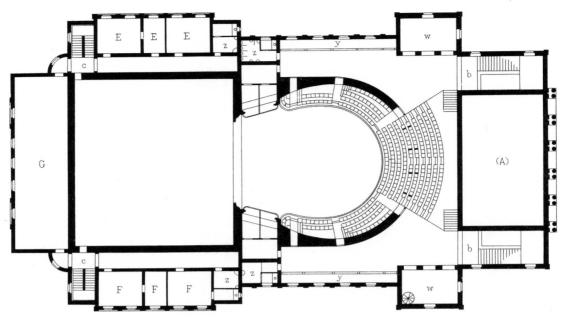

PL. 99

PLAN, II TIER.

Grundriss, II Rang.

Plan, 2ᵉ Loges.

PL. 99

A. Lounge, (Erfrischungssaal, Foyer.)   C. General Management, (Verwaltung, L'Administration.)   F. Rehearsal Room, (Probe Saal, Salle de Répétition.)
B. Balcony, (Balkon, Balcon.)   D. Scene Store, (Coulissen Magazin, Dépôt des Décors.)   G. Stores, (Magazin, Dépôt.)
          E. Dressing Room, (Ankleideraum, Loge des Artistes.)

a. I Tier Stairs, (I Rang Treppe, Escalier des 1ᵉˢ)   c. Service Stairs, (Personal Treppe, Escalier de Service.)   y. Cloak Counter, (Kleiderablage, Vestiaire.)
b. II Tier Stairs, (II Rang Treppe, Escalier des 2ᵈᵉˢ)   w. Bar, (Anrichtetisch, Buffet.)   z. Lavatory, (Retirade, Toilette.)

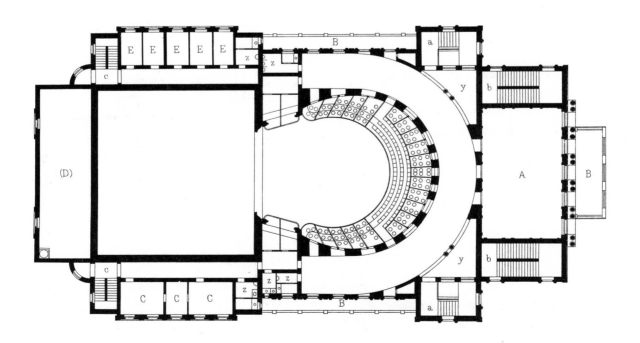

PLAN, I TIER.

Grundriss, I Rang.

Plan, 1ᵉ Loges.

PL. 98

Edwin O. Sachs ed:

Feet.

"LESSING" THEATRE, BERLIN.

Von der Hude.

Mètres.

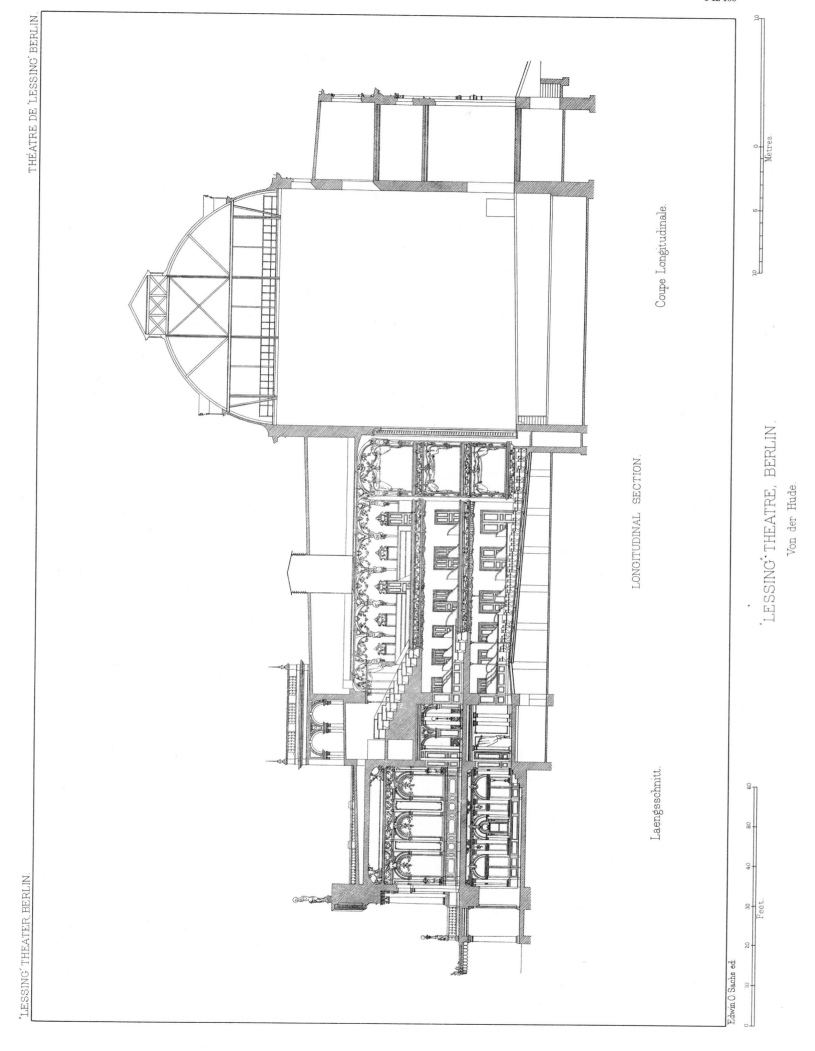

PL. 100

"LESSING" THEATRE, BERLIN.

Von der Hude.

LONGITUDINAL SECTION.

Coupe Longitudinale.

Laengsschnitt.

THÉATRE DE LESSING BERLIN.

"LESSING" THEATER BERLIN.

Edwin O. Sachs ed.

FRONT ELEVATION.

Vorder Ansicht.   Façade Principale.

PL. 101

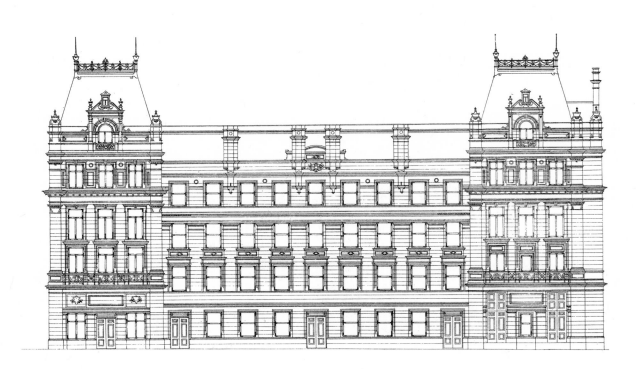

SIDE ELEVATION.

Seiten Ansicht.   Façade Latérale.

PL. 102

Edwin O. Sachs ed:

0 5 10   20   30   40   50

Feet.

"HER MAJESTY'S" THEATRE, LONDON.

C. J. Phipps.

0   5   10   20

Mètres.

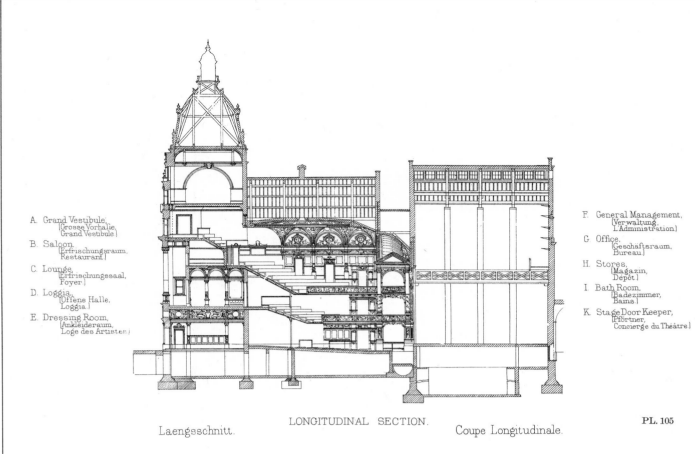

A. Grand Vestibule,
(Grosse Vorhalle,
Grand Vestibule.)

B. Saloon.
(Erfrischungsraum,
Restaurant.)

C. Lounge,
(Erfrischungssaal,
Foyer.)

D. Loggia,
(Offene Halle,
Loggia.)

E. Dressing Room,
(Ankleideraum,
Loge des Artistes.)

F. General Management,
(Verwaltung,
L'Administration.)

G. Office,
(Geschäftsraum,
Bureau.)

H. Stores,
(Magazin,
Dépôt.)

I. Bath Room,
(Badezimmer,
Bains.)

K. Stage Door Keeper,
(Pförtner,
Concierge du Théâtre.)

Laengsschnitt.   LONGITUDINAL SECTION.   Coupe Longitudinale.   PL. 105

a. Stall Stairs,
(Parkett Treppe, Escalier des Stalles)

b. Pit Passage,
(Parterre Gang, Couloir du Parterre)

c. I Tier Stairs,
(I Rang Treppe, Escalier des 1res.)

d. II Tier Stairs,
(II Rang Treppe, Escalier des 2des)

e. III Tier Stairs,
(III Rang Treppe, Escalier des 3mes)

f. Private Box Stairs,
(Logen Treppe, Escalier des Loges.)

g. Service Stairs,
(Personal Treppe, Escalier de Service)

p. Box Office,
(Kasse, Caisse.)

s. Stage Door,
(Bühnen Eingang, Entrée du Théâtre.)

w. Bar,
(Anrichte tisch, Buffet.)

y. Cloaks,
(Kleiderablage, Vestiaire.)

z. Lavatory,
(Retirade, Toilette.)

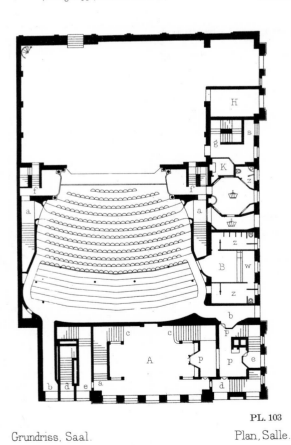

PL. 103

Grundriss, Saal.   Plan, Salle.

PLAN, AREA.

Grundriss, I Rang.   Plan, 1er Loges.

PL. 104

PLAN, I TIER.

25   0   25   50
Feet.

"HER MAJESTY'S" THEATRE, LONDON.

C. J. Phipps.

10   0   10
Mètres.

FRONT ELEVATION.

Vorder Ansicht.   Façade Principale.   PL. 106

A. Main Entrance, (Haupt Eingang, Grande Entrée.)   D. Saloon, (Erfrischungsraum, Restaurant.)   G. Green Room, (Unterhaltungsraum, Foyer des Artistes.)
B. Grand Vestibule, (Grosse Vorhalle, Grand Vestibule.)   E. Dressing Room, (Ankleideraum, Loge des Artistes.)   H. Stage-door Keeper, (Pfoertner, Concierge du Théâtre.)
C. Lobby, (Vorraum, Dégagement.)   F. General Management, (Verwaltung, L'Administration.)   I. Stage Manager, (Regie, Direction de la Scène.)

K. Stores, (Magazin Dépôt.)   L. Caretaker, (Hausmeister, Concierge de L'Administration.)

a. Stalls Stairs, (Parkett Treppe, Escalier des Stalles.)   d. III Tier Stairs, (III Rang Treppe, Escalier des 3mes)   p. Box Office, (Kasse, Caisse.)
b. Pit Stairs, (Parterre Treppe, Escalier du Parterre.)   e. Service Stairs, (Personal Treppe, Escalier de Service.)   s. Stage Door, (Bühnen Eingang, Entrée du Théâtre.)
c. II Tier Stairs, (II Rang Treppe, Escalier des 2des)   f. Office Stairs, (Treppe zur Verwaltung, Escalier de l'Administration)   w. Bar, (Anrichtetisch, Buffet.)
y. Cloaks, (Kleiderablage, Vestiaire.)   z. Lavatory, (Retirade, Toilette.)

PLAN, AREA.   PL. 107   PLAN, I TIER.   PL. 108

Grundriss, Saal.   Plan, Salle.   Grundriss, I Rang.   Plan, 1 Loges.

Edwin O. Sachs ed:

Feet.

Feet.

"LYRIC" THEATRE, LONDON.

C. J. Phipps.

Metres.

Metres.

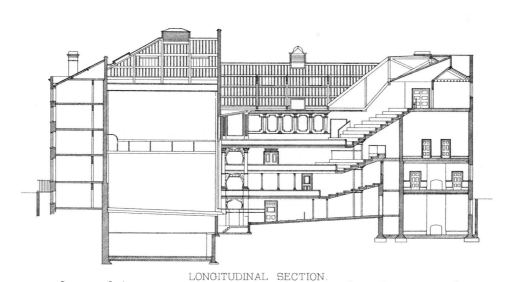

Laengsschnitt.   LONGITUDINAL SECTION.   Coupe Longitudinale.   PL. 111

A. Lounge, (Erfrischungssaal, Foyer.)   D. Saloon, (Erfrischungsraum, Restaurant.)
B. Office, (Geschäftsraum, Bureau.)   C. Wardrobe Room, (Kleiderkammer, Costumes.)   E. Dressing Room, (Ankleideraum, Loge des Artistes.)

c. II Tier Stairs, (II Rang Treppe, Escalier des 2 des)   e. Service Stairs, (Personal Treppe, Escalier de Service.)   w. Bar, (Anrichtetisch, Buffet.)
d. III Tier Stairs, (III Rang Treppe, Escalier des 3 mes)   f. Office Stairs, (Treppe zur Verwaltung, Escalier de l'Administration) y. Cloak Counter, (Kleiderablage, Vestiaire.)
                                   z. Lavatory, (Retirade, Toilette.)

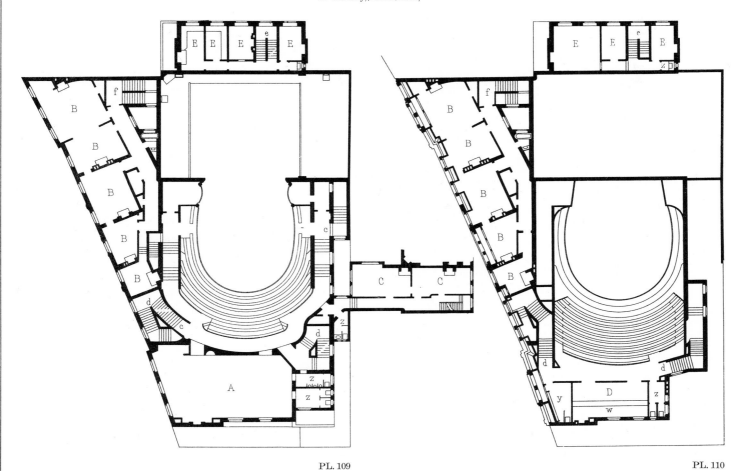

PL. 109   PL. 110

PLAN, II TIER.   PLAN, III TIER.
Grundriss, II Rang.   Plan, 2° Loges.   Grundriss, III Rang.   Plan, 3° Loges.

25   0   25   50
Feet.   10   0   10
                                                     Mètres.

"LYRIC" THEATRE, LONDON.
C. J. Phipps.

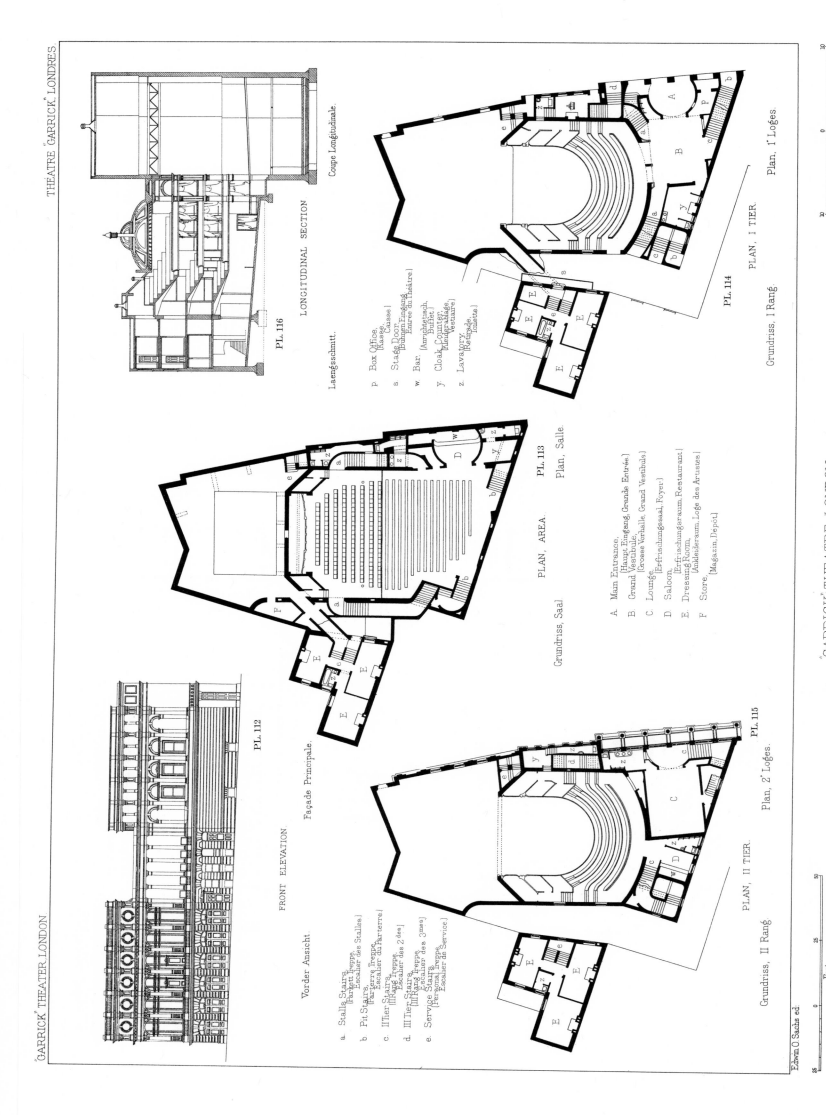

PL. 112

FRONT ELEVATION

Façade Principale.

Vorder Ansicht

a. Stalls Staircase. [Parkett Treppe. Escalier des Stalles.]
b. Pit Stairs. [Parterre Treppe. Escalier du Parterre.]
c. II Tier Stairs. [II Rang Treppe. Escalier des 2des.]
d. III Tier Stairs. [III Rang Treppe. Escalier des 3mes.]
e. Service Stairs. [Personal Treppe. Escalier de Service.]

PL. 116   LONGITUDINAL SECTION

Laengsschnitt.   Coupe Longitudinale.

p. Box Office. [Kasse. Caisse.]
s. Stage Door. [Bühnen Eingang. Entrée du Théâtre.]
w. Bar. [Ausschank. Buffet.]
y. Cloak Counter. [Kleiderablage. Vestiaire.]
z. Lavatory. [Retirade. Toilette.]

PL. 113   PLAN, AREA.

PLAN, Salle.

Grundriss, Saal.

A. Main Entrance. [Haupt Eingang. Grande Entrée.]
B. Grand Vestibule. [Grosse Vorhalle. Grand Vestibule.]
C. Lounge. [Erfrischungssaal, Foyer.]
D. Saloon. [Erfrischungsraum, Restaurant.]
E. Dressing Room. [Ankleideraum. Loge des Artistes.]
F. Store. [Magazin, Depot.]

PL. 114   PLAN, I TIER.

PLAN, 1 Loges.

Grundriss, I Rang.

PL. 115   PLAN, II TIER.

PLAN, 2 Loges.

Grundriss, II Rang.

Edwin O. Sachs ed.

Feet.

Mètres.

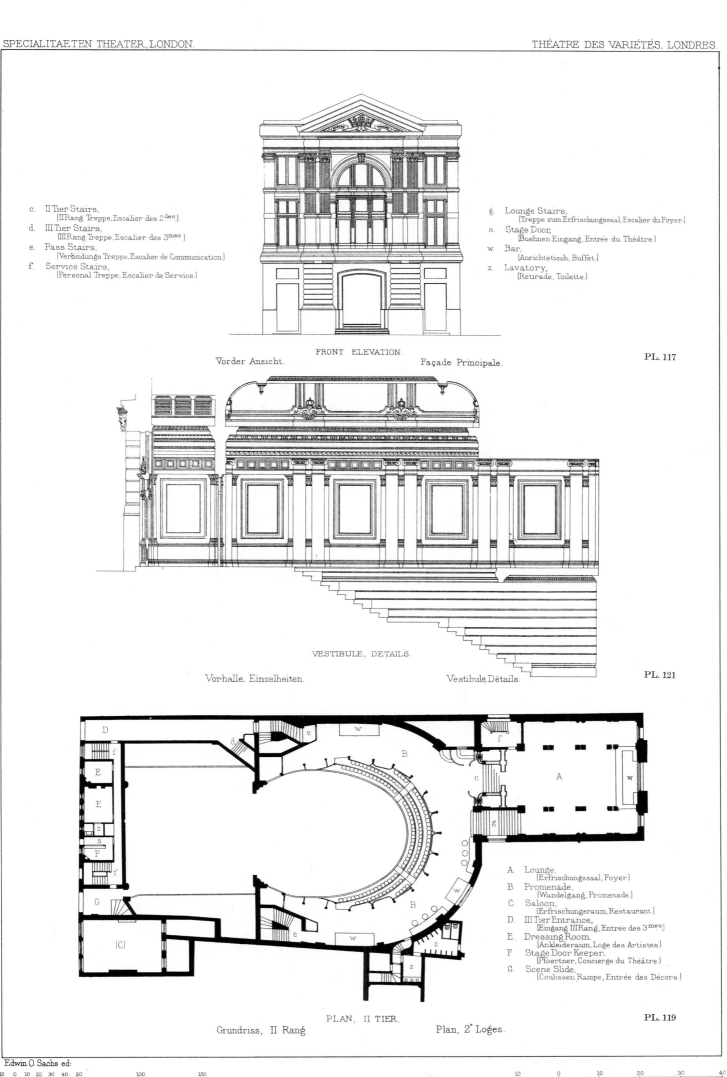

c. II Tier Stairs,
    (II Rang Treppe, Escalier des 2des.)
d. III Tier Stairs,
    (III Rang Treppe, Escalier des 3mes.)
e. Pass Stairs,
    (Verbindungs Treppe, Escalier de Communication.)
f. Service Stairs,
    (Personal Treppe, Escalier de Service.)

g. Lounge Stairs,
    (Treppe zum Erfrischungssaal, Escalier du Foyer.)
s. Stage Door,
    (Buehnen Eingang, Entrée du Théâtre.)
w. Bar,
    (Anrichtetisch, Buffet.)
z. Lavatory,
    (Retirade, Toilette.)

FRONT ELEVATION.

Vorder Ansicht.   Façade Principale.   PL. 117

VESTIBULE, DETAILS.

Vorhalle, Einzelheiten.   Vestibule, Détails.   PL. 121

A. Lounge,
    (Erfrischungssaal, Foyer.)
B. Promenade,
    (Wandelgang, Promenade.)
C. Saloon,
    (Erfrischungsraum, Restaurant.)
D. III Tier Entrance,
    (Eingang III Rang, Entrée des 3mes.)
E. Dressing Room,
    (Ankleideraum, Loge des Artistes.)
F. Stage Door Keeper,
    (Pfoertner, Concierge du Théâtre.)
G. Scene Slide,
    (Coulissen Rampe, Entrée des Décors.)

PLAN, II TIER.

Grundriss, II Rang   Plan, 2e Loges.   PL. 119

Edwin O. Sachs ed:

Feet.

Feet.

Feet.

Mètres.

Mètres.

Mètres.

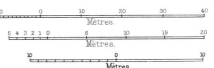

"EMPIRE" VARIETY THEATRE, LONDON.

T. Verity, F. T. Verity.

LONGITUDINAL SECTION.

Laengsschnitt.   Coupe Longitudinale.   PL. 120

A. Saloon,
    (Erfrischungsraum, Restaurant.)
B. Pit Lobby,
    (Parterre Vorraum, Dégagement du Parterre.)
C. Workshop,
    (Werkstatt, Atelier.)
D. Engineer,
    (Maschinenmeister, Ingénieur.)

E. Dressing Room,
    (Ankleideraum, Loge des Artistes.)
F. Scene Store,
    (Coulissen Magazin, Dépôt des Décors.)
G. Stores,
    (Magazin, Dépôt.)
H. Cellar,
    (Keller, Caves.)
I. Area,
    (Lichthof, Cour.)

a. Stalls Stairs,
    (Parkett Treppe, Escalier des Stalles.)
b. Pit Stairs,
    (Parterre Treppe, Escalier du Parterre.)
e. Pass Stairs,
    (Verbindungs Treppe, Escalier de Communication.)
f. Service Stairs,
    (Personal Treppe, Escalier de Service.)

w. Bar,
    (Anrichtetisch, Buffet.)
y. Cloaks,
    (Kleiderablage, Vestiaire.)
z. Lavatory,
    (Retirade, Toilette.)

PLAN, AREA.

Grundriss, Saal.   Plan, Salle.   PL. 118

Edwin O. Sachs ed.

"EMPIRE" VARIETY THEATRE, LONDON.

T. Verity, F. T. Verity.

25   0   25   50
Feet.

10   0   10
Mètres.

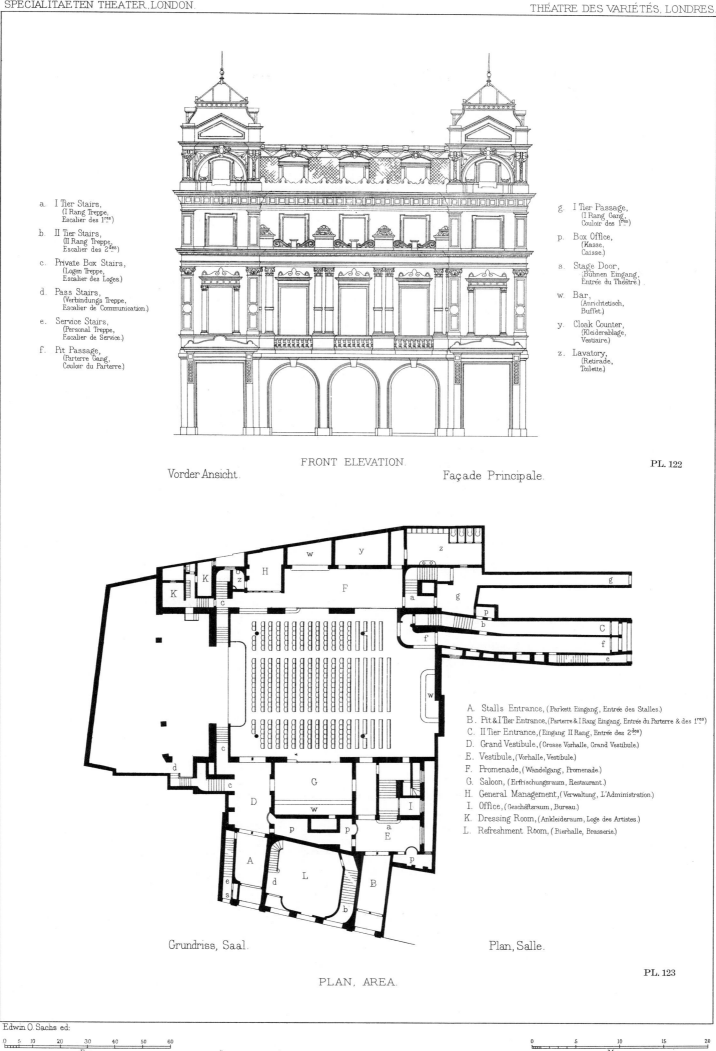

a. I Tier Stairs,
    (I Rang Treppe,
    Escalier des 1res.)

b. II Tier Stairs,
    (II Rang Treppe,
    Escalier des 2des.)

c. Private Box Stairs,
    (Logen Treppe,
    Escalier des Loges.)

d. Pass Stairs,
    (Verbindungs Treppe,
    Escalier de Communication.)

e. Service Stairs,
    (Personal Treppe,
    Escalier de Service.)

f. Pit Passage,
    (Parterre Gang,
    Couloir du Parterre.)

g. I Tier Passage,
    (I Rang Gang,
    Couloir des 1res.)

p. Box Office,
    (Kasse,
    Caisse.)

s. Stage Door,
    (Bühnen Eingang,
    Entrée du Théatre.)

w. Bar,
    (Anrichtetisch,
    Buffet.)

y. Cloak Counter,
    (Kleiderablage,
    Vestiaire.)

z. Lavatory,
    (Retirade,
    Toilette.)

FRONT ELEVATION.

Vorder Ansicht.   Façade Principale.

PL. 122

A. Stalls Entrance, (Parkett Eingang, Entrée des Stalles.)
B. Pit & I Tier Entrance, (Parterre & I Rang Eingang, Entrée du Parterre & des 1res.)
C. II Tier Entrance, (Eingang II Rang, Entrée des 2des.)
D. Grand Vestibule, (Grosse Vorhalle, Grand Vestibule.)
E. Vestibule, (Vorhalle, Vestibule.)
F. Promenade, (Wandelgang, Promenade.)
G. Saloon, (Erfrischungsraum, Restaurant.)
H. General Management, (Verwaltung, L'Administration.)
I. Office, (Geschäftsraum, Bureau.)
K. Dressing Room, (Ankleideraum, Loge des Artistes.)
L. Refreshment Room, (Bierhalle, Brasserie.)

Grundriss, Saal.   Plan, Salle.

PL. 123

PLAN, AREA.

Edwin O. Sachs ed:

Feet.

Feet.

Metres.

Metres.

"OXFORD" VARIETY THEATRE, LONDON.

Oswald C. Wylson, Charles Long.

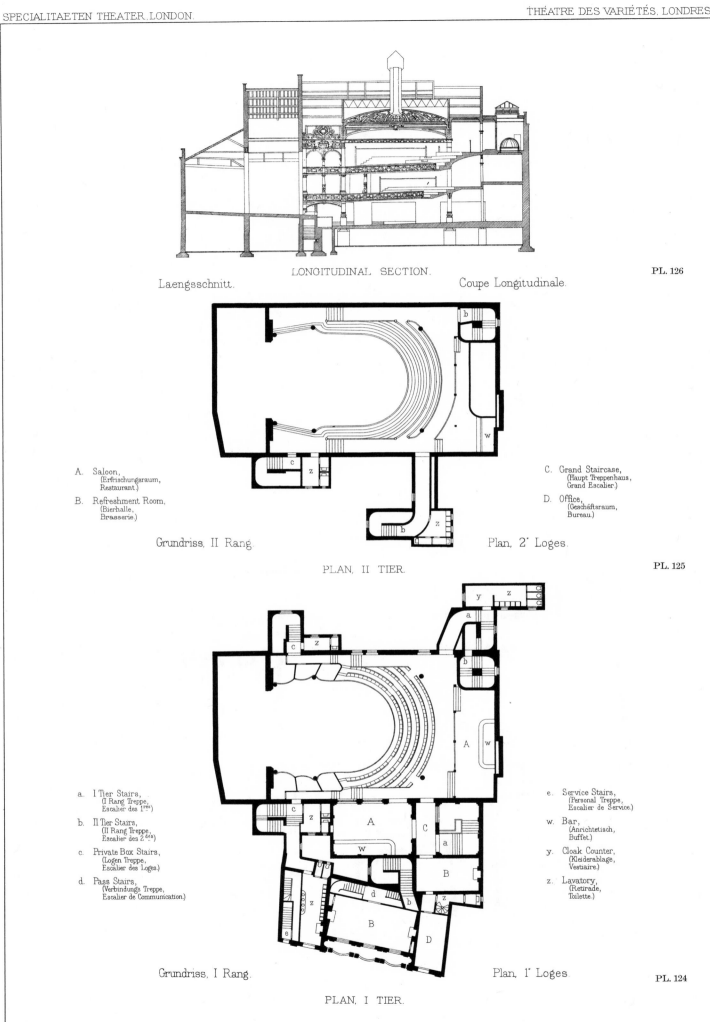

LONGITUDINAL SECTION.

Laengsschnitt.   Coupe Longitudinale.   PL. 126

A. Saloon,
    (Erfrischungsraum,
    Restaurant.)

B. Refreshment Room,
    (Bierhalle,
    Brasserie.)

C. Grand Staircase,
    (Haupt Treppenhaus,
    Grand Escalier.)

D. Office,
    (Geschäftsraum,
    Bureau.)

Grundriss, II Rang.   Plan, 2ᵉ Loges.

PLAN, II TIER.   PL. 125

a. I Tier Stairs,
    (I Rang Treppe,
    Escalier des 1ʳᵉˢ)

b. II Tier Stairs,
    (II Rang Treppe,
    Escalier des 2ᵈᵉˢ)

c. Private Box Stairs,
    (Logen Treppe,
    Escalier des Loges.)

d. Pass Stairs,
    (Verbindungs Treppe,
    Escalier de Communication.)

e. Service Stairs,
    (Personal Treppe,
    Escalier de Service.)

w. Bar,
    (Anrichtetisch,
    Buffet.)

y. Cloak Counter,
    (Kleiderablage,
    Vestiaire.)

z. Lavatory,
    (Retirade,
    Toilette.)

Grundriss, I Rang.   Plan, 1ᵉ Loges.   PL. 124

PLAN, I TIER.

Edwin O. Sachs ed:

25   0'   25   50
                 Feet.

10   0   10
        Mètres.

"OXFORD" VARIETY THEATRE, LONDON.

Oswald C. Wylson, Charles Long.

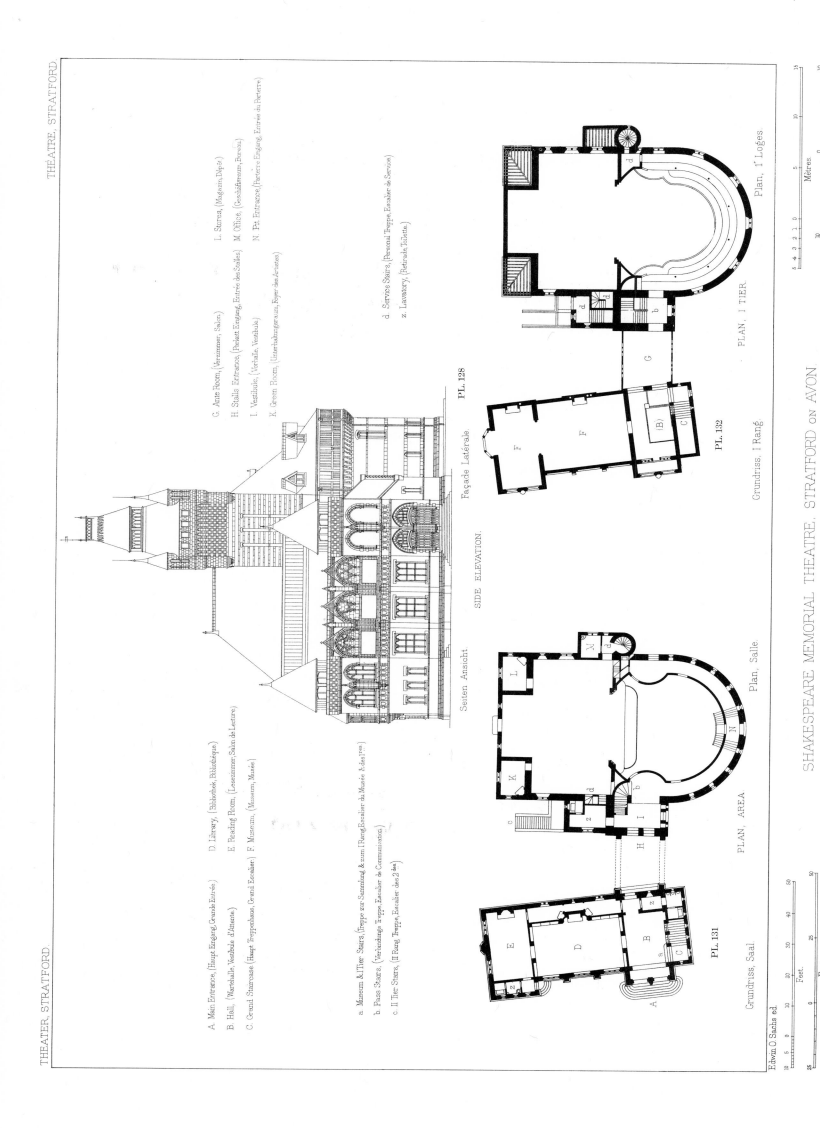

A. Main Entrance, (Haupt Eingang, Grande Entrée.)

B. Hall, (Wartehalle, Vestibule d'Attente.)

C. Grand Staircase (Haupt Treppenhaus, Grand Escalier.)

D. Library, (Bibliothek, Bibliothèque.)

E. Reading Room, (Lesezimmer, Salon de Lecture.)

F. Museum, (Museum, Musée.)

G. Ante Room, (Vorzimmer, Salon.)

H. Stalls Entrance, (Parkett Eingang, Entrée des Stalles.)

I. Vestibule, (Vorhalle, Vestibule.)

K. Green Room, (Unterhaltungsraum, Foyer des Artistes.)

L. Stores, (Magazin, Dépôt.)

M. Office, (Geschäftsraum, Bureau.)

N. Pit Entrance, (Parterre Eingang, Entrée du Parterre.)

a. Museum & I Tier Stairs, (Treppe zur Sammlung & zum I Rang Escalier du Musée & des 1 res.)

b. Pass Stairs, (Verbindungs Treppe, Escalier de Communication.)

c. II Tier Stairs, (II Rang Treppe, Escalier des 2 tres.)

d. Service Stairs, (Personal Treppe, Escalier de Service.)

z. Lavatory, (Retirade, Toilette.)

PL. 128

Seiten Ansicht.   SIDE ELEVATION.   Façade Latérale.

PL. 132

PLAN, I TIER.   Grundriss, I Rang.   Plan, I Rang.

Plan, I Loges.

PL. 131

Grundriss, Saal.   PLAN, AREA.   Plan, Salle.

SHAKESPEARE MEMORIAL THEATRE, STRATFORD ON AVON

W F Unsworth

Edwin O Sachs ed.

Feet.

Feet.

Métres.

Métres.

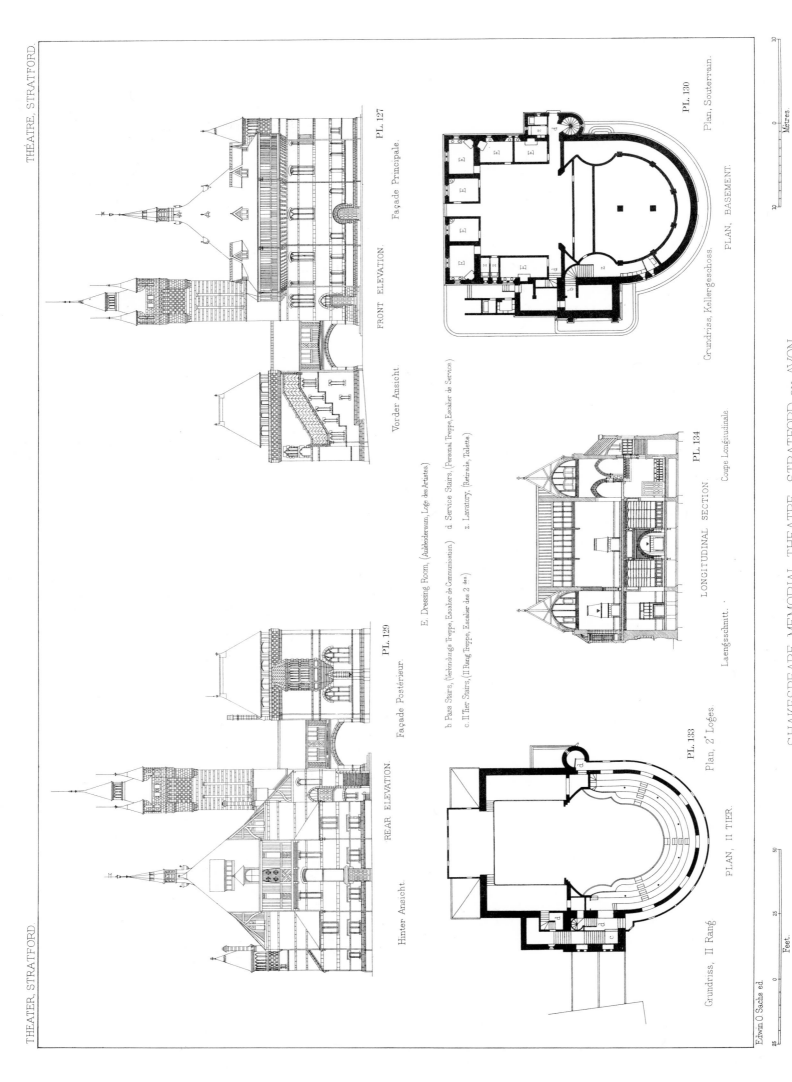

PL. 127

FRONT ELEVATION.

Façade Principale.

Vorder Ansicht.

PL. 130

Plan, Souterrain.

Grundriss, Kellergeschoss.

PLAN, BASEMENT.

PL. 129

REAR ELEVATION.

Façade Postérieur.

Hinter Ansicht.

E. Dressing Room, (Ankleideraum, Loge des Artistes.)

b Pass Stairs, (Verbindungs Treppe, Escalier de Communication.)

c. II Tier Stairs, (II Rang Treppe, Escalier des 2 ^{des}.)

d Service Stairs, (Personal Treppe, Escalier de Service.)

z. Lavatory, (Retirade, Toilette.)

LONGITUDINAL SECTION.

PL. 134

Coupe Longitudinale.

Laengsschnitt.

PL. 133

Plan, 2' Loges.

Grundriss, II Rang

PLAN, II TIER.

SHAKESPEARE MEMORIAL THEATRE, STRATFORD on AVON

W. F. Unsworth

Edwin O Sachs ed

Feet.

Mètres.

PL. 135

Querschnitt.

Coupe Transversale.

TRANSVERSE SECTION.

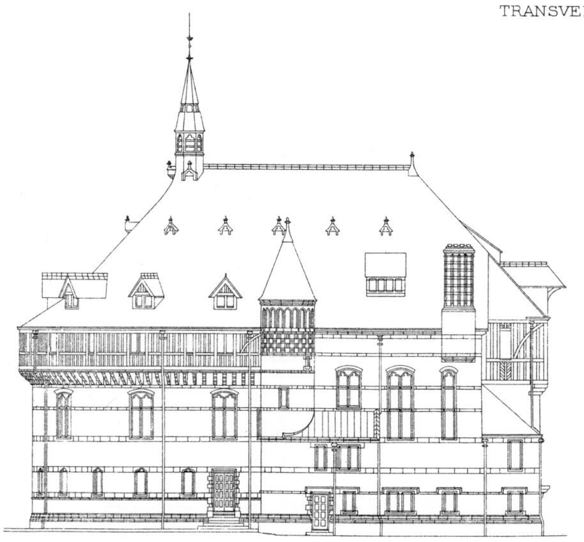

PL. 128

PL. 134

SIDE ELEVATION.

LONGITUDINAL SECTION.

Seiten Ansicht.

Façade Latérale.

Laengsschnitt.

Coupe Longitudinale.

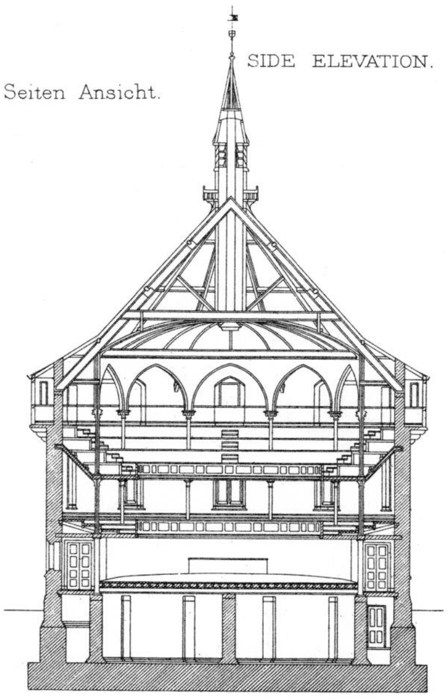

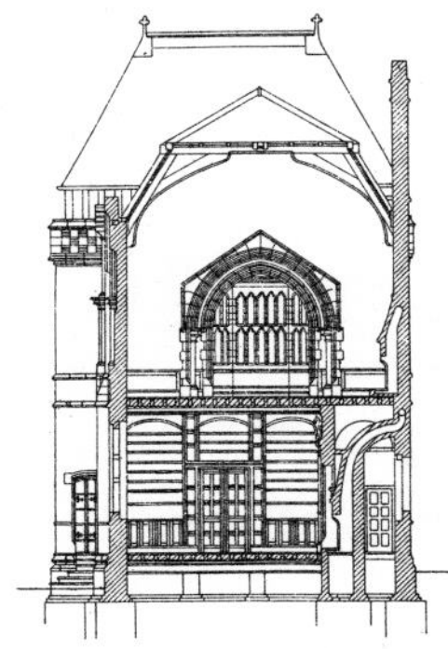

TRANSVERSE SECTIONS.

Querschnitte.

PL. 135

Coupe Transversales.

Edwin O. Sachs ed:

25   0   25   50

Feet.

10   0   10

Mètres.

SHAKESPEARE MEMORIAL THEATRE, STRATFORD ON AVON.

W. F. Unsworth.

Vorder Ansicht.   FRONT ELEVATION.   Façade Principale.   PL. 136

A. Stalls Entrance,
      (Parkett Eingang, Entrée des Stalles.)
B. Pit Entrance,
      (Parterre Eingang, Entrée du Parterre.)
C. I & II Tier Entrance,
      (Eingang I & II Rang, Entrée des 1res et 2des.)
D. Lobby,
      (Vorraum, Dégagement.)

E. Saloon,
      (Erfrischungsraum, Restaurant.)
F. Treasury,
      (Hauptkasse, Bureau des Comptes.)
G. Shops,
      (Laden, Magazins.)
H. Entrance to Concert Hall,
      (Eingang zum Concertsaal, Entrée, Salle de Concert.)

I. Dressing Room,
      (Ankleideraum, Loge des Artistes.)
K. Workshop,
      (Werkstatt, Atelier.)
L. Band Room,
      (Musiker, Musiciens.)
M. Scene Store,
      (Coulissen Magazin, Dépôt des Décors.)

a   Stalls Passage,
      (Parkett Gang, Couloir des Stalles.)
b   Pit Passage,
      (Parterre Gang, Couloir du Parterre.)
c   I Tier Stairs,
      (I Rang Treppe, Escalier des 1res.)
d   II Tier Stairs,
      (II Rang Treppe, Escalier des 2des.)

e   III Tier Stairs,
      (III Rang Treppe, Escalier des 3mes.)
f   Pass Stairs,
      (Verbindungs Treppe, Escalier de Communication.)
g   Private Box Stairs,
      (Logen Treppe, Escalier des Loges.)
h   Service Stairs,
      (Personal Treppe, Escalier de Service.)
i   Lift,
      (Aufzug, Ascenseur.)
k   Stairs to Concert Hall,
      (Treppe zum Concertsaal, Escalier, Salle de Concert.)
p   Box Office,
      (Kasse, Caisse.)
w   Bar,
      (Anrichtetisch, Buffet.)

y   Cloaks,
      (Kleiderablage, Vestiaire.)
z   Lavatory,
      (Retirade, Toilette.)

PLAN, AREA.   PL. 137

Grundriss, Saal.   Plan, Salle.

Edwin O. Sachs ed:

25   0   25   50
      Feet.

GRAND THEATRE, LEEDS.

George Carson.

10   0   10
      Mètres.

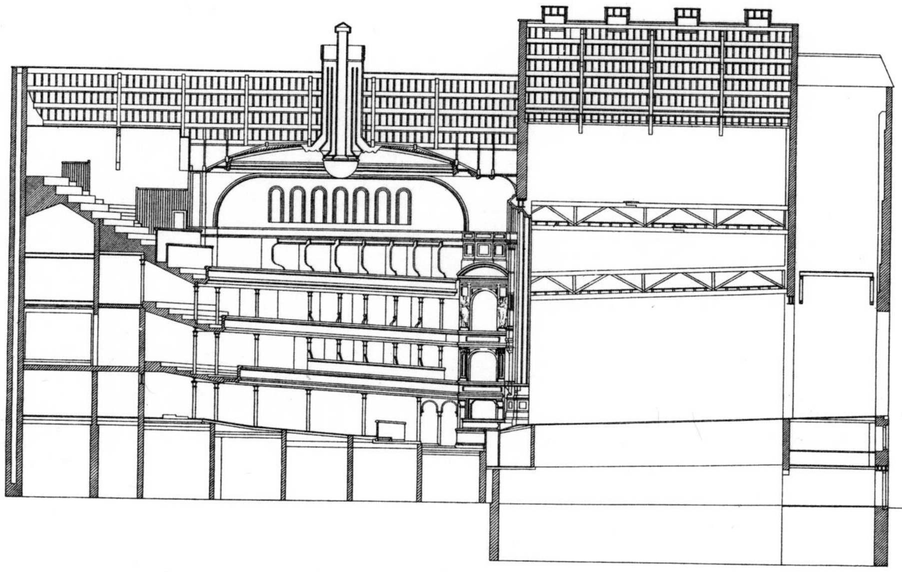

Laengsschnitt.　　　LONGITUDINAL SECTION.　　　Coupe Longitudinale.　　　**PL. 139**

A. Grand Staircase,
　　(Haupt Treppenhaus, Grand Escalier.)
B. Saloon,
　　(Erfrischungsraum, Restaurant.)
C. Smoking Room,
　　(Rauchsaal, Fumoir.)

D. Lobby
　　(Vorraum, Dégagement.)
E. Wardrobe Room,
　　(Kleiderkammer, Costumes.)
G. Ballet Room,
　　(Tanz Saal, Foyer de la Dance.)
H. Rehearsal Room,
　　(Probe Saal, Salle de Répétition.)

I. Dressing Room,
　　(Ankleideraum, Loge des Artistes.)
K. Concert Hall,
　　(Concertsaal, Salle de Concert.)
L. Supper Room,
　　(Speise Saal, Salle à Manger.)

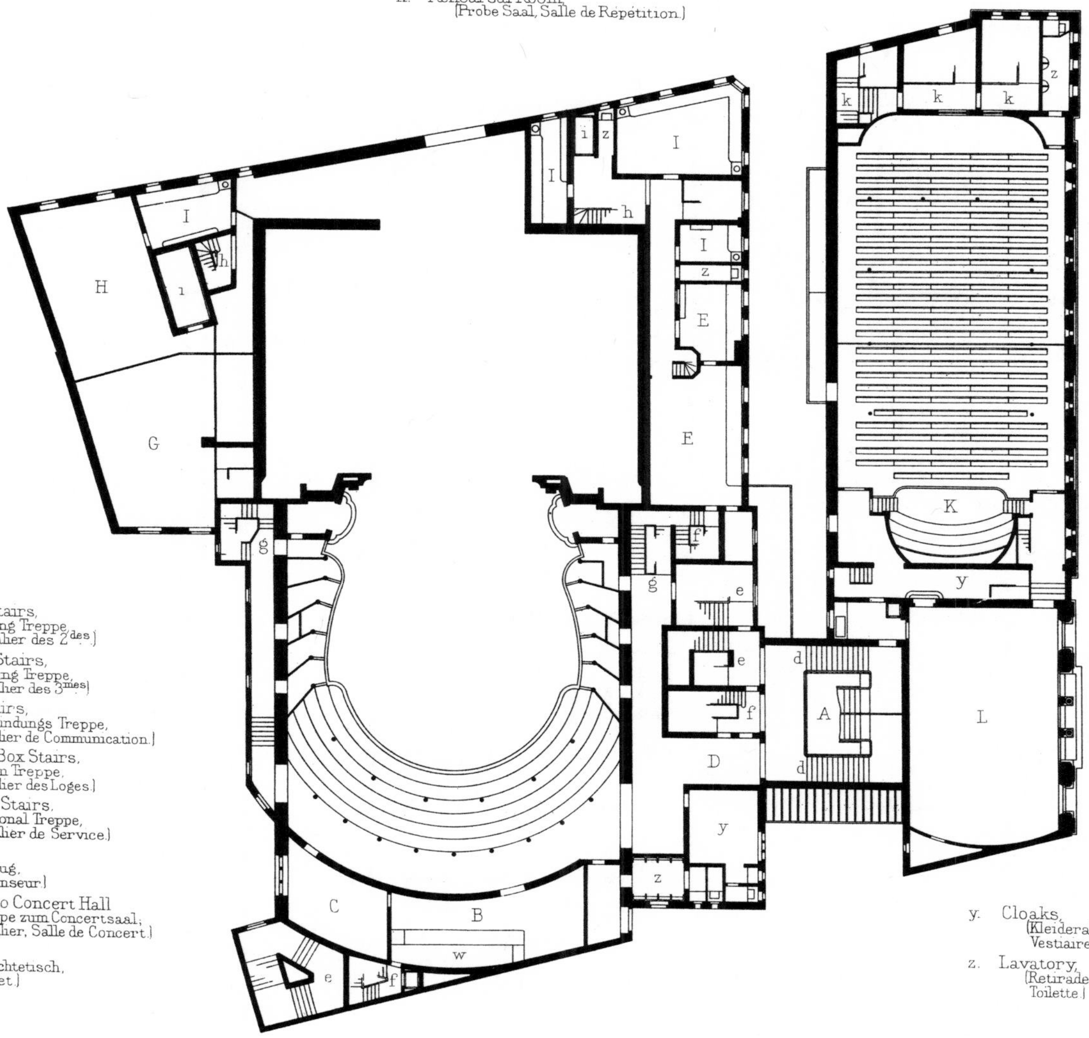

d. II Tier Stairs,
　　(II Rang Treppe,
　　Escalier des 2des.)
e. III Tier Stairs,
　　(III Rang Treppe,
　　Escalier des 3mes.)
f. Pass Stairs,
　　(Verbindungs Treppe,
　　Escalier de Communication.)
g. Private Box Stairs,
　　(Logen Treppe,
　　Escalier des Loges.)
h. Service Stairs,
　　(Personal Treppe,
　　Escalier de Service.)
i. Lift,
　　(Aufzug,
　　Ascenseur.)
k. Stairs to Concert Hall,
　　(Treppe zum Concertsaal,
　　Escalier, Salle de Concert.)
w. Bar,
　　(Anrichtetisch,
　　Buffet.)

y. Cloaks,
　　(Kleiderablage,
　　Vestiaire.)
z. Lavatory,
　　(Retirade,
　　Toilette.)

PLAN, II TIER.　　　　　　　　　　　　　　　　　**PL. 138**

Grundriss, II Rang.　　　　　　Plan, 2e Loges.

Feet.　　　　　GRAND THEATRE. LEEDS.　　　　　Mètres.

George Carson.

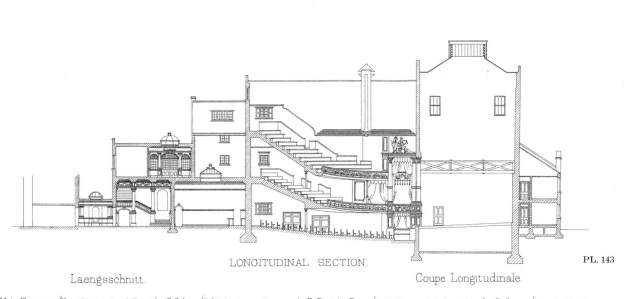

LONGITUDINAL SECTION.   PL. 143

Laengsschnitt.   Coupe Longitudinale.

A. Main Entrance, (Haupt Eingang, Grande Entrée.)   C. Saloon, (Erfrischungsraum, Restaurant.)   E. Dressing Room, (Ankleideraum, Loge des Artistes.)   G. Stores, (Magazin, Dépôt.)

B. Grand Vestibule, (Grosse Vorhalle, Grand Vestibule.)   D. Lobby, (Vorraum, Dégagement.)   F. Scene Stores, (Coulissen Magazin, Dépôt des Décors.)   H. Office, (Geschäftsraum, Bureau.)

a. Stalls Entrance, (Parkett Eingang, Entrée des Stalles.)   e. Private Box Stairs, (Logen Treppe, Escalier des Loges.)   s. Stage Door, (Buehnen Eingang, Entrée du Théâtre.)

b. Pit Entrance, (Parterre Eingang, Entrée du Parterre.)   f. Service Stairs, (Personal Treppe, Escalier de Service.)   w. Bar, (Anrichtetisch, Buffet.)

c. I Tier Stairs, (I Rang Treppe, Escalier des 1ˢᵉˢ.)   p. Box Office, (Kasse, Caisse.)   y. Cloaks, (Kleiderabgabe Vestiaire.)

d. II Tier Stairs, (II Rang Treppe, Escalier des 2ᵈᵉˢ.)   z. Lavatory, (Retirade, Toilette.)

PL. 141   PL. 140   PL. 142

PLAN, I TIER.   PLAN, AREA.   PLAN, II TIER.

Grundriss, I Rang.   Plan, 1ˢ Loges.   Grundriss, Saal   Plan, Salle.   Grundriss, II Rang   Plan, 2ᵉ Loges.

Edwin O. Sachs ed.

25 ___ 0 ___ 25 ___ 50
Feet.

10 ___ 0 ___ 10
Mètres.

"NEW" THEATRE, CAMBRIDGE.

Ernest Runtz.

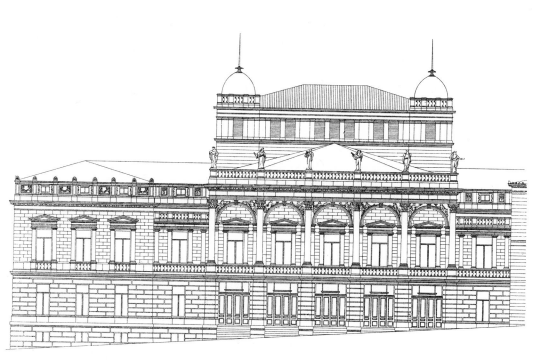

FRONT ELEVATION.

Vorder Ansicht.   Façade Principale.   PL. 144

A. Grand Vestibule, (Grosse Vorhalle, Grand Vestibule.)   C. Refreshment Room, (Bierhalle, Brasserie.)   F. Scene Store, (Coulissen Magazin, Dépôt des Décors.)
B. Lobby, (Vorraum, Dégagement.)   D. Green Room, (Unterhaltungsraum, Foyer des Artistes.) G. Store, (Magazin, Dépôt.)
                                                          E. Dressing Room, (Ankleideraum, Loge des Artistes.)

a. I Tier Stairs, (I Rang Treppe, Escalier des 1res)   p. Box Office, (Kasse, Caisse.)
b. II Tier Stairs, (II Rang Treppe, Escalier des 2mes)   d. Pass Stairs, (Verbindungs Treppe, Escalier de Communication.)   y. Cloak Counter, (Kleiderablage, Vestiaire.)
c. Service Stairs, (Personal Treppe, Escalier de Service.)   z. Lavatory, (Retirade, Toilette.)

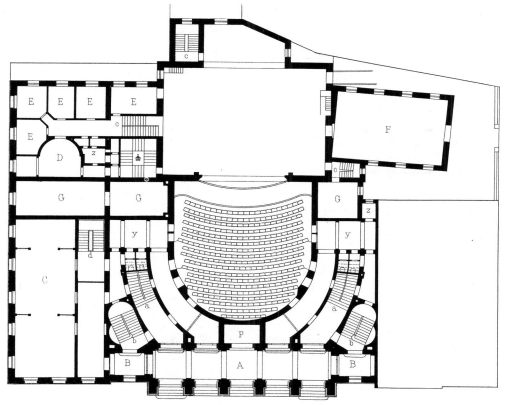

PLAN, AREA.

Grundriss, Saal.   Plan, Salle.   PL. 145

Feet.

Feet.

NATIONAL THEATRE, ATHENS.

E. Ziller.

Mètres.

Mètres.

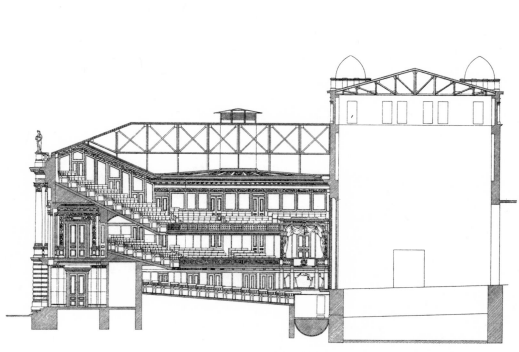

LONGITUDINAL SECTION.   PL. 147

Laengsschnitt.   Coupe Longitudinale.

A. Lounge, (Erfrischungssaal, Foyer.)   C. Lobby, (Vorraum, Dégagement.)   E. Dressing Room, (Ankleideraum, Loge des Artistes.)
B. Promenade, (Wandelgang, Promenade.)   D. Green Room, (Unterhaltungsraum, Foyer des Artistes.)   F. Scene Store, (Coulissen Magazin, Dépôt des Décors.)

a. I Tier Stairs, (I Rang Treppe, Escalier des 1res)   c. Service Stairs, (Personal Treppe, Escalier de Service.)   y. Cloak Counter, (Kleiderablage, Vestiaire.)
b. II Tier Stairs, (II Rang Treppe, Escalier des 2mes)   z. Lavatory, (Retirade, Toilette.)

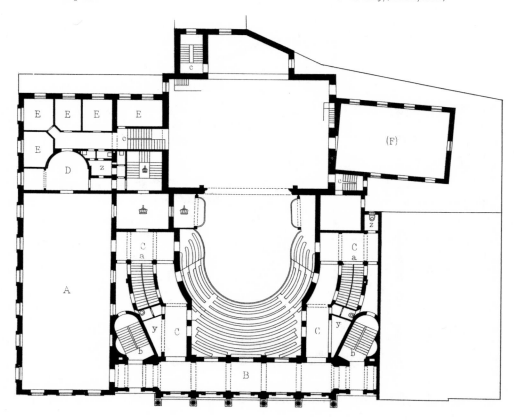

PLAN, I TIER.   PL. 146

Grundriss, I Rang.   Plan, I Loges.

0 5 10   20   30   40   50
Feet.

25   0   25   50
Feet.

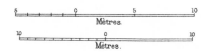

NATIONAL THEATRE. ATHENS.
E. Ziller.

5   0   5   10
Mètres.

10   0   10
Mètres.

FRONT ELEVATION.   PL. 148

Vorder Ansicht.   Façade Principale.

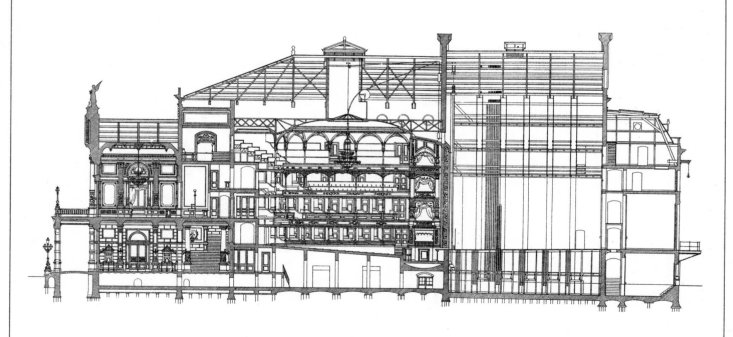

LONGITUDINAL SECTION.   PL. 152

Laengsschnitt.   Coupe Longitudinale.

Edwin O. Sachs ed.

MUNICIPAL THEATRE, ROTTERDAM.

J. Verheul.

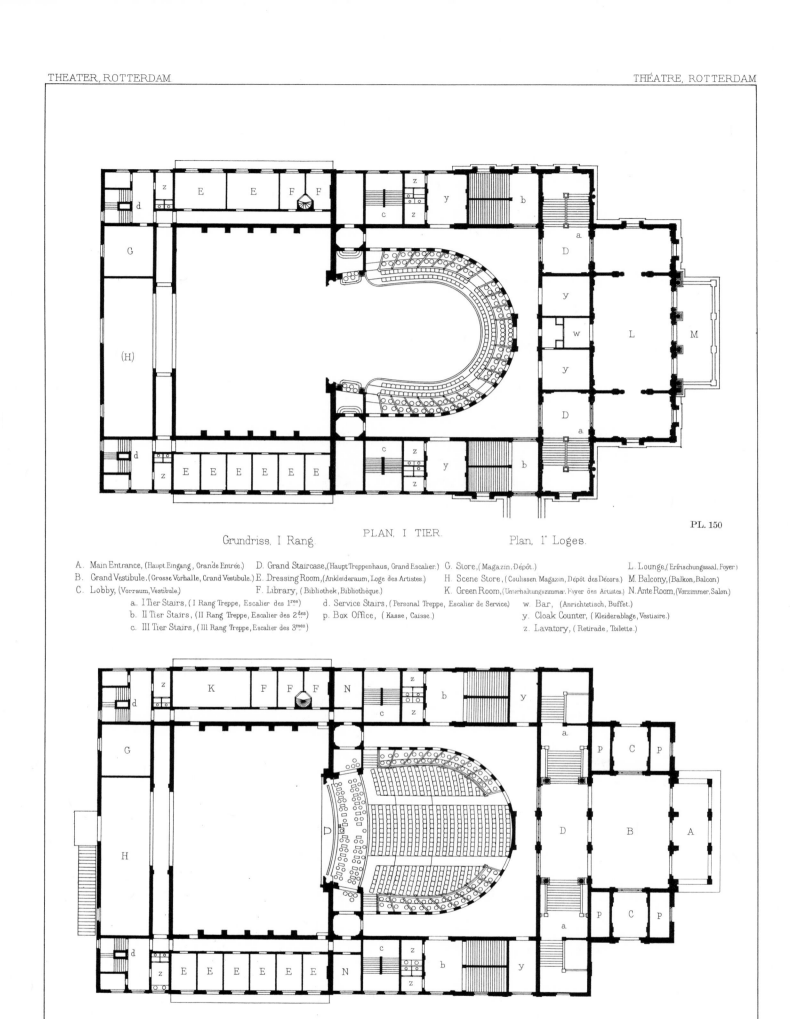

Grundriss, I Rang.   PLAN, I TIER.   Plan, I' Loges.

PL. 150

A. Main Entrance, (Haupt Eingang, Grande Entrée.)   D. Grand Staircase,(Haupt Treppenhaus, Grand Escalier.)   G. Store,(Magazin, Dépôt.)   L. Lounge,(Erfrischungssaal, Foyer.)
B. Grand Vestibule. (Grosse Vorhalle, Grand Vestibule.)   E. Dressing Room,(Ankleideraum, Loge des Artistes.)   H. Scene Store, (Coulissen Magazin, Dépôt des Décors.)   M. Balcony,(Balkon, Balcon.)
C. Lobby, (Vorraum, Vestibule.)   F. Library, (Bibliothek, Bibliothèque.)   K. Green Room,(Unterhaltungszimmer, Foyer des Artistes.)   N. Ante Room,(Vorzimmer, Salon.)

a. I Tier Stairs, (I Rang Treppe, Escalier des 1res)   d. Service Stairs, (Personal Treppe, Escalier de Service.)   w. Bar, (Anrichtetisch, Buffet.)
b. II Tier Stairs, (II Rang Treppe, Escalier des 2des)   p. Box Office, (Kasse, Caisse.)   y. Cloak Counter, (Kleiderablage, Vestiaire.)
c. III Tier Stairs, (III Rang Treppe, Escalier des 3mes)   z. Lavatory, (Retirade, Toilette.)

PL. 149

Grundriss, Saal.   PLAN, AREA.   Plan, Salle.

25 ... 0 ... 25 ... 50
Feet.

MUNICIPAL THEATRE, ROTTERDAM.
J. Verheul.

10 ... 0 ... 10
Mètres.

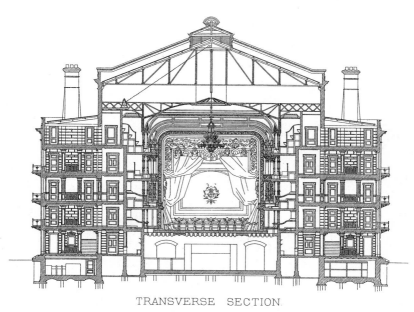

TRANSVERSE SECTION.   PL. 153

Querschnitt.   Coupe Transversale.

E. Dressing Room, (Ankleideraum, Loge des Artistes.)   G. Store, (Magazin, Dépôt.)   N. Ante Room, (Vorzimmer, Salon.)

b. II Tier Stairs, (II Rang Treppe, Escalier des 2des.)   d. Service Stairs, (Personal Treppe, Escalier des 2des.)   y. Cloak Counter, (Kleiderablage, Vestiaire.)

c. III Tier Stairs, (III Rang Treppe, Escalier des 3mes.)   w. Bar, (Anrichtetisch, Buffet.)   z. Lavatory, (Retirade, Toilette.)

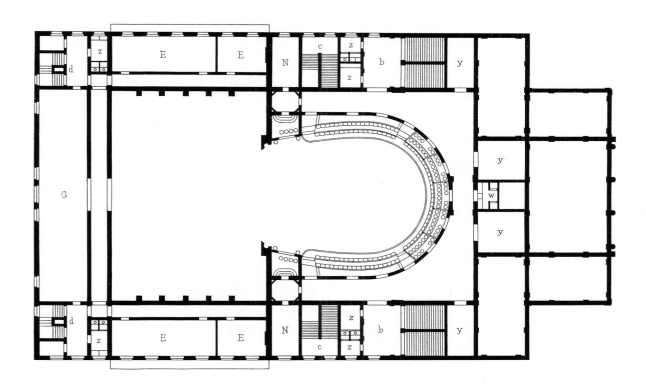

PLAN. II TIER.

Grundriss, II Rang.   Plan, 2e Loges.   PL. 151

25   0   25   50
Feet.

MUNICIPAL THEATRE, ROTTERDAM.

J. Verheul.

10   0   10
Mètres.

FRONT ELEVATION.　　　　　　　PL. 154

Vorder Ansicht.　　　　　　Façade Principale.

A. Lounge,
　(Erfrischungssaal,
　Foyer.)

B. Hall,
　(Wartehalle,
　Vestibule d'Attente.)

C. Ante Room,
　(Vorzimmer,
　Salon.)

D. Grand Staircase,
　(Haupt Treppenhaus,
　Grand Escalier.)

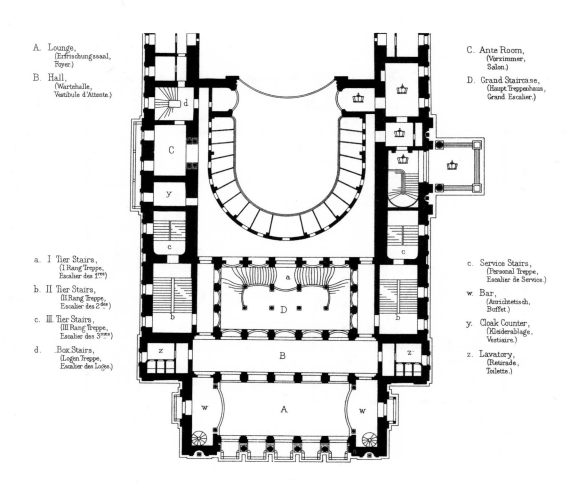

a. I Tier Stairs,
　(I Rang Treppe,
　Escalier des 1res)

b. II Tier Stairs,
　(II Rang Treppe,
　Escalier des 2des)

c. III Tier Stairs,
　(III Rang Treppe,
　Escalier des 3mes)

d. Box Stairs,
　(Logen Treppe,
　Escalier des Loges.)

c. Service Stairs,
　(Personal Treppe,
　Escalier de Service.)

w. Bar,
　(Anrichtetisch,
　Buffet.)

y. Cloak Counter,
　(Kleiderablage,
　Vestiaire.)

z. Lavatory,
　(Retirade,
　Toilette.)

PLAN, I TIER.

Grundriss, I Rang.　　　　Plan, 1er Loges.　　　PL. 157

Edwin O. Sachs ed:

25　　0　　25　　50
Feet.

10　　0　　10
Mètres.

NATIONAL THEATRE, BUCHAREST.

G. Sterian.

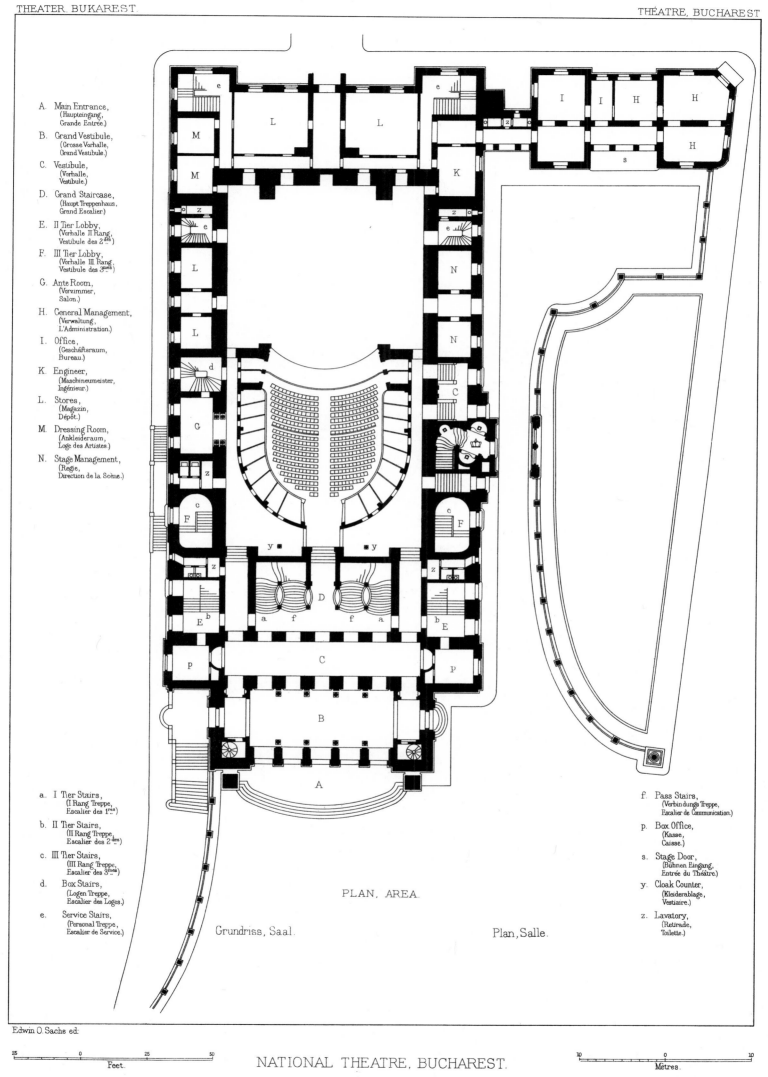

A. Main Entrance,
(Haupteingang,
Grande Entrée.)

B. Grand Vestibule,
(Grosse Vorhalle,
Grand Vestibule.)

C. Vestibule,
(Vorhalle,
Vestibule.)

D. Grand Staircase,
(Haupt Treppenhaus,
Grand Escalier.)

E. II Tier Lobby,
(Vorhalle II Rang,
Vestibule des 2des.)

F. III Tier Lobby,
(Vorhalle III Rang,
Vestibule des 3mes.)

G. Ante Room,
(Vorzimmer,
Salon.)

H. General Management,
(Verwaltung,
L'Administration.)

I. Office,
(Geschäftsraum,
Bureau.)

K. Engineer,
(Maschineumeister,
Ingénieur.)

L. Stores,
(Magazin,
Dépôt.)

M. Dressing Room,
(Ankleideraum,
Loge des Artistes.)

N. Stage Management,
(Regie,
Direction de la Scène.)

a. I Tier Stairs,
(I Rang Treppe,
Escalier des 1res.)

b. II Tier Stairs,
(II Rang Treppe,
Escalier des 2des.)

c. III Tier Stairs,
(III Rang Treppe,
Escalier des 3mes.)

d. Box Stairs,
(Logen Treppe,
Escalier des Loges.)

e. Service Stairs,
(Personal Treppe,
Escalier de Service.)

f. Pass Stairs,
(Verbindungs Treppe,
Escalier de Communication.)

p. Box Office,
(Kasse,
Caisse.)

s. Stage Door,
(Bühnen Eingang,
Entrée du Théâtre.)

y. Cloak Counter,
(Kleiderablage,
Vestiaire.)

z. Lavatory,
(Retirade,
Toilette.)

PLAN, AREA.

Grundriss, Saal.

Plan, Salle.

Edwin O. Sachs ed:

25 0 25 50
Feet.

10 0 10
Mètres.

NATIONAL THEATRE, BUCHAREST.

G. Sterian.

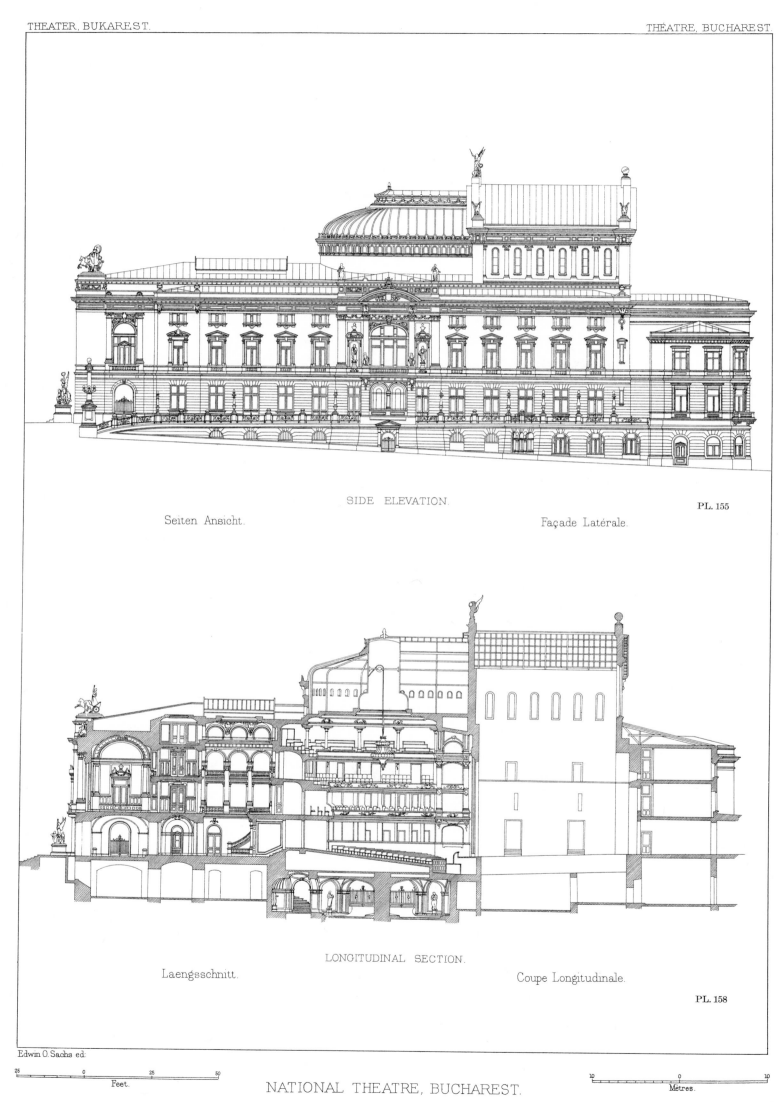

SIDE ELEVATION.

Seiten Ansicht.   Façade Latérale.

PL. 155

LONGITUDINAL SECTION.

Laengsschnitt.   Coupe Longitudinale.

PL. 158

Edwin O. Sachs ed.

25   0   25   50
Feet.

10   0   10
Mètres.

NATIONAL THEATRE, BUCHAREST.

G. Sterian.

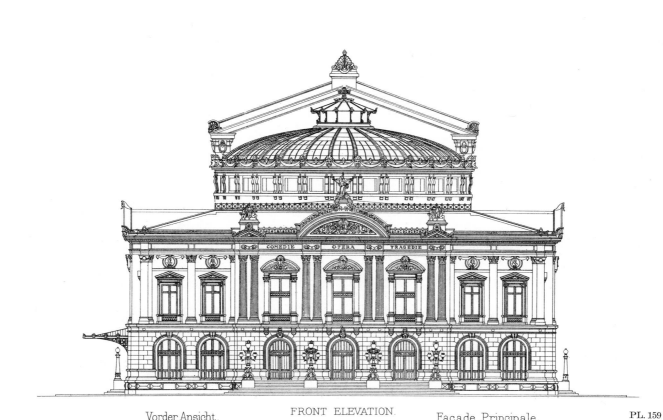

Vorder Ansicht.   FRONT ELEVATION.   Façade Principale.   PL. 159

A. Main Entrance,
    (Haupt Eingang, Grande Entrée.)
B. Grand Vestibule,
    (Grosse Vorhalle, Grand Vestibule.)
C. Lobby,
    (Vorraum, Dégagement.)
D. Hall,
    (Wartehalle, Vestibule d'Attente.)

a. I Tier Stairs,
    (I Rang Treppe, Escalier des 1res.)
b. II Tier Stairs,
    (II Rang Treppe, Escalier des 2des.)

E. Saloon,
    (Erfrischungsraum, Restaurant.)
F. Police,
    (Polizei, Sergents de Ville.)
G. Scene Store,
    (Coulissen Magazin, Dépôt des Décors.)

c. III Tier Stairs,
    (III Rang Treppe, Escalier des 3mes.)
d. Service Stairs,
    (Personal Treppe, Escalier de Service.)

H. Green Room,
    (Unterhaltungsraum, Foyer des Artistes.)
I. Stage Management,
    (Regie, Direction de la Scène.)
K. Stores,
    (Magazin, Dépôt.)
L. Engineer,
    (Maschinenmeister, Ingénieur.)

y. Cloak Counter,
    (Kleiderablage, Vestiaire.)
z. Lavatory,
    (Retirade, Toilette.)

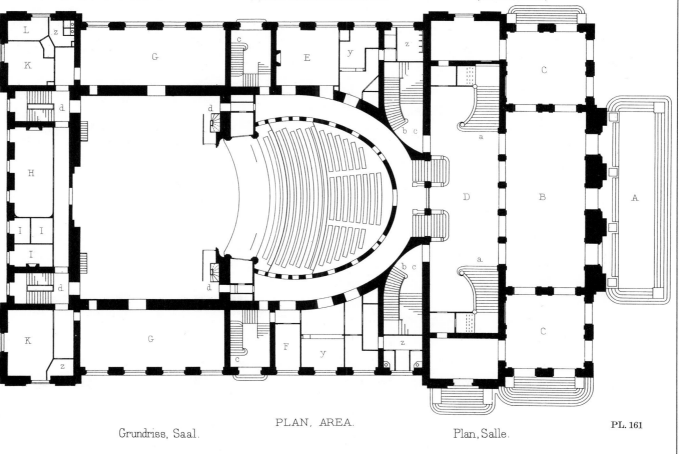

Grundriss, Saal.   PLAN, AREA.   Plan, Salle.   PL. 161

Edwin O. Sachs ed.

25   0   25   50
Feet.

MUNICIPAL THEATRE, GENEVA.
J. E. Goss.

10   0   10
Mètres.

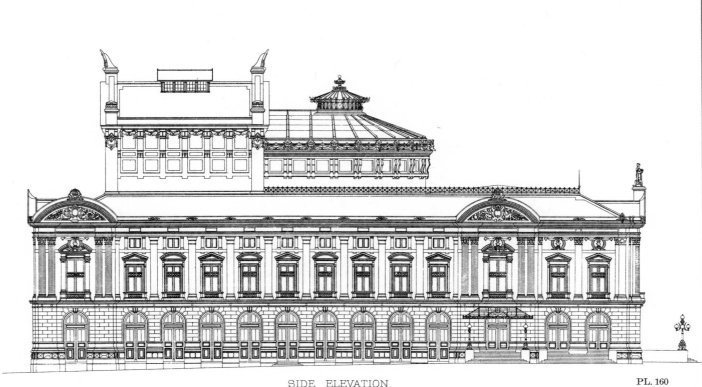

SIDE ELEVATION.   PL. 160

Seiten Ansicht.   Façade Latérale.

A. Lounge,
      (Erfrischungssaal, Foyer.)
B. Saloon,
      (Erfrischungsraum, Restaurant.)
C. Smoking Room,
      (Rauchsaal, Fumoir.)

D. Hall,
      (Wartehalle, Vestibule d'Attente.)
E. Ante Room,
      (Vorzimmer, Salon.)
F. Accident Room,
      Kranken, Zimmer, Laboratoire du Médecin.)

G. Scene Store,
      (Coulissen Magazin, Dépôt des Décors.)
H. Stage Management,
      (Regie, Direction de la Scène.)
I. Dressing Room,
      (Ankleideraum, Loge des Artistes.)

b. II Tier Stairs,
      (II Rang Treppe, Escalier des 2des.)
c. III Tier Stairs,
      (III Rang Treppe, Escalier des 3mes.)

d. Service Stairs,
      (Personal Treppe, Escalier de Service.)

y. Cloak Counter,
      (Kleiderablage, Vestiaire.)
z. Lavatory,
      (Retirade, Toilette.)

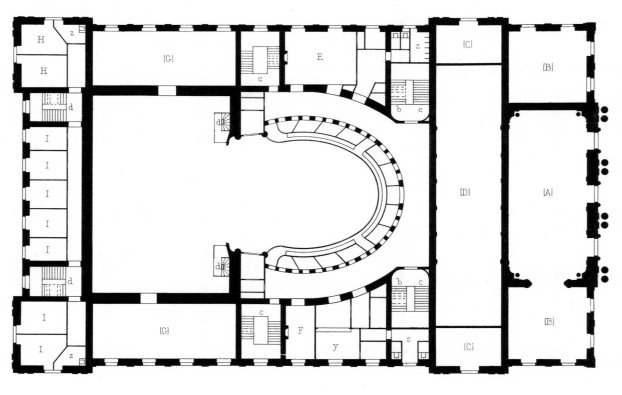

PLAN, II TIER.   PL. 162

Grundriss, II Rang.   Plan, 2e Loges.

Edwin O. Sachs ed.

25   0   25   50
Feet.

MUNICIPAL THEATRE, GENEVA.
J. E. Goss.

10   0   10
Métres.

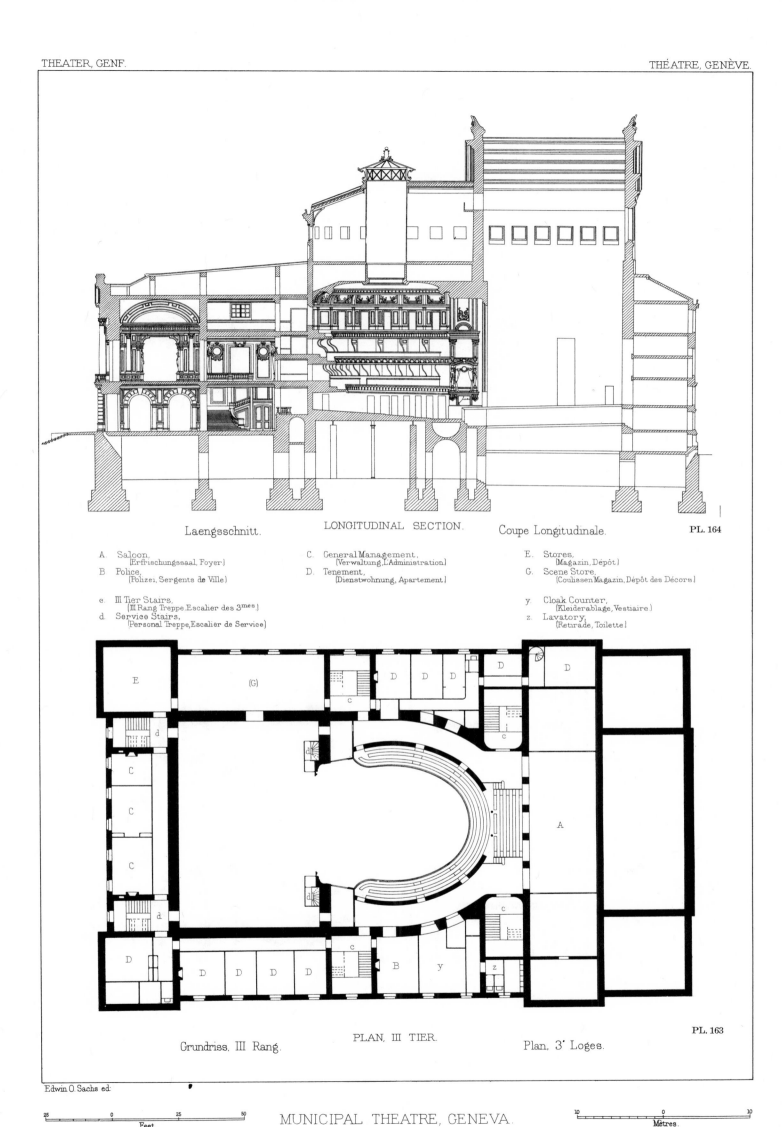

Laengsschnitt. LONGITUDINAL SECTION. Coupe Longitudinale. PL. 164

A. Saloon,
    (Erfrischungssaal, Foyer)
B. Police,
    (Polizei, Sergents de Ville)

c. III Tier Stairs,
    (III Rang Treppe, Escalier des 3mes.)
d. Service Stairs,
    (Personal Treppe, Escalier de Service)

C. General Management,
    (Verwaltung, L'Administration)
D. Tenement,
    (Dienstwohnung, Apartement)

E. Stores,
    (Magazin, Dépôt)
G. Scene Store,
    (Coulissen Magazin, Dépôt des Décors)

y. Cloak Counter,
    (Kleiderablage, Vestiaire)
z. Lavatory,
    (Retirade, Toilette)

Grundriss, III Rang. PLAN, III TIER. Plan, 3' Loges. PL. 163

Edwin O. Sachs ed.

25 0 25 50
Feet.

10 0 10
Mètres.

MUNICIPAL THEATRE, GENEVA.
J. E. Goss.

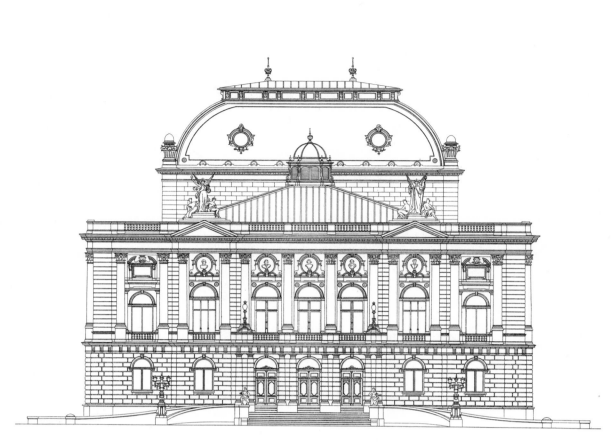

Vorder Ansicht.　　　FRONT ELEVATION.　　　Façade Principale.

PL. 165

A. Lounge,
       (Erfrischungssaal, Foyer.)
B. Balcony,
       (Balkon, Balcon.)

a.. I Tier Stairs,
       (I Rang Treppe, Escalier des 1res.)
b. II Tier Stairs,
       (II Rang Treppe, Escalier des 2des.)
c. III Tier Stairs,
       (III Rang Treppe, Escalier des 3mes.)

C. Office,
       (Geschaeftsraum, Bureau.)

d. Pass Stairs,
       (Verbindungs Treppe, Escalier de Communication.)
e. Service Stairs,
       (Personal Treppe, Escalier de Service.)

D. General Management,
       (Verwaltung, L'Administration.)
E. Dressing Room,
       (Ankleideraum, Loge des Artistes.)

w. Bar,
       (Anrichtetisch, Buffet.)
y. Cloak Counter,
       (Kleiderablage, Vestiaire.)
z. Lavatory,
       (Retirade, Toilette.)

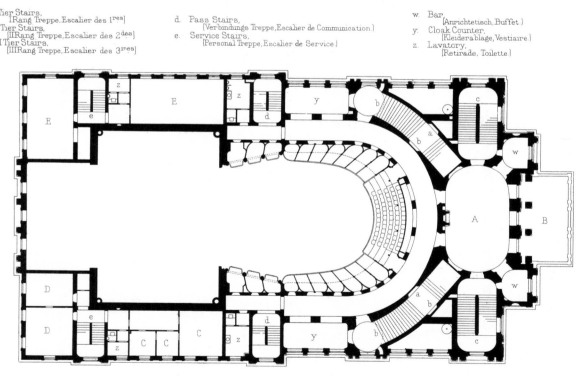

PLAN, II TIER.

PL. 167

Grundriss, II Rang.　　　Plan, 2' Loges.

Edwin O. Sachs ed.

Feet.

Feet.

Metres.

Metres.

MUNICIPAL THEATRE, ZÜRICH.

Ferdinand Fellner, Hermann Helmer.

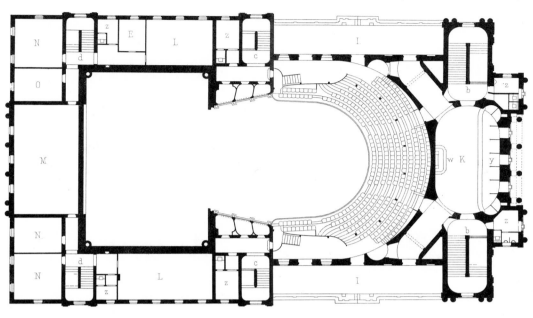

PL. 168

Grundriss, III Rang.   PLAN, III TIER.   Plan, 3˟ Loges.

A. Main Entrance,
      (Haupt Eingang, Grande Entrée.)
B. Grand Vestibule,
      (Grosse Vorhalle, Grand Vestibule.)
C. Lobby,
      (Vorraum, Dégagement.)
D. III Tier Lobby,
      (Vorraum III Rang, Vestibule des 3˟ᵉˢ)
E. Dressing Room,
      (Ankleideraum, Löge des Artistes.)

a. I Tier Stairs,
      (I Rang Treppe, Escalier des 1ʳᵉˢ)
b. II Tier Stairs,
      (II Rang Treppe, Escalier des 2ᵈᵉˢ)
c. III Tier Stairs,
      (III Rang Treppe, Escalier des 3ᵐᵉˢ)

F. Scene Store,
      (Coulissen Magazin, Dépôt des Décors.)
G. Fire Service,
      (Feuerwehr, Service des Pompiers.)
H. Stage Door Keeper,
      (Pfoertner, Concierge du Théâtre.)
I. Balcony,
      (Balkon, Balcon.)

d. Pass Stairs,
      (Verbindungs Treppe, Escalier de Communication.)
e. Service Stairs,
      (Personal Treppe, Escalier de Service.)
p. Box Office,
      (Kasse, Caisse.)
s. Stage Door,
      (Buehnen Eingang, Entrée du Théâtre.)

K. Saloon,
      (Erfrischungsraum, Restaurant.)
L. Supers Room,
      (Statisten, Comparses.)
M. Chorus Room,
      (Musik Saal, Foyer des Choristes.)
N. Rehearsal Room,
      (Probe Saal, Salle de Répétition.)
O. Library,
      (Bibliotek, Bibliothèque.)

w. Bar,
      (Anrichtetisch, Buffet.)
y. Cloak Counter,
      (Kleiderablage, Vestiare.)
z. Lavatory,
      (Retirade, Toilette.)

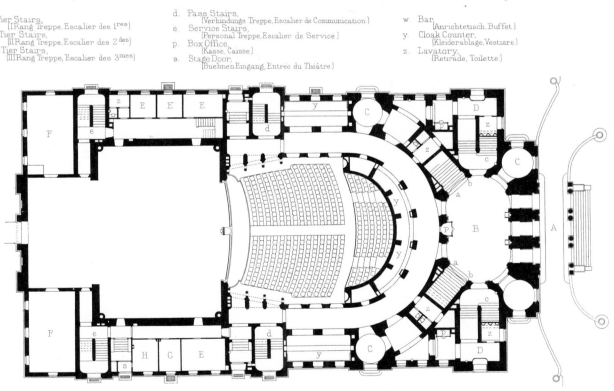

PLAN, AREA.

Grundriss, Saal.   Plan Salle.   PL. 166

Edwin O. Sachs ed:

Feet.

Mètres.

MUNICIPAL THEATRE, ZÜRICH.

Ferdinand Fellner, Hermann Helmer.

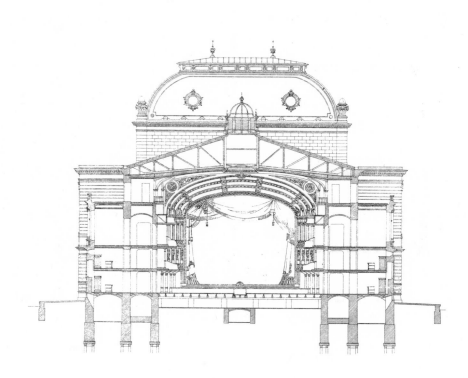

TRANSVERSE SECTION.   PL. 170

Querschnitt.   Coupe Transversale.

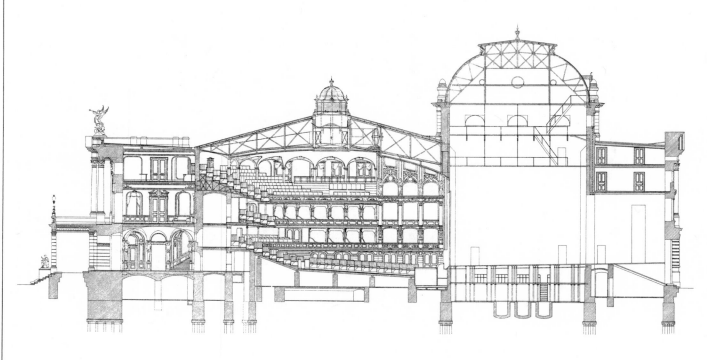

LONGITUDINAL SECTION.

Laengsschnitt.   Coupe Longitudinale.

PL. 169

Edwin O. Sachs ed.

MUNICIPAL THEATRE, ZÜRICH.

Ferdinand Fellner, Hermann Helmer.

DATE DUE

GAYLORD			PRINTED IN U.S.A.